Letters
from
Redgrave Hall

The Bacon Family

1340–1744

The Bacon family in front of Redgrave Hall, c. 1676 (reproduced by courtesy of Peter and Sarah Holt-Wilson).
(see page xxvii)

Letters
from
Redgrave Hall

THE BACON FAMILY

1340–1744

Edited by

DIARMAID MacCULLOCH

General Editor

A. HASSELL SMITH

The Boydell Press

Suffolk Records Society
VOLUME L

A Suffolk Records Society publication
First published 2007
The Boydell Press, Woodbridge

ISBN 978 1 84383 286 7

Issued to subscribing members for the year 2006–07

The Boydell Press is an imprint of Boydell & Brewer Ltd
PO Box 9, Woodbridge, Suffolk IP12 3DF, UK
and of Boydell & Brewer Inc.
668 Mt Hope Avenue, Rochester, NY 14620, USA
website: www.boydellandbrewer.com

A catalogue record for this book is available
from the British Library

This publication is printed on acid-free paper

Printed in Great Britain by
Antony Rowe Ltd, Chippenham, Wiltshire

CONTENTS

ILLUSTRATIONS

DAVID DYMOND

General Editor of Volumes XXXIV to L
1992 – 2007

As the Society celebrates its first fifty years and as many volumes, it is also time to record our gratitude to one whose dedicated, expert and detailed work has ensured the high standards which all expect of our publications. This year's volume on the Bacon family's letters is the last of fifteen to appear under the co-ordinating editorship of David Dymond. We now pay tribute to him at the end of his long and distinguished service in this crucial role.

The job of the general editor is at best demanding and sometimes onerous. Proposed texts come through him for Council to accept or decline politely. The author whose text joins the queue may need the help of a specialist in the field, though often David's wide knowledge and experience enables him to fulfil the intermediate role. His attention to detail – other people's detail, too – is exceptional. When the printers have the final version there will be proofs to check, and work on future titles continues in order to keep the annual volumes appearing on time.

As the Staff Tutor in Local and Regional History for the Board of Continuing Education at the University of Cambridge for many years, David frequently heard of work in progress relating to Suffolk. He has therefore been well-placed to steer researchers towards publishing in our series. During his tenure, volumes have been published on documents from the fourteenth to the nineteenth centuries, demonstrating David's competence across six centuries.

David joined the Council in 1966, and in 1972 produced *The County of Suffolk surveyed by Joseph Hodskinson, published in 1783,* as our volume XV. His *Norfolk Landscape* appeared in 1985. While co-ordinating our series, he was, as one in the top flight of local historians, chairman of the British Association for Local History for which he wrote *Writing Local History* (1981), its second edition in 1999 called *Researching and Writing Local History*. He edited *The Register of Thetford Priory 1482–1540*, two volumes of nearly 900 pages, for the Norfolk Record Society and the British Academy in 1995 and 1996, and, most recently, *The Churchwardens' Book of Bassingbourn 1496–c.1540* as Cambridgeshire Record Society's volume 17.

David was elected a Fellow of the Society of Antiquaries of London in 1964, and in 2000, received both a Cambridge PhD by submission of published works and an Honorary LittD of the University of East Anglia for services to history and education in the region.

We extend our warmest thanks and congratulations to David for all that he has done to further the aims of our Society in the scholarly publication of historical records and are delighted that he remains willing to serve as a member of Council.

John Blatchly
Chairman

PREFACE

This text has been a long time in the making, for I first saw a microfilm of the University of Chicago's Regenstein Library collection of Bacon letters in the early 1970s, while working for my doctorate on Elizabethan Suffolk. I made much use of them in my doctorate, which later became my first monograph, and realised their value as a unit, despite the fragmentary nature of the collection and the previous use which had been made of them. It was 1996 before I saw the originals in Chicago. Further commitments have made another decade pass before all has been safely gathered in.

Gratitude must go to the Suffolk Records Society for their patience with the gestation of this volume, particularly to the tactful solicitations of David Dymond, David Sherlock and Peter Northeast, and particular thanks to Dr John Blatchly, who with his characteristic energy and generosity constructed the genealogical table included in this edition and, together with David Sherlock, suggested and provided illustrations of Redgrave Hall. I am most grateful to Mrs Joye Rowe, Professor Alan Simpson and Professor Joachim Weintraub for their invaluable help in the planning of this project, and also to the staff of the Joseph P. Regenstein Library in the University of Chicago for making available to me photo-copies and microfilms for the main task of transcription. I am also indebted to the Seeley Historical Library in the University of Cambridge, England, and to Professor Hassell Smith of Norwich for lending me microfilms at an early stage of my work; Professor Smith has also given me much generous editorial advice while I was preparing the edition. In 1996 Suzy Taraba and her colleagues at the Regenstein made me very welcome and were extremely helpful as I checked the originals in the Library, and I was the recipient of a generous grant from the British Academy which assisted with my travelling costs in getting to Chicago. The text and pictures of four of the letters are reproduced by kind permission of the Director of Chicago University Library, and other illustrations are reproduced by kind permission of Peter and Sarah Holt-Wilson and the National Monuments Record, Swindon.

This edition is a gift in token of love and gratitude to my mother Jennie MacCulloch, and to my late father Nigel MacCulloch, a faithful parish priest in Suffolk and constant enthusiast for its history.

Diarmaid MacCulloch
St Cross College, Oxford
Lent 2006

ABBREVIATIONS

Bacon handlist	*University of Chicago Library: handlist of Bacon family manuscripts* (List and Index Society, 1991)
Bald, *Donne and the Drurys*	R.C. Bald, *Donne and the Drurys* (Cambridge, 1959)
BL	British Library
Cal. Hatfield MSS	*Calendar of the Manuscripts ... preserved at Hatfield House ...* (24 vols., HMC, 1883–1976)
CPR	*Calendar of Patent Rolls*
Complete peerage	*Complete peerage of England, Scotland, Ireland, etc. ...*, ed. G.E.C[okayne, revised V. Gibbs] (13 vols., London, 1910–49)
Freeman Bullen, 'Beneficed clergy, 1551–1631'	R. Freeman Bullen, 'Catalogue of beneficed clergy of Suffolk, 1551–1631', *PSIA* 22 (1936), 294–333
1561 visitation, ed. Corder	*The visitation of Suffolk 1561*, ed. J. Corder (Harleian Society, new series vols. 2 and 3, 1981 and 1984)
HMC	Historical Manuscripts Commission
HMC Gawdy	*Report on the manuscripts of the family of Gawdy, formerly of Norfolk*, ed. Walter Rye (HMC, 1885)
Hill, *Julius Caesar*	L.M. Hill, *Bench and bureaucracy: the public career of Sir Julius Caesar, 1580–1636* (Stanford, 1988)
History of Parliament 1509–58	*History of Parliament: The House of Commons 1509–1558*, ed. S.T. Bindoff (3 vols., Secker and Warburg, 1982)
History of Parliament 1558–1603	*The History of Parliament: The House of Commons 1558–1603*, ed. P.W. Hasler (3 vols., Her Majesty's Stationery Office, 1982)
LP	*Letters and Papers Foreign and Domestic, of the Reign of Henry VIII, 1509–47*, ed. J.S. Brewer *et al.* (21 vols. and 2 vols. addenda, 1862–1932)
MacCulloch, *Suffolk*	D. MacCulloch, *Suffolk and the Tudors: politics and religion in an English county 1500–1600* (Oxford, 1986)
Moor	E. Moor, *Suffolk words and phrases* (London: R. Hunter, 1823; repr. with new introduction by S. Ellis, London: David and Charles, 1970)
Morant, *Essex*	P. Morant, *The history and antiquities of the county of Essex* (2 vols., London, 1768, repr. with new introduction by G.H. Martin, Halifax, 1978)
Nathaniel Bacon papers	*The papers of Nathaniel Bacon of Stiffkey*, ed. A.H. Smith, G.M. Baker, R.W. Kenny, V. Morgan, J. Key and B. Taylor (4 vols. to date, Norwich: Centre of East Anglian Studies, and Norfolk Record Society, vols. 46, 49, 53, 64, 1979–2001)

PRO	see TNA
Nf.	Norfolk
ODNB	*Oxford Dictionary of National Biography*
PSIA	*Proceedings of the Suffolk Institute of Archaeology*
Simpson, *Wealth of the gentry*	A. Simpson, *The wealth of the gentry, 1540–1660: East Anglian Studies* (University of Chicago Press, 1961)
Smith, *County and court*	A.H. Smith, *County and court: government and politics in Norfolk 1558–1603* (Oxford, 1974)
Storey, 'Culford Hall'	G. Storey, 'Culford Hall: near Bury St Edmunds', in *People and places: an East Anglian miscellany* (Lavenham, 1973), pp. 94–198
Suffolk in the XVIIth century	*Suffolk in the XVIIth century: the Breviary of Suffolk by Robert Reyce, 1618*, ed. Lord Francis Hervey (London, 1902)
TNA (formerly PRO)	The National Archives (formerly Public Record Office)

INTRODUCTION

This is an edition in full transcription of all the letters, 261 in number, to be found in the Bacon Manuscripts held in the Joseph Regenstein Library of the University of Chicago (MSS 4054–4307, 4487); it is the first time that they have been so presented. The wider collection, which consists mainly of a rich assemblage of court rolls, manorial records and other estate muniments, represents the remains of the family archive accumulated at Redgrave Hall, Suffolk, site of a former monastic grange of Bury St Edmunds abbey; after the dissolution of the monasteries, this became the home of the senior line of the Bacon family founded on the prosperity of Sir Nicholas Bacon [here styled Nicholas Bacon I], Lord Keeper of the Great Seal to Queen Elizabeth I. Bacons lived there until 1701,[1] when the distinguished lawyer Sir John Holt (1642–1710), bought the estate and, dying childless, left it to his brother Rowland. The house was much altered in the eighteenth century, although it retained the core of the building created by Lord Keeper Bacon (see Pl. 1). The bulk of the Redgrave archive was sold by the Holt-Wilson family at Sothebys from April 1921, and after the Second World War Redgrave Hall was demolished. Although I remember the ruins as a distant prospect from the Botesdale–Diss road when I was a boy in the 1950s and 1960s, nothing remains of the main buildings today.[2]

The bulk of the collection offered at Sothebys was bought by the University of Chicago, arriving there in 1925. Over the next few years, a series of strays which had been sold as separate lots by Sothebys, or which had been detached from the main archive a few decades before the main sale, were added to the Redgrave collection. In addition, certain letters included in the Redgrave sequence of correspondence are not integral to the collection, but have been acquired by the Regenstein Library because of their Bacon connection.[3] These are strays from the widely dispersed archive of Lord Keeper Bacon's younger son Nathaniel Bacon from Stiffkey Hall, Norfolk (see letters **78, 89, 90, 92, 159 [4129A, 4139A, 4139B, 4140A, 4205A]**). The petition of Mary Warren to Bishop Joseph Hall, no. **4265**, also appears to be an addition to the collection. Letter **90 [4139B]** was the gift of the Newberry Library in Chicago to the Regenstein Library in 1972. The whole collection has been meticulously catalogued by the Regenstein Library, and the catalogue is now a publication in the List and Index Society series.[4] For this edition, I have created a sequential numbering from **1** to **261** in strict chronological order (including reconstructed dates, some of these educated guesses, for undated material), but in referring to the items I have appended the Chicago piece-number in square brackets, since this will locate the items in the List and Index Society handlist.

Several historians have benefited from the material presented in these letters

---

1   E.R. Sandeen, 'The building of Redgrave Hall, 1545–1554', *PSIA* 29 (1961–3), pp.1–33, at p. 30.
2   Bald, *Donne and the Drurys*, pp. 5–6. On Sir John Holt see *ODNB, s.v.* Holt, John.
3   See *Nathaniel Bacon papers* I, 305, n. 335, for discussion of no. **4139A**, printed *ibid*. I, 200–1.
4   *Bacon handlist*: see List of Abbreviations above.

Plate 1: *Redgrave Hall as it appeared* c.*1850 after its eighteenth-century extension, with a group who are probably members of the Holt family in the foreground. The frontal view is reminiscent of the point of view in the late seventeenth-century painting of Redgrave Hall, and reveals the turret which had replaced the central turret on the older part of the house. Photograph by Hallam Ashley. Reproduced by kind permission of the National Monuments Record: T. Baxendale negative no. BB85/1029.*

and in the rest of the Redgrave collection. Ernest R. Sandeen devoted much attention to the archive in the course of producing his University of Chicago doctoral
thesis 'The Building activities of Sir Nicholas Bacon' (1959), and much of his
material can easily be consulted in articles published in the United Kingdom.[5] The
Redgrave archive in general was also the basis of the study of the first Sir Nicholas
Bacon in Alan Simpson's *The wealth of the gentry* and of R.C. Bald's *Donne and
the Drurys*. Later it was used by Robert Tittler in his biography, *Nicholas Bacon:
the making of a Tudor statesman* (1976).

Now at last, then, in Chicago the Redgrave archive has found a secure home
where it is treated with all the care and professionalism which characterises a
major library. It was little used by historians while it was still in its original home,
although various substantial subtractions were made from it. The correspondence
preserved in the Chicago collection is now quite selective. Batches have been
preserved relating to particular incidents and items of business; one can visu-
alise them as bundles in boxes, tied together with sheep-skin thongs or, in later
years, lawyers' pink tape. In one case, we can be certain that we are looking at
a bundle preserved together to relate to a particular item of business: the **192–8
[4238–43]** sequence of letters is a coherent unit, and letter **191 [4237]** is shown
by its endorsement from Sir Edmund Bacon to have served as a wrapper to that
correspondence. The sequences in the present collection, therefore, represent the
remnant of an archive, originally carefully ordered in topical bundles, after the
bundles had been selectively ransacked for the sale-room or for the interest of
antiquarians.

What has been lost? An inventory of the Redgrave muniment room and audit
house in 1658 mentions '25 old letters sowed together of Mr. Jo. Donne', correspondence which must have been generated by the great poet's friendship with Sir
Robert and Lady Drury of Hawstead. Even at that early date, these letters were
evidently perceived to have a special value; probably none of the present items
relating to John Donne were included in that bundle. Correspondence between
Sir Edmund Bacon of Redgrave and the scholarly diplomat Sir Henry Wotton
was put into print in 1661; there can be little doubt that this came from Redgrave.
Some correspondence of the Bacon family was taken in the eighteenth century
to Kimberley Hall (Norfolk) and has now become British Library Additional
MSS 39218–39252. As late as 1920, when that great Suffolk antiquary the Rev.
Edmund Farrer was sorting the Redgrave collection, he noted 'an enormous quantity (which was, I have been told, 150 years ago much larger) of state documents,
connected mostly with Lord Keeper [Sir Nicholas] Bacon's official life'. Sadly
and tantalisingly, very little of this material remains in the collection today.[6] It is
more than likely that some of the manuscripts which have only gone missing in
the twentieth century will one day appear again in public.[7]

At the heart of the collection is the founder of the Redgrave estate after its long
years as part of the possessions of Bury St Edmunds abbey, the first Sir Nicholas

---

5 Sandeen, 'The building of Redgrave Hall', which includes photographs of the surviving remnant
of the Tudor Hall in 1958, and E.R. Sandeen, 'The building of the sixteenth-century Corpus Christi
College Chapel', *Proceedings of the Cambridge Antiquarian Society* 55 (1962), 23–35. See also
*The Sir Nicholas Bacon collection: sources on English society 1250–1700. An exhibition at the
Joseph Regenstein Library at the University of Chicago, April–June, 1972* (Chicago, 1972).
6 Bald, *Donne and the Drurys*, pp. 3–5.
7 Professor Hassell Smith tells me that his frequent efforts to locate further survivals of Redgrave
material have so far not produced any results.

Bacon (1510–79). This son of the abbot of Bury's sheepreeve, a self-made lawyer of immense energy and talent and with wide cultural interests, was a major figure in the establishment of English Protestantism, achieving his highest office in the reign of Elizabeth I as her first Lord Keeper of the Great Seal. At his death his eminence was recognised with a magnificent funeral and a burial place in St Paul's cathedral next to the tomb of John of Gaunt.[8] He had two families: his sons by his Suffolk-born first wife Jane Ferneley (d. 1552) were Nicholas II (*c.* 1540–1624), Nathaniel (1546?–1622) and Edward (1548/9–1618), and sons by his brilliant and forceful second wife Anne Cooke (*c.*1528–1610) were Anthony (1558–1601) and the famous philosopher-lawyer Francis (1561–1626). Lord Keeper Bacon at first envisaged Redgrave as one of his principal residences, along with a house nearer the capital, Gorhambury House. Redgrave was the house which his eldest son, also Nicholas [II], inherited on his death; his younger son Nathaniel was set up in the very idiosyncratic house which the Lord Keeper built at Stiffkey in Norfolk, while Edward established himself at Shrubland Hall near Ipswich after being married to the heiress of Shrubland.[9]

In his last years, Lord Keeper Bacon chose to spend most of his time at Gorhambury, and he had too many sons and too much affection for them to allow his great estates throughout the south-east of England to remain as a unit. He gave the three sons of his first marriage a rigorous training in the running of county affairs, and they all remained country squires of distinctly Puritan outlook, a great contrast to their alarmingly talented younger half-brothers Anthony and Francis. The eldest, Nicholas II, although achieving the honour of becoming Premier Baronet of England in James I's reign, was probably something of a disappointment to his father, not the material for a statesman and sometimes dilatory in doing what the Lord Keeper saw as his duty, as several letters reveal. Nathaniel did rather better, inheriting his father's capacity for hard work and attention to detail, and possessing a sense of duty which made him one of the leading administrators of Elizabethan Norfolk. Edward was also lacking in exceptional qualities, but they all played their part in the Puritan oligarchy which over several generations dominated East Anglian politics from the 1570s through to the Restoration of Charles II.[10]

In 1591 Sir Nicholas Bacon II built a further mansion nearer Bury St Edmunds, Culford Hall, replacing a house which he had acquired for himself after his father's death; this move to acquire a second home in the same county was throughout the kingdom characteristic of energetic gentry families with designs on local power, and it was undoubtedly connected to Bacon's own ambitions in local government, reflecting his wish to be prominent among the leading gentry of the Bury area who ran the Liberty of St Edmund (the administrative unit which survived until 1974 as the separately administered county of West Suffolk). No doubt Sir

---

8   Simpson, *Wealth of the gentry*, pp. 1–139, is a concise biography and economic study of Bacon, and see also MacCulloch, *Suffolk*, index refs. *s.v.* Bacon, Sir Nicholas (d. 1579), and R. Tittler, *Nicholas Bacon: the making of a Tudor statesman* (1976).

9   A.H. Smith, 'The gardens of Sir Nicholas and Sir Francis Bacon: an enigma resolved and a mind explored', in A. Fletcher and P. Roberts (eds.), *Religion, culture and society in early modern Britain* (1994), pp. 125–60, and A.H. Smith, 'Concept and compromise: Sir Nicholas Bacon and the building of Stiffkey Hall', in C. Harper-Bill, C. Rawcliffe and R.G. Wilson (eds.), *East Anglia's history: studies in honour of Norman Scarfe* (Woodbridge, 2002), pp.159–89. See also *ODNB*, *s.v.* Bacon, Sir Nathaniel.

10 MacCulloch, *Suffolk*, pp.102–3.

Plate 2: *The tomb of Sir Nicholas Bacon, first baronet, who died in 1624, in Redgrave parish church. This outstanding monument was by Nicholas Stone and Bernard Janssen and made in Sir Nicholas's lifetime, as the inscription emphasises, together with his distinguished descent from Bures and Butts. He lies in armour, clearly proud both of his knightly ancestry on his wife's side, and of his military service to his country, which is nevertheless revealed in letter 103 [4150] as not always what it should have been. Reproduced by kind permission of the National Monuments Record: CC65/34D.*

Nicholas felt that it was a good match cementing his family more firmly into this group when also in 1591–2 he arranged the marriage of his eldest daughter Anne (1572–1624) to Robert Drury of Hawstead, just outside Bury St Edmunds. Robert Drury (1575–1615) was a young man of military inclinations from a family of far greater antiquity among the Suffolk gentry than the Bacons. He was among the clients of the queen's erratic favourite the earl of Essex, who knighted him in the same year of 1591 during the English campaign in France. Like many in the Essex circle, Drury was a fashionable young man with financial problems, in his case inherited from his soldier-administrator father. Relations with his father-in-law eventually proved tense: during his years of military campaigns in the 1590s, the new Lady Drury spent much of her time living with her father at Culford. Later she settled down with her husband and there is every sign in this correspondence that the marriage eventually became a happy one.[11]

Sir Robert Drury died in 1615, and his widow did not remarry; they had no surviving children. She died on 5 June 1624, and her executors were her brothers

---

11 On the politics of the purchase of Culford, MacCulloch, *Suffolk*, pp. 40–41; on the marriage, Storey, 'Culford Hall', pp. 108–12.

Sir Edmund Bacon and Nicholas Bacon III; hence her papers ended up in the Bacon archive at Redgrave.[12] Lady Drury's younger brother Nathaniel Bacon (ninth son of the family and an artist of real talent) was given Culford Hall as a marriage portion when in 1614 he married Jane Meautys, the widow of Sir William Cornwallis, and it was to the Cornwallis family that Culford was to pass on Nathaniel's death without living issue. Redgrave therefore reverted to being the capital mansion of Sir Nicholas Bacon II, and he was buried in the parish church there in 1624 with a sumptuous monument which still remains (see Pl. 2).[13] The later letters in the sequence relate to his son and heir Sir Edmund Bacon and to his successors at Redgrave, ending with a small number of early eighteenth-century items which postdate the sale of the Redgrave estate to Sir John Holt.

It cannot be claimed, then, that this is a continuous record of the inhabitants of Redgrave Hall through the two-century span of the collection. It represents no more than a series of snapshots of one of Tudor and Stuart Suffolk's great families; but these are precious fragments indeed, considering how much has been lost from the private archives of the county during this period. The letters have here been arranged to form a sequence from the Bacon Collection MSS **[4054–4307]**, and this edition includes one further stray, here numbered as **7 [4487]**, so overall the sequence has been renumbered as letters **1–261.** One other document described in the *Bacon handlist*, no. **4363**, as a letter from John Jurdon to Roger Jurdon, is not in fact a letter, but an extract of the will of Roger Jurdon, and so has not been included in the edition.

THE MAKE-UP OF THE PRESENT COLLECTION

1–4, 6, 8 [4054–4058, 4060]: Early fragments

The first few letters represent strays from archives of the predecessor estates of the Bacon family, particularly the Bures estates which passed into the Butts family and came to the Bacons through the marriage of Sir Nicholas Bacon II, the first Baronet, to Anne Butts (d. 1616), daughter and heir of Edmund Butts of Thornham, Norfolk, and of his wife Anne (d. 1609), daughter of Henry Bures of Acton, Suffolk.[14] It is possible that if letter **2 [4055]** does form part of the original Redgrave collection as it arrived in Chicago in 1925, the Bacons had found it among these earlier archives, or had even noticed it among the collections of friends of theirs in a completely different archive. They may have kept or acquired it because they were interested in the name Edmund Bacon, and hoped that he might be an ancestor to boost their distressingly recent status as gentlemen.

Certainly Sir Nicholas Bacon II was particularly conscious of the importance of his descent from two ancient East Anglian families, Butts and Bures. He stressed this descent prominently on the tomb which he erected to himself and his Butts heiress wife in his own lifetime; such genuinely ancient gentility provided him with more convincing reasons to lie on his tomb in the full armour of a knight than might be provided by the spectacular legal career of his father (see Pl. 2). One wonders whether the survival of the magnificent medieval Bures monumental brasses in the Suffolk parish church of Acton through all the storms

---

[12] Bald, *Donne and the Drurys*, p. 156.
[13] Storey, 'Culford Hall', pp. 113–27.
[14] *ODNB, s.v.* Bacon, Sir Nicholas.

of the Reformation was thanks to the solicitude of the Bacons, who for more than a century were at the heart of the Puritan county establishment which was not otherwise favourably disposed towards relics of a popish past. It is noticeable that Sir Nicholas Bacon II provided his mother-in-law Anne Butts with a brass at Redgrave whose magnificence is unusual for a brass of the late sixteenth century, and may be a deliberate gesture of emulation to the brasses of her ancestors by marriage preserved at Acton.

5–13 [4059, 4487, 4061–64]: Correspondence of Nicholas Bacon I relating to government financial business
In 1540 Nicholas Bacon, the rising lawyer who was already marked out as a member of the evangelical and largely Cambridge-educated clique who were taking an increasingly prominent role in royal administration, became solicitor of the Court of Augmentations. This was the government department responsible for dealing with the windfall of property coming to the Crown as a result of Henry VIII and Edward VI's dissolutions of monastic houses and chantries; the appointment gave plenty of opportunities for personal profit, so it was central to his developing prosperity, taking him far beyond his already profitable private career as a lawyer. He bought Redgrave in 1545 and soon began replacing the decayed grange-house of the Bury monks, ruthlessly exploiting redundant ecclesiastical buildings both then and during the reign of Edward VI, to the extent that during Edward's reign he even cannibalised redundant altar-stones from local parish churches for his new home.[15] In 1547 he had become Attorney of the Court of Wards and Liveries, giving him another opportunity for massive profit, because the Court used the feudal rights of the Crown to exploit the estates of those who were royal tenants-in-chief and who had inherited their estates while still minors. Despite his evangelical convictions, he retained his office through the reign of Catholic Queen Mary, as is demonstrated by letter **12 [4064]**: his usefulness to the Crown outweighed his commitment to a Protestantism which the queen would have found obnoxious, and like his evangelical brother-in-law the future Elizabethan statesman William Cecil, he chose to keep quiet about his religious outlook in these difficult years. The major theme of the letters is official financial business relating to East Anglia; letter **7 [4487]** provides a rare glimpse of the administrative arrangements for the dissolution of a religious house, in this case the major chantry college at Wingfield.

14–29, 31–35 [4066–4082, 4084, 4086–88]: The projected marriage of William Yaxley, 1565–67
This sequence of letters takes us to the years in which Nicholas Bacon I's career had reached its apogee, and documents one of his few unsuccessful schemes. One of the architects of the Protestant religious settlement of 1558–9, Bacon had been knighted by Queen Elizabeth and made Lord Keeper of the Great Seal, a substitute title for Lord Chancellor of England, in tacit recognition that his humble origins made the title of Lord Chancellor socially inappropriate. Now from 1565 he was engaged in a scheme for a marriage alliance between his youngest daughter Elizabeth and a wealthy young Suffolk gentleman from a rather longer-established family, William Yaxley, whose wardship he had in effect sold to himself around

---

[15] Simpson, *Wealth of the gentry*, pp. 46–56.

the time of his departure from the Court of Wards.[16] The Lord Keeper was clearly enthusiastic for this scheme and cherished it closely: in letter **23 [4075]** he refers to it as 'this maryage with me'! His instructions to his servants Francis Boldero and George Nunn (letters **24** and **26 [4077** and **4079]**) sound distinctly reminiscent of the instructions to ambassadors which litter the State Papers of Tudor monarchs.

The marriage might have seemed an obvious dynastic match: like the new Bacon dynasty at Redgrave, the Yaxleys were a self-made family of East Anglian lawyers, albeit from a couple of generations before the Bacons, and they were near neighbours at Yaxley Hall. The new problem which lurks behind this correspondence, even though significantly never articulated in it, was religion. While Bacon was one of the symbols of the new Protestant regime created by the Elizabethan Settlement of religion, William Yaxley's surviving widowed mother Margaret and his aged uncle Miles Spencer, archdeacon of Sudbury, were clearly religious traditionalists, hostile to the developing Reformation – Spencer, indeed, was the chief surviving obstacle to the furtherance of Protestant reformation in the diocese of Norwich up to his death in 1570.[17] It was probably principally because of religion that the negotiations failed: Mrs Yaxley and the formidably devious Archdeacon Spencer proved a match for one of the most acute legal brains in Tudor England. Looking through the correspondence, one wonders whether the real aim of William Yaxley's relatives was to spin out the marriage negotiations until Yaxley was of age, at which time Bacon as his legal guardian could no longer get the advantage of his marriage elsewhere if a Bacon marriage deal did not prove successful.

30, 33, 36–88 [4083, 4085, 4089–4139]: Correspondence between Lord Keeper Bacon and the Redgrave household 1567–75
This material forms a fairly continuous sequence which occupies nearly a fifth of the whole correspondence, and it covers a wide range of subjects, ranging from a possible marriage for Lord Keeper Bacon's younger son Nathaniel (letter **36 [4089]**), through improvements to the gardens and estate at Redgrave, to matters of national and East Anglian politics. The letters provide a fascinating witness to the Lord Keeper's attempts to train up his son and heir Nicholas II as a worthy successor to his own talents in domestic and political administration. Letter **72 [4124]** is the first recorded time when a delicate mission with national implications was entrusted to the younger Nicholas Bacon: this was a visit at the end of 1572 to Philip Howard, the eldest son of England's premier nobleman Thomas Duke of Norfolk, who that summer had been executed on charges of high treason. The postman in this mission was no less a figure than the earl of Sussex, and the Lord Keeper told his son to keep the visit discreet. Letter **74 [4126]** provides an example of the younger Bacon being given a letter to read but told to send it on without showing that he had read it.

However, the elder Nicholas's letters frequently betray an impatience with the slowness of his pupil, impatience which on the evidence of the letters is wholly understandable: after all, this was no callow youth, but a Cambridge graduate in his late twenties moving into his early thirties. The first surviving note chiding Nicholas Bacon II for his reluctance to reply in detail and with sufficient care comes in June 1569 (letter **44 [4097]**). Sometimes the details are matters of estate

---

16 Simpson, *Wealth of the gentry*, pp. 84–8.
17 MacCulloch, *Suffolk*, pp. 164, 185.

management. An example of Nicholas II's sloth occurs at letter **54 [4108]**, when in October 1570 arbitrators in a land dispute said that they had not been briefed about the lands in question. Letter **60 [4114]** provides an example of the younger Nicholas's cavalier attitude to the length of time a survey would take. At letter **77 [4129]**, the Lord Keeper is irritated that a wood has been left unfenced: he growls to his servant Francis Boldero that 'It was some fawlt in my sonne and James Vale that I was not advertysed of it before this tyme' – frank words to a servant, who was obviously more trusted than the son.

Worse still, Nicholas junior was also both capricious and lacking in energy in his apprenticeship as a county politician. Letter **73 [4125]** brings a telling-off to him for not being at the assizes. Letter **54 [4108]** provides independent evidence that senior magnates of the county also found the younger Nicholas annoyingly unbusinesslike in his preparation for a legal dispute. The Lord Keeper's brother-in-law William Cecil likewise shared his opinion of the Bacon boys' efficiency: in 1579, trying to sort out problems connected with old Sir Nicholas's will, he wrote stingingly to Nicholas II and Nathaniel that 'I thought my selfe not well used to be differed so longe of some kind of answere' from either of them, and added menacingly that he had 'forborne' to let the brothers' recently widowed mother know about their negligence.[18] Throughout the previous two decades, young Nicholas must have dreaded the words 'I marvel', which in the correspondence always portend some acid rebuke for negligence from the Lord Keeper. However, he might have taken comfort from the fact that on one occasion in the letters **(24 [4077])**, that omnicompetent veteran of Bacon estate management, Francis Boldero, was also on the receiving end of the phrase.

There is only one holograph letter from the Lord Keeper in this sequence, written on the extremely confidential matter of possible line-ups in the county election for knights of the shire (county members of Parliament) when his son Nicholas II had taken upon himself to stand for the county in 1572 (letter **64 [4118]**; see Pl. 3). This is one of the most interesting letters in the whole sequence, providing a rare glimpse of a senior Tudor politician meditating on how to gain the maximum possible advantage from a large parliamentary electorate with its own opinions and agendas. Sir Nicholas's handwriting is an extremely peculiar version of secretary hand, instantly recognisable, and in his later years its lack of development made it extremely old-fashioned by Elizabethan standards. The Lord Keeper's other letters are written by a sequence of clerk/secretaries. At the end of the 1560s (letter **42 [4095]** and thereabouts), he acquired a new clerk, John Osborne of Harkstead (Suffolk), who was noticeably much more up-to-date than his predecessors in punctuation, making liberal use of full stops, capitals and commas. Osborne proved an outstanding secretary who also drew the plans for (and perhaps designed) all Sir Nicholas Bacon I's buildings.[19] In Osborne's hand it is particularly difficult to decide whether to transcribe 'you' or 'ye', and I have not satisfied myself that I have been consistent on this. In letter **43 [4096]** we can witness the evolution of the word 'tawdry' in the clerk's second thoughts on the spelling of the Liberty of St Audrey; might there even be a rare specimen of the Lord Keeper's sense of humour here, provoked by a moment of irritation at the arbitrary action of an officer of that Liberty?

---

[18] See Nicholas's and Nathaniel's letters to the Lord Treasurer, *Nathaniel Bacon papers* II, 77–9, 81–2, and Burghley's letter of reproof, *ibid.*, 93–5. See also *ibid.*, 100–7.

[19] Smith, 'Concept and Compromise', pp. 174–5.

88–129 [4139–76] and some later items: Business correspondence of Sir Nicholas Bacon II and his family, after 1579

There is much more patchy survival in this material dating after the death of the Lord Keeper in 1579, and much of it is to do with legal disputes and administrative business concerned with wills. One of the more interesting items is letter **103 [4150]**, a letter from the deputy lieutenants of Suffolk to their fellow deputy lieutenant Bacon, written at the height of the national crisis in which England was menaced by the Spanish Armada in 1588. In the middle of such an emergency, Sir Nicholas Bacon II seems to be displaying a pointless touchiness about the allocation of troops, and his fellow deputies are having a hard time being polite in the face of such boneheaded behaviour. Letter **125 [4171]** (see Pl. 6) is a valuable letter about the manoeuvring for election to Parliament, this time in 1601, with a hint of trouble in the previous election; once more, as in Lord Keeper Bacon's letter of 1572 (**64 [4118]**), this brief note provides a spotlight on events otherwise unrecorded. Letter **108 [4154]** provides the first introduction to the Drury family. Sir William Drury, who died in 1590 from wounds resulting from a duel fought in France with Sir John Borough, left considerable debts. He had been made receiver of royal revenues in Essex, Hertfordshire, Middlesex and London, and from 1587 had been running into financial trouble as a result of his financial incompetence.[20] His death spelt financial disaster for the consortium of prominent Suffolk knights who were his sureties: Nicholas Bacon II, William Waldegrave, William Spring, Robert Jermyn and John Higham (three of them had also been Bacon's irritated colleagues among the deputy lieutenants of 1588).

From the beginning, Sir Nicholas Bacon II as the young Sir Robert Drury's father-in-law took the leading role among the sureties for Drury's debts, and in the end he assumed the sole liability; Drury came to trust him more than his own mother, now remarried to the Kentish magnate Sir John Scott.[21] Letter **111 [4158]** preserves the anxious atmosphere among the sureties, as Bacon negotiated acrimoniously with the Scotts. In 1592 Sir Robert married Sir Nicholas Bacon II's daughter Anne, and in 1594 an agreement finally secured Bacon Sir Robert Drury's wardship from Sir John Scott, in return for a payment which represented Lady Drury's jointure; from then on, Bacon was in charge of the Drury estates.[22] Further controversies between Bacon and Drury were resolved by the arbitration of Sir John Popham during 1601 (see letter **123 [4168]**: the agreements are Chicago Bacon Collection MSS nos. **4338–4339**). In several items in this sequence of letters (letters **101, 121, 126, 137, 156 [4146, 4170, 4173, 4185, 4204]**), the great lawyer Sir Edward Coke emerges both as professional consultant and long-standing family friend.

For all Sir Nicholas Bacon II's faults, he and his wife and family shared the deep Puritan piety which characterised so many leading East Anglian magistrates, and of which his brother Nathaniel has often been seen as a prime example. Letter **160 [4206]** provides a rather touching example of this piety in action: a letter from the chief inhabitants of the small central Suffolk parish of Wyverston, showing how Sir Nicholas was prepared to give them a say in the choice of their parish minister even though the patronage lay with him alone. He had appointed the

---

[20] *History of Parliament 1558–1603* II, 59.

[21] Bald, *Donne and the Drurys*, pp. 20–23.

[22] *Bacon handlist*, no. **4392**; Bald, *Donne and the Drurys*, pp. 25–26. The 1592 marriage agreements are Bacon Collection MSS, nos. 4390–91, and the 1594 agreement nos. 4321–22.

new minister to preach two trial sermons to the villagers, and the villagers (some signing with marks only) wrote to Sir Nicholas to signify their approval of the candidate's performance in the pulpit. However nominal the villagers' consent might have been, this was an example of Reformed Protestantism in action, an acknowledgement of the principle that a godly congregation, however humble, should have a say in the choice of a godly minister alongside the upper ranks of society. John Calvin would have approved of the careful mixture of aristocracy and democracy to which the letter gives witness. This is not the only instance of such action in the Bacon family, and one wonders whether it might reflect the practice of Lord Keeper Bacon in the previous generation. There are two recorded instances of Nicholas II's brother Nathaniel giving the inhabitants of Norfolk parishes in his patronage the choice of a new minister, at Whissonsett in 1606 and Hemsby in 1616.[23]

130–38, 147–84 [4178–4187, 4196–4230]: Business and personal correspondence of Sir Robert and Lady Drury, 1604–1621

By 1607 Sir Robert Drury had gained complete control of his troubled inheritance, and had escaped the burden of debt left him by his father. The tensions which had threatened his marriage also seem to have gone with the resolution of his quarrels with his father-in-law, and the tone of his correspondence with his wife is of close and relaxed affection.[24] He became a leading courtier, a familiar presence at the court of James I. It is in this sequence of letters that we find the greatest interaction in the collection between local affairs and national politics, and R.C. Bald has ably placed these fragments of Sir Robert's correspondence in the context of other surviving evidence of his political and diplomatic activities. From his father Sir William, Sir Robert inherited a house in the west suburbs of London, near Covent Garden, Drury House, which has given its name to the road passing its entrance gate, Drury Lane.

Once more, despite the Drurys' place in the upper reaches of fashionable metropolitan society, there is much evidence of their continuing close and interested involvement in church affairs. Letters **130–31 [4178–9]**, letters from the East Anglian clergyman Thomas Daynes to Lady Anne Drury, are two specimens of fawning clerical prose which are not calculated to leave the modern reader with a favourable impression of a Puritan clergyman. One wonders what effect they had on Lady Drury. Certainly from now on, we find a growing association between the Drurys and a rather different breed of clergy who (although still firm in their Reformed Protestantism) were much more prepared than Daynes to accept the Church of England as they found it, and who were also clergy of considerable intellectual and literary distinction. The Drurys did indeed turn to the great Puritan seminary of Emmanuel College Cambridge for young star clergy, but these clergy tended to drift from their Puritan roots in their later careers. Lady Drury took the initiative in securing Joseph Hall (1574–1656), Fellow of Emmanuel College Cambridge, for the rectory of Hawstead; he was instituted on 2 December 1601.[25] The future Bishop William Bedell (baptised 1572, died 1642), referred to in letter

---

23 D.J. Lamburn, 'The influence of the laity in appointments of clergy', in *Patronage and recruitment in the Tudor and early Stuart Church*, ed. C. Cross (Borthwick Studies in History 2, York, 1996), p. 107.

24 On the improvement in his fortunes, Bald, *Donne and the Drurys*, p. 33, and on marriage tensions, pp. 31, 49.

25 Bald, *Donne and the Drurys*, p. 50.

130 [4178] when he was rector of St Mary's Bury St Edmunds, was an Emmanuel man and friend to Joseph Hall; Hall's successor at Hawstead, Ezekiel Edgar, instituted 4 July 1608, was also an alumnus of Emmanuel.[26]

Most prominent of all in this collection of clerical luminaries was John Donne (1572–1631), poet, brilliant preacher and in later life dean of St Paul's cathedral. Donne and Sir Robert Drury may have known each other at Cambridge, and certainly through Cambridge they would have had many acquaintances in common, for instance Sir Henry Wotton, who was also a close friend of Sir Robert's brother-in-law Sir Edmund Bacon. The connection seems to have been made by the time of the tragic death of Sir Robert and Lady Drury's daughter Elizabeth in 1609, when Donne seems to have composed verses for her monument which can still be seen in Hawstead church, and he also composed a 'Funeral Elegie' for her which he printed at the end of *The Anatomy of the World* (1611). But R.C. Bald ascertained a longer-standing connection: William Lyly (*c.* 1550–1603), who lived at Hawstead and, according to Joseph Hall, exerted a baleful influence over Sir Robert Drury. He was a long-time double agent in the pay of Sir Francis Walsingham who was active from the 1580s in penetrating the circles of conspiracy among Roman Catholic exiles. He married John Donne's elder sister Anne as her second husband.[27]

After the contact made around the death of Elizabeth Drury, Donne accompanied Sir Robert on his journey abroad in 1611–12 (see letter **150 [4199]**).[28] One of the purposes of this mission was to explore the possibility of a marriage between the Elector Palatine Friedrich V and Princess Elizabeth the daughter of James I, a cause dear to the heart of godly Protestants in England, since the Elector Palatine was one of the chief champions of Reformed Protestantism in central Europe. One surviving letter (**154 [4202]**) refers to the time which the Drurys spent at the electoral court at Heidelberg, soon to be destroyed in the catastrophe which overtook the Elector Palatine in the Thirty Years' War. The marriage which resulted from this embassy was one of the turning-points in British history: from it, after many misadventures and turns of fortune, sprang the royal line which took the British throne in 1714 in the person of George I.

There is much of miscellaneous interest in this correspondence, which becomes particularly full around the time of Sir Robert Drury's death in 1615. The Drurys were great enthusiasts for horses, which would have endeared them to that enthusiastic patron of Newmarket, King James I; letter **163 [4209]** illustrates particularly well the care which horses received, especially since they were going to enable Sir Robert to make a good showing in the royal hunt at Royston. Letter **153 [4201]** is of particular importance, since it is the most detailed description known of the last illness of that major statesman of late Elizabethan and Jacobean England, Lord Treasurer Robert Cecil, earl of Salisbury, son to Lord Keeper Bacon's close colleague and brother-in-law William Cecil Lord Burghley. It gives a good idea of the horrors and futilities of contemporary medicine, even for someone so favourably placed as the Lord Treasurer of England. A source of horror in a different fashion in these seventeenth-century letters is provided by examples of the characteristic vile writing hand of lawyers, for instance Robert Mawe (letters **109**

---

[26] Bald, *Donne and the Drurys*, pp. 51–2, 64. On Bedell and Hall, see *ODNB*.

[27] Bald, *Donne and the Drurys*, pp. 69–84.

[28] Surviving correspondence from Drury and Donne from this journey preserved elsewhere is described in Bald, *Donne and the Drurys*, pp. 89–103.

[see Pl. 4], **116 [4157, 4163]**) and Serjeant John Godbold (**207 [4253]**), not to be outdone by some clerics like Richard Brabon (**171, 176 [4217, 4224]**). It is worth noting that Brabon felt nothing odd in larding his letters to Lady Drury with Latin tags and phrases: evidently the high level of education which the old Lord Keeper and his wife Lady Anne had so prized two generations before was still maintained in the Bacon line.

139–46 [4188–4195]: Correspondence relating to Charles Gawdy, 1608–1609
This small group is a single file of papers. Charles Gawdy, the son of Sir Bass-ingbourn Gawdy (the younger of two Bassingbourn Gawdys) of West Harling, Norfolk (1560–1606) was a close relative of the Bacons: his father had married Dorothy Bacon, Sir Nicholas Bacon II's daughter, as his second wife and on Sir Bassingbourn's death, he became a ward of Sir Nicholas Bacon between 1606 and 1610, having lands devised to him by the will of his grandfather (and no doubt also godfather) Sir Charles Framlingham of Debenham.[29] The letters of young Gawdy, which are his apprenticeship in budgeting, requesting funds from his guardian for various purchases, are in the naïve italic hand and poor spelling of a teenager, and his grasp of finance is also painfully adolescent. Some of the letters reveal that he had exhausted the sympathy of tradesmen in Bury St Edmunds. In the tart words of the Gawdy family's latest biographer Joy Rowe on the marriage of Bassingbourn Gawdy to Dorothy Bacon, 'The six children of this marriage inherited less of their mother's family's sobriety and financial acumen than of the high spirits and improvidence of their Gawdy relations.'[30]

185–244 [4231–90] and some earlier items: Correspondence relating to Sir Edmund Bacon, 1623–49
Sir Edmund Bacon succeeded his father Sir Nicholas II at Redgrave in 1624 as second Baronet. It is a peculiarity of Sir Edmund that all the letters we have addressed from him, for instance **179, 185, 189, 196 [4220, 4231, 4235, 4244]** are holograph, even though they are a mixture of personal and official business of varying levels of importance. Why did he not trust a secretary? By contrast, it is interesting in letter **188 [4234]** to see a very aged Suffolk Puritan magnate, Sir John Higham (who was probably in his nineties when the letter was written in 1626), employing a secretary who adopts the latest letter-writing layout. The Uriah Heep-like spelling of 'umble' from the Drurys' London supplier of groceries, wine and liveries, Richard Elton (letters **195, 203, 204 [4241, 4249, 4250]**), probably arouses the wrong resonances in us.

Within this section of letters, **157 [4186]** and **206–44 [4252–4290]** represent correspondence beginning in 1638 relating to the Hungate and Caesar estates, with one earlier letter from Lady Anne Caesar. Lady Caesar, by birth one of the family of Woodhouse of Waxham in Norfolk, was granddaughter to Lord Keeper Bacon and still much involved with the Bacon family; she was successively widow of Henry Hogan and William Hungate. She then married the distinguished lawyer Sir Julius Caesar (baptised 1558, died 1636) as her third husband (and his second wife) in 1615, about a fortnight after the death of Sir Robert Drury; the bride

---

29 *Bacon handlist*, nos. **4404–7**, are a set of accounts by Sir Nicholas Bacon for this wardship. Sir Charles Framlingham's will is TNA (PRO), Prerogative Court of Canterbury wills 49 Scott, f. 79.
30 *ODNB, s.v.* Gawdy Family.

was given away by her uncle, the great lawyer Sir Francis Bacon.[31] The family servant George Gardiner's endorsements of this batch of letters (letter **206 [4252]** onwards), shows that they must have been examined and arranged in 1648; they are not always correctly dated in these endorsements. There was reason enough to sort out this correspondence carefully, since it related to family quarrels about property, particularly in their Essex estate of Fremnalls in Downham, which involved Sir Edmund Bacon and the Woodhouses.

The legal complications of administering the Caesar estates were overtaken and made much worse by the outbreak of civil war in 1642, as is evidenced by the troubles of Richard Humphrey, facing the exactions of the Essex County Committee in 1643 (letter **211 [4257]**). It cannot have been enjoyable for Sir Edmund and the Woodhouses to have to cope with the complaints of the Humphreys and Caesars, however justified, as East Anglia slid into war around them during 1643. Worse still is the situation depicted in letters **236–37 [4282–83]**, where the sudden outbreak of the second English Civil War in 1648 and the upheavals surrounding the siege of Colchester suddenly imperilled the already tangled legal situation at Fremnalls: stock on the ground there might be confiscated as the rebellion was suppressed.

245–61 [4291–4307]: Correspondence relating to the heirs and successors of Sir Edmund Bacon, 1651 onwards

Sir Edmund the second baronet died on 10 April 1649 without issue and was succeeded as third baronet by his brother Robert, who died in December 1655.[32] Some of the correspondence (**246–51 [4292–97]**) concerns the sale of the manor of Foxearth in Essex, that property which had passed from the Bures family to the Butts and then the Bacons, and symbolised their chief claim to ancient lineage, to pay the debts and anticipation of expenditure on forthcoming legacies of Sir Robert. The third baronet is the last of the Bacons to be represented directly in the correspondence. The fourth and last baronet of the senior Redgrave Bacon line, Sir Edmund, succeeded his grandfather the third baronet Sir Robert in 1655, Edmund's father Robert having died in the lifetime of Sir Robert. With Sir Edmund's death in 1685 the fourth baronet had no heirs male of his body to inherit, for in a degree of tragic loss astonishing even by seventeenth-century standards of infant mortality, all his six sons had predeceased him, as had two of his six daughters.[33] The baronetcy was inherited by Robert Bacon of Egmere (Norfolk), grandson of the third baronet through a younger son, and this fifth baronet died in 1704. Evidently with his home in Norfolk, Sir Robert had no especial attachment to or use for Redgrave Hall, and before his death he sold the property to Lord Chief Justice Sir John Holt; Redgrave passed for ever from the possession of the Bacons. Nor does Sir Robert seem to have had enough interest in the Bacon family's illustrious Tudor and Jacobean past to sort out and retain anything but

---

[31] Bald, *Donne and the Drurys*, p. 156; *ODNB*, s.v. Caesar, Sir Julius.

[32] Genealogical information in this paragraph is conflated from G.E. Cokayne (ed.), *The Complete baronetage* (6 vols., London, 1900–9), I, 2, and P. Townend (ed.), *Burke's peerage, baronetage and knightage* (2 vols., London, 1970), I, 149.

[33] Cokayne and Townend respectively have five sons and ten daughters and six sons and ten daughters. Using the Registers of Redgrave Parish Church and comparing entries there with the account in W. Betham (ed.) *The baronetage of England* (5 vols., London, 1801–5), John Blatchly corrects these variant figures to six and six.

recent family correspondence from among the deeds and legal papers which the new owner acquired in the Hall's muniment room. The final few letters bring the sequence from Redgrave beyond the ownership of the Bacons into the time of the heirs of Sir John Holt.

Note on the Frontispiece and Jacket Illustrations

The splendid image of the Bacon family in front of their home (which I have obtained through the good offices of John Blatchly, and which we reproduce by kind permission of the present owners, Peter and Sarah Holt-Wilson), can be dated to the time of the fourth Baronet, Sir Edmund Bacon and, by considering the children depicted, may be assigned to or around 1676.[34] At this stage no Bacon sons survived, but there were still five daughters alive, and five young women can be seen in the painting. The grouping before the house seems to centre in the foreground on Sir Edmund on horseback: with his right hand he gestures an order to a figure also on horseback and holding a falcon, perhaps a steward – for by now there was no son and heir to portray. A servant restrains a greyhound behind the second figure's horse.

Slightly further back two bare-legged children have a picnic, not altogether under the eye of the family chaplain and rector of the parish. With the series of deaths of sons, there seems to be no time at which two sons could thus be depicted, and it is likely that these are two small daughters. Philippa and Jane Bacon were respectively aged four and three in 1676, the latter dying that August. Behind the chaplain stand arrayed three females who appear to be older daughters, all dressed in blue. These should correspond to Frances, then aged 16, Elizabeth, aged 9, and Susannah, aged 8. They are confronted on the right-hand side of the picture by an older woman in black. One would normally expect such a figure to be a widow, perhaps a grandmother, but given the number of deaths of children which Lady Bacon had experienced, we may suppose that this is intended to represent her. Indeed, the picture may be intended as a family commemoration of the death of little Jane in 1676, which would explain the mourning garb of her mother. Lesser figures, the most humble of which rather puzzlingly takes the absolute foreground before the baronet, cannot be identified.

The house itself, apart from the outer balustrade and gateway to the court-yard which appear seventeenth-century, is shown much as its Tudor builders left it, displaying all the strict symmetry which always characterised Lord Keeper Bacon's building. This regard for centrally presented designs was clearly deliberate on his part, and may reflect his humanist insistence on the importance of avoiding extremes, expressed in his distinctive choice of family motto, *Mediocria firma* – 'strength lies in the middle ground'.

The statue of the 'Water-Bearer' stood in front of Redgrave Hall even after its rebuilding. It is likely to have formed part of the garden layout which Lord Keeper Bacon was creating at Redgrave in the late 1560s (see **37 [4090]**), because water displays and canals, built with the advice of the experienced creator of such ensembles Edmund Withipoll of Ipswich, comprised a prominent feature of the layout. The statue appears in the 1676 picture of the old Hall, amid the trees on the left and near the single-storey building on that side: it was no doubt moved into a new position at the time of the eighteenth-century rebuilding.

---

34 Here I am particularly indebted to Dr Blatchly for his detective work on the dating of the picture.

Genealogical Table of the Bacon Family

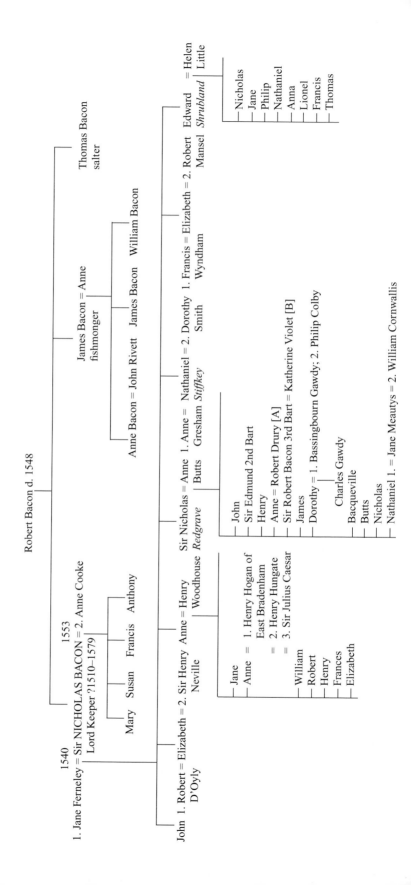

[A] 1. William Drury of Hawstead = Elizabeth, daughter of Sir William Stafford = 2. Sir John Scott of Nettlestead

ROBERT = Anne Bacon

Elizabeth Drury d. 1609

Elizabeth = William Cecil

Frances = 1. Nicholas Clifford
2. Sir William Wray of Glentworth

[B] SIR ROBERT BACON 3rd Bart, d. 1655 = Katherine Violet

Robert

Philippa

Sir Edmund 4th Bart, d. 1685 = Elizabeth daughter of Sir Robert Crane of Chilton, d. 1690

They had six sons who died without issue and six daughters, two dying without issue

Editorial Methods

The letters are presented in chronological order where known or ascertainable, with my own numbering 1–261, which means that sometimes they do not strictly follow the sequence of numbering in the Chicago listing. After the number assigned them in this edition, the Chicago piece number is given in square brackets. A full list of the letters with my numbering, the Chicago piece-numbers and the relevant page-numbers in this edition is given below on p. 3.

To secure as much uniformity as possible with A. Hassell Smith's and Gillian M. Baker's *The papers of Nathaniel Bacon of Stiffkey*, broadly similar rules of transcription and a similar set of symbols and editorial conventions have been adopted here. I extend my thanks to the editors for their generous permission to reproduce a version of their explanatory text on these matters.

DATES in headings are given in New Style as far as it concerns the division of the year, but left in Old Style for 1 January to 25 March in transcriptions of text. Headings for letters from continental Europe give the Old Style/New Style equivalent dates where known.

ORIGINAL SPELLING has been retained in all full transcripts, with the following exceptions: the modern use of *i* and *j* has been adopted, and the final *j* in occasional words has been transcribed *i*; the modern use of *u* and *v* has been adopted; y^e has been transcribed *the*; and *lettre* and its various abbreviations have been transcribed *letter*.

CAPITALISATION has been modernised. Initial *ff* has been transcribed *F*, or in mid-sentence *f*, and in certain abbreviations, e.g. *Norff*, *ff* has been transcribed *f*. (Note: in specific cases where the sense could be in doubt, upper case has been used, e.g. Act, Court, Bench, Hundred, etc.)

PUNCTUATION has been added or deleted where the sense of the text would otherwise be in doubt.

DOCUMENTS IN LANGUAGES OTHER THAN ENGLISH have been provided with a summary indication of content in translation.

LATIN QUOTATIONS AND OTHER NON-ENGLISH WORDS, shown in italics in the English texts, have been translated in a footnote where it will assist reading.

FORENAMES AND SURNAMES have been transcribed in all cases and have not been modernised. Abbreviated Christian names have been extended except in cases where the abbreviation is ambiguous (e.g. *Edw.* could be Edward or Edwin) and the identity of the person is in doubt. Initials have been retained in all cases.

PLACE-NAMES have been transcribed in all transcripts and in passages quoted from documents which have been summarised. If necessary, the modern equivalent has been placed in square brackets after the name. Place-names have been modernised in calendars.

ARABIC NUMERALS have ordinarily been used in all cases, with no indication of instances where the original used Latin numerals. (Note: in dates *th* has been omitted as has the superior *o*.)

ADDRESSES have been abbreviated to omit such common phrases as *give these with speed* or to omit *Suffolk* when a place-name is also given. Omission marks have not been used in the transcription of addresses.

SUSPENSIONS AND CONTRACTIONS have normally been expanded and modernised, with the following exceptions: where the extension is in doubt; where the abbreviation is continued into modern usage, for example *etc., viz., gent., esq., St*; the superior letters denoting amounts of money which have been transcribed £ *s d* and placed on the line; apparently meaningless abbreviation signs, usually associated with *ll*, *m* or *n* at the end of words, which have been disregarded. The abbreviated form '*acon*' at the end of words such as 'comendacon' has been expanded as '*ation*', e.g. 'commendation'. Sir Nicholas Bacon I frequently uses an idiosyncratic 'z' form of final 's' which has been transcribed 's'.

It has not always proved possible, however, to avoid inconsistencies in the expansion of suspensions and contractions. In general, the principle has been followed that where the addition of a letter (or letters) will help the reader (i.e. if it conforms to modern usage or will not distort the sense or pronunciation of a word), it has been added; if the addition of a letter will serve only to confuse the reader, the abbreviation has been disregarded.

> e.g. *hono^r* has been transcribed *honour*
> BUT *cont^{r}y* has been transcribed *contry*, i.e. country; *com'ission* has been transcribed *commission*; *com'pany* has been transcribed *company*; *cañe* has been transcribed *canne*; *fam'e* has been transcribed *fame*.

& has been transcribed *and* (in English) or *et* (in Latin or Norman French).

M^r has been transcribed *Mr* (as the point in time at which *Mr* becomes a title in its own right – as opposed to Master – seems to lie somewhere in the reign of Queen Elizabeth I),
BUT *M^{rs}* and *M^{res}* have been transcribed *Mistres*.

Symbols and Conventions

* *	indicates words which have been inserted.
** **	indicates words which have been inserted within an insertion.
~~words, text~~	indicates words which have been deleted.
/	indicates the conclusion of a marginal annotation.
«»	indicates period within which an undated manuscript must fall, e.g. **10 March 1580/1 «» 1584**.
italics	indicates editorial comment outside the text.
[*italics*]	indicates editorial comment within the text.
[*sic*]	draws attention to mistake in the text.
[*?*]statute	indicates doubt about the transcription of a word or number.
[*word illegible*]	indicates a word that cannot be read.
[*word deleted*]	indicates a deleted word that cannot be read.
[the other]	indicates missing words (through damage to MS) which have been supplied, or the elucidation of doubtful words.
[?the other]	as above, but there is doubt about the first word (no space between question mark and following word).
[? the other]	as above, but there is doubt about both words (space between question mark and following words).
[*? two words*]	indicates missing words that cannot be supplied.
[*and*] the lo[*r*]ds	indicates words or letters omitted in MS which have been supplied.
[ ]*f[ff]*.	indicates numbers of folios in an individual item after its transcription.
< >	indicates a letter in the Redgrave collection omitted and briefly calendared here, since it is printed in the *Nathaniel Bacon papers*.

Letters
from
Redgrave Hall

1340–1744

University of Chicago, Joseph P. Regenstein Library
Bacon Collection, MSS 4054–4307

The Redgrave Letters, 1–261

Nos. in this vol.	Nos. in Bacon Coll.	Page(s) below	Nos. in this vol.	Nos. in Bacon Coll.	Page(s) below
1–4	4054–7	4	104	4150A	64
5	4059	6	105–8	4151–4	64
6	4058	7	109	4157	67
7	4487	8	110	4155	68
8–9	4060–1	9	111–13	4158–60	69
10	4063	9	114	4162	71
11	4062	10	115	4161	71
12–31	4064–84	11	116–20	4163–7	72
32	4086	26	121	4170	75
33	4085	27	122	4169	75
34–46	4087–99	27	123	4168	76
47	4101	34	124	4172	76
48	4100	34	125	4171	77
49–67	4102–21	35	126–31	4173–9	78
68	4121A	46	132	4181	82
69–70	4122–3	46	133	4180	83
71	4123A	49	134–7	4182–5	83
72–7	4124–9	49	138–56	4187–4204	86
78	4129A	52	157	4186	96
79–80	4130–1	52	158	4205	96
81	4138	53	159	4205A	96
182–7	4132–7	54	160–73	4206–19	97
88	4139	57	174–5	4221–2	106
89–90	4139A & B	57	176	4224	107
91	4140	57	177	4223	108
92	4140A	58	178	4225	108
93–7	4141–5	58	179	4220	109
98	4147	60	180–95	4226–41	110
99	4156	61	196	4244	120
100	4148	61	197–8	4242–3	121
101	4146	62	199–261	4245–4307	122
102–3	4149–50	63			

1. **[4054]** *John Malwaryn to Andrew de Bures, 8 September [c. 1340].*[1] *Informs him that he has appointed his servant James Taverner to act as his attorney in land transactions in the manor of Thrandeston and receive dues for the same for the benefit of Malwaryn.*

Honors et reverences, trescher Sieure et amy. Vuillez [s]avoir qe iay ordeigne Jak Taverner mon vadlet per[? *four words*] ycelle p[? *two words*] des parcelles destor abein vif come mors al manoir de Traundeston en manere come il verra mensh' estre pur mon presence et pur receivre les devers de mesme le veie a mon oeps namee ferme et estable ceo qil ferra en mon nom midron des choses suisditz a s'r ceo ieo hu' sa facce une lettre per me. Et S'e vuillez foi et credence a lui doner de ceo qil vous dirra touchauntz les choses suisdites. Treshonore S'e le sance espirit vous eo en garde. Escript a Londres le 8 io'r de Septembr'

Signed: Le v're John Malwaryn. *In secretary's hand?*
Endorsed: A mons'e Andr' de Bures
1 f.

2. **[4055]** *Edmund Bacun to his steward or servant Thomas Gorges [c. 1350].*[2] *Informs him that Thomas de Wytheham has asked him for favour for the rent on which he has been distrained since the death of Lady Beaumond. Orders him to ascertain the amount of the rent in the past and in the future and pardon him eight shillings of it, while taking sureties for the payment of the rest by the coming Michaelmas.*

A Thomas Gorges Edmoun Bacun salutes. S'r sachetes qe Thomas de Wytheham ad taunt parle a moy qe ieo luy ay grauntte sil face grees de la rente pur quoy il est destreint cest ascauver du temps qe la dame de Beaumound fust mortes tauntes qala fin de moun terme qe dounkes luy lirrai en peeses. Dountes ie[o v]ous maunkes qe vous enquersetes cumbien amounteret ceo qest arere et ceo qest avenir pur moun temps. Et de cele summe luy relessetes *8 souses* les queux ieo luy ay pardones et du remenaunt de le denere prise bone seurete pur la quele vous meymes voletes respoundre a payer a la seint Michel prochein avenir. Dounkes la destresce feste sur luy pur cele encheson. Factes del mercr'. Et ceo ne lessetes. Adieux.

In secretary's hand.
1 f.

3. **[4056]** *Lionel Earl of Ulster to John atte More, bailiff or steward of his feudal fees in the counties of Essex, Hertfordshire, Huntingdonshire and Cambridgeshire, 7 April 1361. Note of the homage done by Robert de Bures for the Earl's lands and tenements at Foxearth [Essex], and order that no distress be made on him for those lands.*

---

1   Date suggested in *Bacon handlist*, p. 380, by analogy with material elsewhere in the collection: see especially nos. **2072, 2077, 2080**. **2080** refers to a John Taverner, son of the late Robert Taverner of Bures.

2   Date suggested in *Bacon handlist*, p. 380; the hand is consistent with a mid-fourteenth-century date. It is difficult to find a context for this document, which the Bacons may have acquired because of the surname of one of those named, in their search for respectably ancient ancestry. It may relate to the manor of Witham Parva alias Powershall in Witham (Essex), where a family of Bacon held land in the mid-fourteenth century: see Morant, *Essex* II, 107.

Leone[l fitz] au noble roi lengleterre Conte Dulnestre[3] seign're de Clare et de Connaght a Johan atte More bailiff de nos fees es contees desse[x Her]tford Huntyngdon et Cantebrigge salutes. Pur ce qe mons'r Robert de Bures nous ad fait homage pur terres et tenementes qux il cla[m]e tenir de nous en Foxerth el contee dessex, vous mandons si nulle destress aves pris du dit mons' Robert per celle cause vewes cestes lui facez menctenant deliverer a cestes nos lettres vous eut seront garrant. A dieux. Escr' a nostre Chastiel de Clare[4] le 7 iour daprill lan du regne nostre tresresdoute s'r et pierre le Roi 35te

In secretary's hand.
Addressed: A John atte More Baillif de nos fees es contees dessex Hertford Cantebr' et Hunt'
Endorsed: Mons'r Robert de Bures. [*in sixteenth-century hand*:] Foxherd
1 f.; traces of seal.

4.   [4057] *John Jordon to [?John] Bowde [c. 1521]*[5]

Kosyn Bowde I recomend me on to yow and to Margret y my kensewoman certy-fyeng yow that Master Wynfeld[6] ys kort was the teusday befor May Day and ther the gret stuard and the serveor spake may many gret wordes that Master Wenfeld wold sese yowyr kopy hold and that ye had broke kovinantes with hym and the nexte day after I rode to my master desyryng hym that he wold be good master to yow and me and than he axyt me how I heryt[7] the lond of yow and I scowyt hym that I heryt yt of yow for £9 be the yer, and than he seyd he wold have *the* vantage of the lond for 2 yeres and a half and than I seyd to hym that he had grant the lond to yow fysempyl[8] and be that kovinant and I desyryt hem that he wold be good master to me and that ye xuld nat takyt up so and than he seyd he wold have mony ho of me for he wold nat a byd no lenger and than I desyryt hem that I mout kowe[9] wat xuld plese hym and he axyt me 20 marke. Nevertheless he had £4 of me and yet I cowde nat go throwe with hym for that mony but than he and I a greyt that I and yow xuld waytte on hym at London in hold fystrete the wede-nysday next after the makyng of thys bylle in the mornyng at hys place[10] and ther Master Honfrey[11] to horder the matter a cordyng to ryth and concyens for the recedenc and Sir at the makyng of thys byll *and 4 dayys be for* I was seke and desesyt that I may nan reyde nether well go and ther for yf yt plese yow to speke with Master Honfrey and hym I trost ye xal be throw with hym and I trost to God I wol be at London with yow be 14 dayys after the makyng of thys bylle and I may

---

3   Lionel was third son of King Edward III, and was only styled Earl of Ulster in right of his wife Elizabeth; in the year after this letter was written, he was created Duke of Clarence in allusion to the Honour of Clare, and he was buried in Clare priory after his death in Italy in 1368: *Complete peerage* XII pt. ii, p. 180.

4   Clare castle, the principal seat of the Honour of Clare, which formed one of the chief possessions of the earl of Ulster.

5   John Bowde of Gunton appears in deeds of 1523 and 1524 concerning Gunton and a lease at Laxfield: *Bacon handlist*, nos. **2390–1**.

6   Probably Sir Anthony Wingfield of Letheringham, lord of the manor of Laxfield: see TNA (PRO), C 1/737/37 for a case of 1534–44 with Wingfield as lord.

7   That is, 'hired'.

8   That is, 'in fee simple'.

9   For 'knowe'.

10   Written over erasure ending 'day'.

11   Sir Humphrey Wingfield.

be heyle. Wretyn at Laxfeld the 8 day of May etc. Jhesu kepe yow, be yowyr frend to hys powyr John Jordon. And Sir yf ye lacke mony for to go throw with hym tyl I kom, and *ye* wol go to hon Mster Master Hodyhorn dwellyng yn Crokelane by Fysstrete and by seynt Magnus ye xal reseyve 4 marke of hym for me by thys bylle that ys with yn we yowyr bylle.

Signed in text as above. Holograph. Memorandum in another hand of receipt of 40 shillings: Memorandum recepta de Johanne Jurdon apud London in domo Roberti Beel 40s.
Addressed: Thys bylle be delyveryt to my ryth welle belovyt cosyn Bowde at the Staple Ynne in Holborn
1 f.; traces of seal.

5. [4059] *Peter Brinkley*[12] *to Nicholas Bacon I, 15 April [1539 «» 1543]*

To his lovynge frynd Mr Nicolas Bakon Bryngkeley sendes lowly gretyng in our Lord.

As consernynge your reqwest derectyd to me by your letters, thus it is that seven yeares past or ther abowtte Thomas Kynge the naturall and eldest sonne of Richard Kynge[13] enteryd and toke poscescion of 14 acres of arable lond which for the terme of 3 score yeares shuld longe to the howse of Babwell, the lond beynge lette to ferme for 14s by the yar, and when those 3 score yeares was expyryd, then to remayne to Candelmas gyld holdyn in Bury for ever, the gylde payng 6s 8d to the seyd howse ons in the yar for ever. Now to assure your mastershippe by what tytle he shuld so do, I know not, but upon May Day in the mornyng when he had so donne he cam to me and shewyd me what he had donne: assurynge me furdermore that neyther I nor my successowrs never to rec' 1d more of the isswys or profettes therof. His occasyon (so far as I can remenbre) *was* upon a serteyn brutte that was spredde abrode in our parteis that all such landes as war gevyn to spirituall usis for ever shuld be grantyd to the Kinges maieste onles the next of the bloode shuld enter therupon before May Day but when I had made suche fryndes that I in the ryth of the howse rec' the yearly rent of 14s and beyng furder assuryd of the contynuance therof for the yeares before expressyd I held my pesse and was content. I suppose that when we war dischargyd ther war to cum at the least 39

---

12 Peter Brinkley was warden of Babwell friary (just outside Bury St Edmunds) at its dissolution in 1539: see *Faculty Office registers 1534–1549*, ed. D.S. Chambers (Oxford, 1966), p. 180. He was thereafter a fellow of Wingfield College until its dissolution in 1542, but he may have gone on living at Fornham, and was serving as parish priest at St James's Bury St Edmunds in 1543, among much other preferment (D.J. Peet, 'The mid-sixteenth century parish clergy, with particular consideration of the dioceses of Norwich and York', Cambridge University Ph.D., 1980, p. 316; G. Baskerville, 'Married clergy and pensioned religious in Norwich diocese, 1555', *English Historical Review* 48 (1933), 57, 215). He was still active at Bury in 1546, taking part in the denunciation of Rowland Taylor (*Acts of the Privy Council of England*, ed. J.R. Dasent, 32 vols. (1890–1907), I, 443). A date in 1543 is most likely for this letter.

13 Richard King, merchant, died on 14 April 1514 and was buried in St Mary's, Bury St Edmunds (BL Lansdowne MS 160, f. 137r); his will was proved on 26 May 1514 (Suffolk Record Office Bury St Edmunds, Bury Wills Liber 1 Hoode). Thomas King of Bury St Edmunds, yeoman, Richard's son, was involved during the 1530s in another dispute over his lands at Great Saxham with the abbot of Bury (TNA (PRO), C 1/836/41). The most likely date for the encounter between Thomas King and Warden Brinkley is the spring of 1536, seven years before 1543, just before the dissolution of the smaller monasteries.

yares.[14] And when yow cum your selff in to our parteis I shall gladly waytte on you and geve furder instruccion as our Lord *knowis* *qui te preservet*[15]

Signed: By your beadman Bryngkeley at Fornham Sanctorum 15 die Aprilis. *Holograph.*
Addressed: To the rythe welbelovyd Mr Nicolas Bakon
1 f.; traces of seal.

6. [4058] *Thomas Gawdy*[16] *to* --------- *[c. 1542]*

After my harty recommendacions thes shalbe to advertise yowe that conservnynge the r matter betwyne Gavell and his mother in lawe ther was an end taken before Sir Roger Townisend, Mr John Gates, yowr brother, Mr Sydney and me and as I suppose Mr Edward Calthrope[17] was ther present wich end was that Gavell shold have the lond and paye his mother 4 markes a yere and tied with such condition that iff she was not payed that she shold reentre. The occacion why it was orderid that Gavell shold have the lond was for that the lond laye well for him and his lond wiche is almost all copyholdlond and as conservnynge the title off the lond ther was broughte a copy before us at the end makyng off on Fayrechildes hond[18] off that lond wherby it apperid that Gaels [*sic*] father had the inheritaunce off the lond and not his mother and that copy ded agre word for word w't the corte rolle and no raser in it nor yet interlynynge, also who cowld not coniectre what word cowld be put in the corte rolle wher the raser is that cowld make any title to this Gavell or any taile off the lond to his fathers mother, furder this Gavell seythe that this lond shold be on Mr Sydneis londes hys graundfather, wiche lond was gevin to his mother and father in taile. Iff yowe do well marke the corte rolle wherby the lond in variance was grantyd to old Gavell, it apperit that the lond at the tyme off the grant was in the lordes hondes parte off the demeses and never grantyd before that tyme by copy so that therby it doth apper that the said lond was never Mr Sydneys lond and so then he cowld not make any taile theroff and iff yowe loke well uppon the interlinynge off the copy and the place rasid ther can not be put wordes in that place to make a taile off the lond to Gavells father and mother. Sir at that tyme that the end was mad Gavell was contentyd and so he myghte righte well be iff it be trewe that I am informyd off that the lond is clerly worthe £5 by the yere, so that he shold then have clerly 46s 8d yeylie, [*sic*] and I thinke yowe shall perceyve the quietnes off Gavell in this matter and if he hathe taken the pece off the seyd womans husbond he wold have takyn it off the woman also iff he had not

---

14 Brinkley seems to be mistaken that at least thirty-nine years of the sixty-year term of the original gift by Richard were left when Babwell was 'discharged', i.e. dissolved, in 1539; twenty-one years after Richard's death in 1514 would be 1535.

15 'May he preserve you'.

16 Thomas Gawdy of Shotesham, son of Thomas Gawdy of Harleston: lawyer to the Howard Dukes of Norfolk (see his biography in *History of Parliament 1509–58*, II, 199–201). The names in this letter all suggest a strong connection with the Howard estates, so the copyhold concerned is likely to have been on a Howard manor.

17 In 1525 Edward Calthorpe married Thomasine, daughter and coheir of Thomas Gavell of Kirby Cane (Nf.) and widow of Leonard Copledike of Horham (*1561 visitation*, ed. Corder, pp. 143–4). Calthorpe's Gavell relationship may account for Gawdy's dismissive comment.

18 Possibly John Fairchild of Sibton, gentleman, an old Mowbray servant (see TNA (PRO), SP 1/12, no. 48), escheator in 1508–9 and with various subsequent associations with estates of the Howard family (see TNA (PRO), C 1/452/2, and gift of deer from Framlingham Park, BL Additional MS 17745, m. 12).

a mistaken her name wiche I beleve was skarce honest and also he hathe a subpena ageinst the pore woman for the title off the copy hold as I suppose. Sir I shall leve to write any more off this matter to yowe and referre yt to yowr discression and I dowt not Gavell will leighe corrupcion to my charge and that I have had rewardes and giftes off her. I wold yewe knew the habilite off the woman and by my trowthe I never toke any thinge off her but have gevin her mete drinke and logginge when she hath cume to me for the end off that mater. Sir I trust yow and Mr Ascett[19] will take the payne to see my pore howse when yow cume to Howe[20] and iff I maye knowe when yowe shalbe ther I will be w't yowe and at that tyme I trust to declare to yowe my Lord of Norff: mynd[21] for soche londes as Mettingham Castell[22] held off him by copy copy

Signed: by yowr assuerid frinde Thomas Gaudy. *Holograph.*
1 f.

7. [4487] *Sir Richard Rich to Nicholas Bacon I [May 1542]*[23]
Mr Solycytor I requyre yow to repare to the College of ~~Wynkfel~~ Wykfeld and therof to take a surrender to the Kynges use and of al the poss. of the same and to conclude with hym[24] accordyng to suche articles as doe ensue.

Fyrst ye shal dyliver to the Master of the College al the goodes and carttes the corne and hey of [*sic*] *growyng on* the grounde only exceptyd

Item that the seyd master shal dyscharge the Kyng of al dettes except the dett wyche *the* seyd Master and fo'r brothern of the same college[25] doyth ow to the Duke of Suffolk[26] wyche ys not above the some of £30.

Item ye shal apoynt to the Master for hys pencion yerly £20.

Item to 4 of the bretherne ther every of them £5 wherof yow shal apoynt on to serve the cure and he to have £6 13s 4d.

Item that every conduct ther shal have 40s.

Item as concernyng the dyscharge of other officeres the charges therof shal be at the charge of the Master ther

Item ye shall dyliver the ferme and custodye of the howse to Rychard Freston he paying at suche rent as the same beyng out of lease shal be valued at.

Item to survey the poss. therof and to make certif. accordyngly.

Signed: Rychard Ryche. *Holograph.*
2 ff.

---

19 Perhaps Blennerhasset?
20 In Norfolk.
21 Thomas Howard, 14th Earl of Surrey, 8th (3rd Howard) Duke of Norfolk (1473–1554).
22 The college of secular priests at Mettingham castle; this reference in the past tense suggests that the letter should be dated to the dissolution of the college in 1542. Sir Nicholas Bacon eventually purchased the Mettingham estate: the survey which he commissioned of it in 1562, now BL Additional MS 1450, is discussed in E. Martin, 'Mettingham Castle: an interpretation of a survey of 1562', *PSIA* 37 (1989–91), 115–23.
23 This can be dated by the commission to take the surrender of Wingfield issued on 12 May, the surrender itself on 2 June and the commissioners' certificate in Augmentations, 17 June 1542: *Appendix to the Seventh Report of the Deputy Keeper of the Public Records*, App. II, p. 49.
24 The master of the college was Robert Budd.
25 Four brethren (including Peter Brinkley of no. **5 [4059]**) beside the master signed the deed of surrender on 2 June.
26 Charles Brandon, Duke of Suffolk, was hereditary founder of the college.

8. [4060] *Edmund Butts to George Hoye, 19 June 1543*[27]
Goode George Hoye I commende me unto you desyeringe moste hartelie to sende me the £10 which I should borrowe of you, the which to repaie at my daye in the bille specified I shall not fayle by Godes grace. I have here sent unto [*sic*] a bille of my hande for the assuraunce of your money, for the lone wherof I will make you a suffycient recompence as knoweth God whome I pray to have you in keapynge. Written from Fulham by your frend and lover

Signed: Edmund Butt. *Copy: perhaps mid-sixteenth century.*
Memorandum: This bill made the 19th daie of June in the 35th [*sic*] of the reigne of our sovereigne Lord Kynge Henry the VIIIth wytnesseth that I Edmund Butt gent. doo owe unto George Hoye fermor of Acton yn Suffolk the summe of ten powndes sterlinge to be p'd unto the said Hoye or his assignes at Hallomas next comynge. In wytnes wherof I the said Edmund Butt have subscribed the said bill with my owne hande and sette my seale the daie and yer abovewritton.
1 f.

9. [4061] *Hugh Losse to Nicholas Bacon I, 27 September [1545]*[28]
I beseche you good master Solyster that yt wyll pleace you to delyver to the berer herof Thomas Butcher my servaunt £13 6s 8d for the to parcelles that you bought of me a late in Soffocke. To morowe God wyllyng I most pay as moche money as I can make for certeyn landes that I bought a late of the Kyng. You knowe that the seyd 2 parcelles coste me no lesse then you pay, nor I will take nomore of you be cause you arre on of my good fryndes and thus my letter shall be unto you a suffycyant dyscharge for the receyte therof. And thus the holly gost presarve you in your heleth. From Canons[29] this present Sunday beyng 27 of September

Signed: Yowrs to commaund Hugh Losse *Holograph.*
Addressed: To the right worshipfull Master Bacon Solyster of the Kynges courte of Augmentation
Endorsed by Bacon: Lostes acquytance L[30]
1 f.; remains of seal.

10. [4063] *Officials of the Court of Augmentations to Christopher Peyton, Auditor, and John Eyer, Receiver for Suffolk, 26 November 1550*[31]
After right hartie commendations, where there hathe ben delyvered the 13 daye of January in the 37th yere of the raign of our late soveraign lord Kinge Henrye

---

27 George Hoye of Newton, husbandman, first leased the manor of Acton from Henry Bures, Butts' future father-in-law, on 4 April 1525 for fourteen years, at £54 0s 0d *per annum*: *Bacon handlist*, no. **2393**.

28 The date is derived from the reference to the date 27 September as Sunday. This could also apply to 1551, but is fixed as 1545 by the reference to Bacon's solicitorship, which he relinquished on promotion in Augmentations in 1547.

29 In Middlesex: for Hugh Losse as a Middlesex and London gentleman see e.g. *CPR Edward VI, 1550–53*, pp. 141, 405.

30 Initial appears to be a filing mark from the initial of the writer's surname: compare the address of no. **12 [4064]** below.

31 This is an enclosure in the following letter. There are final receipts from Eyer to Bacon for these two consignments of lead, dated 25 April 1553: *Bacon handlist*, nos. **3312–3313**, and see **3315**. For other transactions about Kenninghall lead involving Bacon (1547, 1549) see *Bacon handlist*, nos. **3273, 3033**.

the Eyght[32] by Mr Eyer unto Nicholas Bacon esquier the Kinges Attorney of the Court of Wardes and Lyveries seven foder of the Kinges Majesties leade than remayng [sic] at Redlingfeild[33] in the countye of Suffolk as by a byll indented made betwen you and the sayd Nicholas for the recept of the sayd lead pleynly apperethe; and where there hathe ben delyvered the 8 daye of August in the fyrst yere of our most gracious soveraign Lord the Kinges Majestie that nowe is[34] by Robert Holdiche esquier unto the sayd Nicholas Bacon five foder of the Kinges Majesties leade than remayning at Kenynghall[35] in the countie of Norfolk as by a byll indented made betwen them twoo lykewise appereth, we (havinge respecte and consideration to the tyme of the recepte of the sayd leade and of the price of leade at that present which was after fower poundes a foder and after whiche rate the Kinge solde then commonly to all men) have thought it good by theise our lettres to requier you Mr Receivour to receive of the sayd Nicholas Bacon for all the sayd leade delivered as well by you as by the said Robart Holdiche amounting to twelve foder after the rate of fower poundes the foder, and there withall to require Mr Audytor upon the sight of Mr Receyvours acquittans and this our warraunte to discharge hym of all the sayd leade. And thes our letters shall be unto you bothe a sufficient warraunte for thexecutinge of the effecte herof. And so hartely fare ye well the 26 daye of Novembre 1550

Signed: Your lovynge frendes Rychard Sakevyle Thomas Moyle Water Myldemaye Rychard Goodrick John Gosnold *Copy, appended to no. 4062 below.*
Addressed: To our loving frendes Mr ~~Aud~~ Awdytor and Mr Receyver of the Countyes of Suff. and Norf. and eyther of them
1 f.

11. [4062] *John Eyer to Nicholas Bacon I, 25 October 1554*[36]

Accordyng to your reqwest I send unto you ~~by this~~ withyn this the copye of the warraunt for the recept of the moneye of you dew unto the Quenes Highnes for 12 fother of lead.[37] I confes that I receyved of you for the same £48 according to the tener of the warraunt and the same ys charged and the Quenes said highnes answered therof in myn accompt of the last yer whearof you may be assewered. For your communycation to be had [sic] my Lord Treasorar[38] I refar yt to your owne wisdom. Thus with my moost hartye ~~recomend~~ recommendations to you and good Mistres Bacon your bedfellowe I praye God send you both your gentill hartes desyers. Scribled in greate haste at Burye the 25 day of October Anno 1554

Signed: Yowrs assewerdly John Eyer *Holograph.*
Addressed: To the worshipfull Mr Nicholas Bacon esqwier the Kynges and Quenes Highnes Attorneye of the Court of the Wardes and Lyvereyes
1 f.

---

[32] 1546.
[33] Redlingfield, a former Benedictine nunnery, dissolved in 1537.
[34] 1547.
[35] Kenninghall Palace, confiscated by the Crown from the duke of Norfolk on his arrest in December 1546.
[36] Eyer was receiver of Augmentations and of other Crown revenues in Norfolk, Suffolk, Cambridgeshire and Huntingdonshire from 1542, and became a servant of Bacon in Elizabeth's reign.
[37] See previous letter, no. **4063** in the Redgrave Collection.
[38] William Paulet, Marquis of Winchester.

12. [4064] *Sir Thomas Pope to Nicholas Bacon I, 17 December 1555*[39]

Mr Bacon, it maye pleas you to understand, I ow Mr Waldegrave[40] threscore poundes payable at Cristmas next. Wherfor I requyre yow to paye unto the sayd Mr Waldegrave threscore poundes parcell of the ~~C~~ hundred poundes you owe me and kepe the rest till I wright my lettres to yow for the same. And this bill shalbe your suffycyen[41] discharge in this behalf. And when I send for the £40 rest of the sayd £100 I wyll send yow your bill of £100 or els delvyer not ~~this moneye~~ the £40. And thus fare ye hartely well. Written at ~~h~~ my lodging the 17 of December Anno 1555

Signed: Your assured frend Thomas Pope *Holograph.*
Addressed: To the right worshipfull his assured loving frend Mr Nycholas Bacon esquyer P[42]
1 f.

13. [4065] *Sir Nicholas Bacon I to Sir Edmund Rous, 18 July 1564*[43]

After my harty commendations. These be to signyfye unto you that I am informed by Mr Denny that you have of late commenced suyte ageynst him at the common lawe upon an oblygation of £7 wherin Sir Anthony Denny his father stoode bownde unto you for the warrantyse of sertayne landes which he excanged with you, which landes being graunted to the Duke of Norfolk by acte of parlament, albeyt (as I am credybly informed) you have bene satisfyed by the saide Duke ~~th~~ towching the same landes and have also bene recompensed by Mr Tamworth exec-utor of the sayde Sir Anthony[44] and recompensed besydes by Mr Denny himselfe, yeat not with standing you doe prosecute your sute upon the sayde oblygation as yf no recompence att all had bene made unto you, for redresse wherof suyte hath bene made to me to grawnte an injunction ageynst you for the staye of this suyte uppon the consyderations aforsayde and also by cawse the matter ys depending before me in the Chauncery yeat ~~undetermyned~~ undecyded. Where the saide Mr Denny offeryth to stande to suche order and dyrection as I shall take conserning the same, which injunction neverthelesse I have for some respecte forborne to graunt, and have rather thowght good fyrst by this my letter to signyfye thus mouche unto you, and therewith all to reqwyer you (this information being trewe) that ye will surceasse and forbare any further to procede in your sayde suyte att the common lawe towching the sayde oblygation untill suche time as the cawse may be harde in the Chawncery where ye maye assure yourself of suche order as

---

39 Pope, a long-standing colleague of Bacon's in administration, and leading official of the Court of Augmentations until its dissolution in 1553, was a member of Mary's Privy Council.
40 Probably Sir Edward Waldegrave of Borley (Essex), a long-standing servant of Mary and by now Chancellor of the Duchy of Lancaster.
41 Apparently for 'sufficient'. The letter forms are not clear.
42 Initial appears to be a filing mark: cf. no. **9 [4061]** above.
43 On Rous, a younger son, see *History of Parliament 1509–58* III, 221–2. He had a troubled and unsuccessful career as a speculator in Crown lands. He suffered particularly from his investment in and sharp practice concerning the estates confiscated by the Crown from the Howard dukes of Norfolk in 1547 and regranted to the Howards by Act of Parliament under Mary I. Proceedings in Rous' chancery suit against Henry Denny, heir of Sir Anthony Denny, can be found at TNA (PRO), C 3/54/8.
44 Apparently John Tamworth of Sandon, Essex (see *History of Parliament 1558–1603* III, 474–5), although Tamworth is not named in Sir Anthony Denny's will, PCC 37 Populwell. He may have substituted as executor for Sir Richard Morison.

the justice and equyte therof shall require, lesse elles yf you should refuse so to do uppon the reqwest of this my letter I should be dryven otherwyse to procede therin then I wolde willingly have cawse to do, whereof I truste you ẏ wyll have consyderatyon. And so I byd you hartely fare well from my howse besydes Charingcrose, the 18 July *Anno* 64.

Draft in secretary's hand.
Endorsed: The coppie of my letter to Sir Edmonde Rowse concerning a matter betwene him and Mr Dennye.
2 ff.

14. [4066] *Archdeacon Miles Spencer to Sir Nicholas Bacon I, 26 August [1564]*

My bounden dutie remembred to your honour. I doo perceive that my nece Yaxleye[45] hathe moved the same for the wardshippe of my cousin hir sonne, for that his yeres draweth faste on and his howses in grete ruine and decaye. I understande your Lordshippe dothe suspende youre determination therin till ye be certefied what I woll doo for him; I have departed with a manor of fyftie poundes by yere in revercion after his mowther, and I have fyftie poundes more wherof I have made my will, and disposed part therof to two of hir sisters children whome I finde at schole fatherles and mowtherless, and theie bothe died intestate and theire elder brother warde wherbie no provision was maide for them. Yf yt shall be your Lordshippes pleasure so baselie to bestowe one of your doughters as of him I will revoke that will and make him sure therof after my dethe, which I woulde not doo but onlie to none other but onlie to your Lordshippe for anye his prefermente, humblie besechinge your Lordshippe to be his good Lorde wherebie he maye hereafter be bounden to serve them whome your Lordshippe shall leave behinde yow, as knowethe the holie ghoste who ever preserve your Lordshippe in helthe and honour. At Bowthorpe this 26 daye of Auguste[46]

Signed: Youre Lordshippes poore Oratoure Miles Spencer. *Autograph.*
Addressed: To the Right Honorable Sir Nicholas Bacone knight Lorde Keper of the Greate Seale
Endorsed in Sir Nicholas Bacon I's hand: Mr Spencer to me for Yaxley.
2 ff.

15. [4067] *Miles Spencer to Sir Nicholas Bacon, 16 June 1565*

My humble dutie remembred to your Lordshippe pleased the same to be advertised I have receyved your letters the 8 of Maii wherby I do perceyve that upon the goode hope you have conceyved that my cosyn Yaxley your warde wyll prove an honest man, your L. is contented to mache hym in maryage wyth your yongest dawghter so that ye maye be enformed how liberally hys mother and I wyll deale wyth hym, it may please *you* as I cowthe better lyke of thys mache then any other: so for thadvertysement therof I wyll deale more lyberally with hym then I wuld if he shuld chaunce to marrye wyth eny other as also for that I dought not but your L. wyll stande veraye good L. to the yongman for the goode affeccion

---

45 Margaret daughter of Robert Stokes, widow of Richard Yaxley. Her son was William Yaxley, the subject of the negotations around which this correspondence revolves.
46 *Bacon handlist* reads the date as 27, but that seems incorrect.

hys late father[47] had alwayes unto your L., and for that your L. is desirous to understand my certeyne determynacion of that I wyll bestowe upon hym, it maye lyke your L. I am contented upon conclusion of thys maryage to assure unto hym of landes to descende after my decesse the yerely valure of one hundred poundes in forme folowing that is to enjoye presently after my decease £40, and £50 in reversion after the decease of hys mother, and the rest beyng £10 to hym after the dethe of a nece of myne and her husband who be elder then hys mother. Towchyng the goodenes of hys mother towardes hym I do thynke for the regarde she hathe to your L. she wyll assure unto hym in reversion all her landes. I beseche your L. to accepte thys myn offer in goode parte, beyng sorye that myn habilite is not answerable to the desyre I have to deale more lyberally wyth hym herin: notwyth-standyng I streche my self ferther for your L. sake towardes hym, as I trust your lordshippe wyll thynke, then otherwise I wuld, havyng two kynnesmen of hys as nere allyed to me as he is hym self being orphans whose parentes departed thys lyff intestate, and lefte ther elder brother warde that in case not able to releve them and therfore as I have at myn owne charges thys 8 yeres kept them to lernyng so must I for pytye sake provide to maynteyne them unto the same. It maye lyke your lordshippe the good affeccion ye bere towardes my kynnesman dothe imbolden me the rather to crave your favour to be shewed towardes hym and hys mother. There is one Thomas Hennyng in Colney whyche is a manor of theires and he is a tenaunte to them and a veray troblesome personne to them and to ther tenauntes and some vexacion I susteyne by hym in the same towne, where I have an other manor in the same towne bothe manors hereafter shall come to hym; if it shall please your L. to be the meane to bryng hym to some resonable order to tende to quietnes of her tenauntes and myn and hereafter to the commodite of my cosyn Yaxley who shall God wyllyng be owner of bothe manors. I have sent the particu-lars of the of the [sic] matter to Mr Wyseman[48] to shewe unto your L. and therfore shall not ~~ferther~~ nede ferther to troble you therin. And thus in rememberaunce of my humble dutie to your goode L. I take my leve. From Norwyche thys 16 of June Anno Domini 1565

Signed: Yours [sic] L. humble orator Miles Spencer. *Autograph.*
Addressed: To the Ryght Honorable hys synguler goode Lord Sir Nicholas Bacon knyght Lord Keper of the Greate Seale of England
Endorsed in Sir Nicholas Bacon I's hand: Doctor Spencer for Yaxley.
2 ff.; seal impression.

16.   [4068] *Sir Nicholas Bacon to Miles Spencer, copy [22 October 1565]*[49]
After my harty comendations. This ys to signyfye unto you that having so mete a messenger I have thowght good now at the last to send you answher of your letter dated the 16 of June last. Trewe yt ys that upon suche good hope as I have conceyved of the yonge man, I do intend by Godes grace ~~y~~ to mache him in maryage with my yongest dowghter yf they bothe shall so lyke and you and his mother also. The neyborwoode, the yong mans good dysposytion and yours and his mothers good inclynation to the matter moveth me very moche. And therfore I intend by God his grace to goo throwghe with yt so that you be so good unnckle

---

47 Richard Yaxley.
48 No doubt Edmund Wiseman, servant to the Lord Keeper (see *CPR Elizabeth I, 1558–60*, p. 304).
49 The date is derived from the reference in no. **17** [**4069**].

unto him, and his mother so good mother as I have juste cawse to thinke you wylbe uppon suche understanding as I have r'h'd [sic] from you bothe. By thoffer contayned in your letter *yt apperes* you are very good ounckle unto him and I beholding unto you bycawse as you wryt you are the rather comine to yt for my sake. And yeat I hope as you maye you wyll do better. My desyre ys that I may be advertyse [sic] from you of the names of the landes that you wyll assure unto him and wher they lye, and which of them you wyll assure in possessyon and which in reversyon. ~~methy~~ [deleted word in Bacon's hand: beginning 'methynks'?]

Copy in secretary's hand.
Endorsed by secretary : The coppye of my letter to Mr Doctor Spencer.
1 f.

17. [4069] *Margaret Yaxley to Sir Nicholas Bacon, 20 November 1565*
Wyth suche dutie as to your honour doo aperteyne thes maye be to signifie unto your L. I have recevyed your letters dated the 22 of October, wherin it hath pleased your L. of your mere goodenes to tender my son the mariage of your L. doughter though he be unworthie and where your L. willed me to lett yow understaund the names of the landes whiche I meane to leve to my son if he do marry your L. doughtor. The manor of Bekerton of the cler yearely valur of one hundred markes. The manor of Wygton £6 3s 4d owte which manor is graunted one anuitie of £3 for terme of lyff. The moitie of ~~of~~ the half manor of Sawley of the clere yerely value of £4 10s. The moitie of the half manor of Kyrby with 2 tenementes in Harwoode of the clere yerely value of 51s 4d. Tenementes in Swyndam £6 3s 4d. One tenement called Menthorpe £4 11s 8d. One tenement in Bisshop Burton 28s 4d. Thes be the landes that I have in Yorkeshire. My purchassed landes in Yexley [sic] in the Countie of Suffolk of the clere yerely value of £15 13s 4d, which I mene to leve hym excepte one anuitie of £5 for terme of lyff. Thus I take my leve at your lordshippe levyng to trouble eny further. From Mellys the 20 day of November 1565.

Signed: Your humble oratrix Margret Yaxlee. *Autograph.*
Addressed: To the Right Honorable and her singler goode Lorde Sir Nicolas Bacon knight Lord Keper of the Grete Seale of England
Endorsed in Sir Nicholas Bacon I's hand: Mistres Yaxley letter.
2 ff.; seal impression.

18. [4070] *Miles Spencer to Sir Nicholas Bacon, 4 December 1565*
My humble dewty remembred to your L. Pleseth the same to be advertysed I have recevyed your L. letters of the 22 of October wherby I perceyve the contynunce of your lordeshippes good favour towardes my nephewe wherof I am right glad desiring of God to gyve hym grace to satysfy your Lordyshippes expectacyon. In answer to your lordeshippes seyd letteres he shall have by me after my death in possessyon the manor of Estcarleton thre myles dystant from Norwich of the clere yerly value of £24, he shall have my manor of Colney twoe myles from Norwich wherof I have made estate to a niece of myne and her husbond duryng ther lyves reservynge to me and myn heyers £10 yerly and that he shall have in possessyon imedyatly after my death, and thre poundes I have purchast of a tene-ment in Colney. He hath a manor in the same towne of Colney which ys ~~as good~~ his motheres joynture and so the hole towne hereafter shalbe his. He shall have

14

the Rectory of Eston fower myles from Norwich which ys £10 by yere after my death in possessyon. This ys accordyng to my former letters wherin I promysed that wyth your Lordeshippes dowter he should have in possessyon after my death forty poundes by yere, and in revercyon the manor of Bowthorpe after his mothers death which ys twoo myles from Norwich and in value £52 by yere and also he shall have in revercyon after my neces death and her husbond the revercyon of Colney which ys £10 by yere which ys threscore *poundes* by yere and better in revercyon. So that in possessyon after my death and revercyon yt shall be better then an hundred poundes by yere. I have gyven to hym landes that dyd perteyn to a chauntry holden of ~~my~~ me by copy belongyng to a prebend I have in Yorke accordyng to a statute made the fyrst yere of Kyng Edward the Syxt; they be worth £6 by yere and do adjoyne to other landes that he shall have by his mother ~~th~~ and as I am informed oon Dotton ~~servant~~ *receyvour* to the quenys maiesty hath gyven informacyon in thexchequyr for the seyd landes ageynst me.[50] Yt may please your Lordeshippe the good affeccyon ye seeme to bere to my nephewe doth imbold me the rather to crave ~~your~~ favour to be shewed towardes hym aswell concernyng these chantry landes yff necessyte requyre as also to be so good lord to hym as I have heretofore moved your lordeshippe to helpe hym that he myght have the leete of Colney by lease or fee ferme or eny other meane. And I wylle bere the charges therof, yt ys but 15d by yere. Besechyng your lordyshippe to consydyr myn abylyte and what my doynges have ben to do any better and thys offer ~~make~~ made to be only with your lordeshippes dowter. Thus comyttyng your lordeshippe to the tuycyon of the holy gost who ever preserve your lordeshippe in honour long to contynewe. Att Norwich the fourth day of December 1565.

Signed: Your Lordyshippes humble orator Miles Spencer. *Autograph; text in a legal hand.*
Addressed: To the Right Honorable and his syngler good Lord Sir Nycholas Bacon knyght Lord Keper of the Great Seale of Inglond
Endorsed in Sir Nicholas Bacon I's hand: Doctor Spencers letter.
2 ff.; seal impression.

19. [4071] *Sir Nicholas Bacon I to Nicholas Bacon II, 11 March 1566*

You shall doo well to cause soome care to be taken of your syster that she spend the day well and vertuusly les els whylst she ~~h~~ seekes hur healthe she myght marr hure manners for the amendment of healthe, good dyet and convenyent exercyce ys that that must help. Methynkes yf she ded bestowe every day sum tyme to lern to wryght amonges other thynges yt wer well doone.

The poomp maker shall have hys charges alowyd when so ever he cum but the sooner he cum the better. Yf he shuld be bownd to performe the woork yt wold be understond whether he be of sooche substaunce as a man may trust to hys bond and what you can lern heryn, sygnyfye by your next letter when he cumes upp,

---

50 Spencer was prebendary of Riccall in York Minster from 1510 until his death. See B. Dobson in G.E. Aylmer and Reginald Cant (eds.), *A history of York Minster* (Oxford, 1977), pp. 94–8. These are possibly the lands referred to as the subject of an Exchequer information included the tenement in Petergate in the city of York, late of a chantry in York Minster whereof Christopher Bentley was last chantry priest, parcel of lands granted to Francis Barker as concealed, 16 Aug. 1566: *CPR Elizabeth I, 1563–66*, no. 2625, p. 476.

for because the depthe ys 28 ~~foote~~ *fadome*[51] I fere he shall hardly be able to doo yt well.

There remeynes in my study a booke in the Saxone language wreton in parchment conteynyng the 5 bookes of Moyses. Thys booke I wold have saffly sent up by the next messenger with grete charge that yt be well lookyd unto. Yt lyythe lowe amongst my wreton bookes.[52] Comend me to your mother and to your wyff. Wreton the 11 of Marche 1565 by

Signed: Your father N. Bacon C.S.[53] *Holograph.*
Addressed in italic hand: To my sonne Nicolas Bacon
2 ff.; seal impression.

20.   [4072] *Francis Boldero and George Nunne to Sir Nicholas Bacon I: schedule of lands offered in the Yaxley/Bacon match, 3 January 1567*

Doctor Spencers londes

The mannor of East Carleton by yere clere	£24
The parsonage of Easton by yere clere	£10

[*Total and note*] £34. He is contented to assure this ~~to~~ ymmediately after his decease to William Yaxley and Elizabeth for terme of their lyves with remaynder to theires of the same William Yaxley etc.

The yerely rent of £10 reserved up on a lease *or graunte* of the mannor of Colney sometyme ~~Spilman~~ Spilmans and other londes there made to John Thomson and Elizabeth his wyff for terme of their lyves   £10
One tenement in Colney with diverse londes there ~~letten to~~ in the tenur of Thomas Denny by yere   £3

[*note to all above paragraphs*] Of all theise he is seased in fee saving of the rent whereof he is seased so long as the reservation doth contynew.

The mannor of Colney sometyme Spilmans after the death of the said Thomson and Elizabeth his wyff wilbe worth over and besides the *said* £10 reserved upon the said lease or ~~in~~ grunt [*sic*] made to them clere   £10
[*note to above paragraph*] He is seased of this in reversion after the death of Thomson and his wyff in fee

[*Total*] £23. [*note added in Nunne's hand*] in lieu of this £23 Mr Doctor is contented to assure his mannor of Hoo and all his landes in Hoo and Swanton of the clere yerely value of £30 and above ymmediatly after his decease to William Yaxley and Elizabeth for terme of thair lyves with remaynders over to theires of William Yaxley etc.

The mannor of Bowthorpe is allready assured by feoffament to dyverse feoffes to the use of Doctor Spencer for terme of lyff, the remaynder to Richard Yaxley and Margaret his wyff parentes of the ward and to theyres of thair twoo bodyes lawfully begotten and for lack of suche heires to the use of Marmaduke Constable

---

51 That is, 'fathoms'.
52 Meaning his manuscripts.
53 *Custos sigilli* or 'keeper of the [great] seal'.

and Elizabeth his wiff and to the heires of thair twoo bodyes lawfully begotten and for lack of suche heire to the use of the ryght heires of Doctor Spencer and is of the clere yerely value of £52

[note to above paragraph] Of this he is seased for terme of his *lyffe* with owt ympechement of wast, the remaynder as appeareth infra.

[second note] The interest of this he will not change for he saith he can not do and undoo.

The copy hold londes in Yorkeshire of clere yerely value of £6

[note to above paragraph] Of this he hath in interest as appear.

[second note] This copy hold is allready grunted to William Yaxley by copy of court roll and so taken up.

Mistres Yaxleyes londes.

Which appere in the particler annexed to the drawttes of thindentur. She agreeth in all all [sic] thinges as the booke is drawn saving she will in no wise make any grunt of any parte of yt in joynture to Mistres Elizabeth and thereupon she stonde.

Remembraunces

Imprimis Doctor Spencer will agre no otherwise to discharge his londes of incombraunces but of suche as have ben done by hymself saving leases and gruntes by copye etc.

Item Doctor Spencer lyketh not to appoynt any tyme of affyance or of marriege with owt assent of the parties and specially bycause Mr Yaxley is so nere his full age. And for your L. saftye he saith yt may be provided for by tendringe of hym a mariage, for he dare not take upon hym to promyse or undertake for his nephew either for the same or for any further ioytur *ioynture [in Nunne's hand]* to be made by hym of any of his own londes.

Verte fol. [in Nunne's hand]

Item towchinge the bondes for performaunce of covenauntes Mr Doctor and Mistres Yaxley meane to sever and ar contented to be bound in reasonable somes severally. So that Doctor Spencer be not compelled to travell owt of Norwiche for any knowlege of recognisaunce or for any assuraunce to be made by hym.

Item towching the survey of Doctor Spencers londes wee have taken a view of them and yt se appeareth that thay will hold their values very well and moar.

Item your L. shall understand that Doctor Spencer ded looke to have ben asserteyned by us of Yaxley Hall to be assured to Mr Yaxley bycause ye there is mentioned no mention made of yt in the booke indenture of covenauntes and besides that as Mr Doctor saith your L. told hym here at Norwiche at your last being there that you would have [word illegible] be Mr Yaxley should have it.

Thus trusting your L. by the consideration of the premisses may understand to what conclusion this lyke to come unto, wee most humble [sic] take our leaves from Norwiche the 3 of January 1566

Signed: Your L. most bounde servauntes Frauncis Boldero George Nunne. In hand of Boldero with corrections by Nunne.

Addressed: To the right honorable and thair singlar good L. and Master the L. Keaper of the Great Seale of Inglond

Endorsed in Sir Nicholas Bacon I's hand: Boldero from Mrs Yaxley and Doctor Spencer
2 ff.

21.   [4073] *Miles Spencer to Sir Nicholas Bacon I, 6 January 1567*

My humble duitie remembred unto your Lordship I have receyved your L. letters of the 6 of Decembre last past according to the contentes wherof I have had conference with your L. officers Frauncys Boldero and George Nonne who have signified unto your L. thalteration of the drawght sent by your L. ~~in~~ wherin was the Maner of Colnye and so manye reversions in the said Maner that I have put in the lue therof the Maner of Herford in Hoo which is without anye Reversion and is worth £30 by yeare and wolbe worth fyvetie poundes with your L. lyttell healp as my nevewe can declare unto your L. and that in hoope that your L. woll depart with Richard Yaxlie his landes unto him. And in case that this offer of his mother and myn be not corespondent to your L. expectation that then your L. wold be so good Lord unto him, that he maye have the preferment of the said landes for that they lye so necessarye for him. And then I would sell the Maner of Est Carleton to satisfie your L. for the same. And as for the copie hould landes in Yorkeshire, I have made unto him a copie therof and am sued in thescheker[54] as my said nevewe can declare unto your L. I besech your L. taccept this myn offre in good part being sorye that myn habilitie is not awnserable to the desyre I have to deale more liberallye with him herein. And thus in remembrance of myn humble duitie unto your good L. I take my leave. From Norwiche this 6 daye of Januarye *Anno* 1566

Signed: Your Lordships humble Orator Miles Spencer. *Autograph.*
Addressed: To the right honorable and his singuler good Lord Sir Nicholas Bacon knight Lord Keaper of the Greate Seale of England
Endorsed in Sir Nicholas Bacon I's hand: Doctor Spencers letter
2 ff.; seal impression.

22.   [4074] *Margaret Yaxley to Sir Nicholas Bacon I, 7 January 1567*

My humbell dutye remembred thes shall syngnyfy [*sic*] unto yowr good Lord-shepe I have receaved yowr letteres dated the 6 of December and thearwythe a drawght of covenantes concernyng the marryage bettwene yowr L. doughter and my sonne. May yt thearfore please yowr L. to understand that I have consydered uppone those arthykelles wythe yowr L. offyceres Fraunces Boldero and Gorge Nonne wherunto I have aggred, savynge in one pointte that is yff yt shall please god to call my sonne William a waye wytheoute yssue that then my sonne Jhon may inheryet my londes, strustyng [*sic*] yowr good L. shall not ther wythe be offended but contynowe in yowr goodnes unto my sonne as yow have hearetofore donne, for the whyche he and his fryndes are bounde to praye for yowr L. Thus wyssyng yowr Lordshepes incresse of honore with contynewell healthe and long lyfe frome Norwche 7 of Januarii

Signed: Yowr L. humbell Oratryxe Margrett Yaxlee. *Autograph.*
Addressed: To the ryght honorrabell and her verye good L. Sir Nicholas Bacone knynght [*sic*] L. Keaper of Greate Seale of Inglond
Endorsed in Sir Nicholas Bacon I's hand: Mistres Yaxleys letter
2 ff.; traces of seal impression.

---

[54] 'The Exchequer'.

23. [4075–6] *Sir Nicholas Bacon I to Miles Spencer and Margaret Yaxley, 11 January 1567*

After my hartie commendations. This is to signyfie to you that I have receyved your lettres, upon consideration whereof and upon talke had with my warde William Yaxley, immedyately upon the reading of your lettres and *also* upon the perusing of the booke whiche you have retorned to me concerning the maryage of my doughter and hym, I do understand two thinges lyke to falle owt clean other wise then I loked for and *otherwyse* in reason (as I thinke) *then in reason* I ought to allowe of. The former is the smalness of my doughters joynture. True it is that I have ben offered for his maryage a thowsande markes and so, I am sewer, I may have for hym, yf this maryage with me taketh not, and for a thowsand mark with my doughter to receyve no more in joynctute but fyfty pounde *or there aboutes* in reversion, after the death of you Mr Spencer, and to have no thing assured in reversion after your death, Mrs. Yaxley, of the landes that you possesse for the betteringe of my doughters ioynctute, semeth in reason to me a veray harde thing to allowe of, specyally, yf God should calle the young man (whiche God forbyde and yet we be all mortall) for during the lyfe of you Mrs*r* Spencer. For so should I be forced to marye my doughter ayen with out any thing in posses-sion, saving the thirdes of the lande of hir husbande. I have for the helpe of this spoken with the young man, and fynde hym some what inclyned to amend her ioynctur with the landes he possesseth, but not to suche a value as the satisfaction of his mariage doth deserve, wherof occasion is offered to me iustely to doubt that there wyll not growe so good end of this as *as I have deservyd nor as* I ded hope of. The second matter *ys yet more hard then the former and that* is this. I have talked with my warde *the young man* to understand howe he is inclyned towarde this matche, letting hym to understand howe he shall growe to his full age shortely, and therefor it is of necessytie for me (as in dede it is) to knowe howe he is disposed in this matter. His answer was, that he coulde not give his consent eyther to mary or to be affyed[55] without the respytt of a yere, whiche you bothe knowe that I can not graunt, except I will putt in daunger the losse of his mariage, whiche I mean not to do. I thought full well that the great care that I have taken for his well bringing up, and the purchasing of lande whiche lyeth veray mete for hym and whiche I ment he showld have hadde, *and more then that too keppe a reasonable reconyng* if he had maryed with my doughter, and other my doinges towardes hym and his, would have bread some better end of this matter, then me thinkes, I shall nowe have cause to loke for, except by this messanger I shall hear other wise from you than of late I have don. I have *therfore* of purpose sent hym down to understand your determynat myndes in this matter. The young man hath moved me that I woulde be content to graunt a libertie of choyce *unto hym to gyve answer of lykyng or myslyking* for a whole yere, from mydsomer next, unto hym. Myn answer was, that so as the lyke libertie might be to my doughter for the lyke tyme I woulde with good will, upon his desyre, assent to yt so that I might have good bandes and assurraunces that if the mariage bytwene them bothe did not take by that daie *by eyther of there refusalles or by dethe or otherwyse* that then I shoulde be paid the 1000 markes whiche I am offered for his marrage, and her thereby to be dischardge of his marrage by me, and to be at libertie to take his choyce where he shall list. *or elles yf you wyll presently bargeyne with me for hys mareyage and geve me the 1000 markes weche I meye receyve there

---

55 Meaning 'betrothed'.

I shall be content to go throw with you.* For certen and determynate answer to thes thinges I have sent down my servant this bearer purposely, to whom I praye you gyve credit.

2.

Suerly yt is not for lyvelode or welth that I have ben contented to come to this matche. For if that hadde ben my marke, I assure you, I ~~have~~ could marye her to one of twyse his lyvinge. But yt was neighborowode and bycause I hadde brought hym up amongest myn own children and as one of myn own sonnes. Well I leave the rest to God and to you. ~~And so right hartely~~ prayeng you that I may have your immedyate and determynate answer to *the contentes of thys letter* bycause the tyme is so short. Thus right hartely fare you well. From my howse nigh Charing Crosse this 11 of Januarye 1566.

Draft in secretary's hand, with corrections by Bacon, including all insertions noted above.
Endorsed in Sir Nicholas Bacon I's hand: The copye of my letter to Doctor Spencer and Mistres Yaxley
4 ff.

24. [4077] *Sir Nicholas Bacon I to Francis Boldero [11 January 1567]*[56]

Boldero, I woulde you shoulde peruse the letter whiche I have sent by Wiseman to Mr D. Spencer and Mistres Yaxley, and thereupon to lett it be sealed and delyvered to Mr Spencer by Wiseman. And withall I woulde that you immedyately with hym repare to Norwiche, and there you and Wiseman to receyve answer of the contentes of this letter, and if you can by writing. And if ye can not, yet by worde whiche I woulde have you and Wiseman reduce into writing. The matters that shoulde be answered be thees. The first whether they will encreasse my doughters ioyncture and, what reason they can make, his marriage being worth a thowsand marke, as in dede I may have for hym, that £50 or thereaboutes *~~or thereab~~* in reversion shoulde be a fytte ioyncture *with the thirdes of hys londes in possessyon*. The second is, whether they wilbe content to be bound to paie me a thowsande markes for his mariage at mydsomer come a yere, if the mariage bytwene my doughter and hym do not take before that tyme *accordyng as there letter ys declaryd. The third ys yf they wyll not be so bownd then whether they wyll bye hys wardshyp and maryage for a 1400 markes or no.*

Your last advertisementes were to brief. For neyther ded you advertise me, who was of counsaill with them in handelinge of that booke, neither what moved them to stand so precysely with the smalnes of my doughters ioyncture, neither what was sayd by you for thincreasse of it. I see except the matter be handled with great care (as in dede the greatnes of the cause doth require) there wilbe muche posting up and down, and to smalle purpose. I would that you shoulde leave all other matters aparte for the well doinge of this. You sent me worde that they woulde be bounde in convenyent summes, for the performaunce of covenauntes, but you wright not in what summes, whiche is to small purpose, and therefor you are to know of them, if the matter go forwarde, whether either of them wilbe bound in one thowsande poundes, and ~~that~~ *oon thyng* specyally in the whole proceding you have to take hedde of, that is, if you can not bring them to my demaundes, yet that you bring them as nere as you can to any of my demaundes [*Bacon continues*

---

[56] Dated by reference to no. **23 [4075–6]**.

holograph to the end] and therof to advertyse me. I marvell you ded not reforme the booke in the hole as you ded one part. I send you a booke nwe[57] wreton and the old also, and let the nwe be reformyd accordyng as they shall be content with yt, yf you see eny lykelynes that the matter shall procede.

Draft in secretary's hand, with corrections by Bacon, including all insertions noted above.
Endorsed in Sir Nicholas Bacon I's hand: A letter to Boldero.
2 ff.

25.   [4078] *Miles Spencer and Margaret Yaxley to Sir Nicholas Bacon I, 15 January 1567*
Right honorable and our singuler good lord, we have receyved your honorable letters, in answere whereunto it may like you tundrestand that wheare your lord-shippe semeth not to be pleased with the smalnes of the joynter specified in the boke which we retorned, we now uppon further consideration have enlarged the same with the Manor of Bikerton and diverse landes and tenementes in Yaxley of the clere yerely value of tenne poundes, which both do amount to the value of £60 by the yere so that all the landes assured by us both amount to the summe of 6 score poundes by yere, as by the draught of the indenture which we retorne to your lordshippe dothe appere, which indenture and the covenauntes therin as it is now penned we do alowe of. And where your lordshippe is contented to graunt to William Yaxley respect until midsomer come a yere, so that you have good bondes and assurance that if the mariage betwen them both doth not take by that day by either of their refusalles or by death or otherwise, that then you shuld be paied 1000 markes and he therby to be discharged and set at liberte to take his choyse, we are contented to be bound by recognisance for the payment of the said 1000 markes in the summe of £800, trusting that you will mitigate that great and huge summe of a 1000 markes which we referre to your goodnes, and also that when Williaz [*sic*] Yaxley shalbe of full age and puttinge in like good and sufficient bondes unto your lordshippe for the same, then our said bondes may be cancelled. In doinge wherof we most humblie desire your lordshippe to signifie us what alowance you wilbe contented to make of such profettes and revenews of his landes which your officers have receyved toward the discharge of the same wherby we may know our owne state the better. This [*sic*] besechinge your good lordshippe to accept this our offer in good parte which I his mother wold not be willinge to promyse to any other man but to your lordshippe, we will cease any longer to troble your honour, committinge the rest unto God and you with our dailie praiers for the preservation of your lordshippe in longe health and honor. From Norwich this 15 of Januarie 1566

Signed: Your humble Orators Miles Spencer [Margaret Yaxlee].[58] *Autograph.*
Addressed: To the right honorable and ther singuler good lord Sir Nicolas Bacon knyght Lord Keper of the Great Seal of Ingland
Endorsed in Sir Nicholas Bacon I's hand: Mr Spencer and Mistres Yaxley
2 ff.; traces of seal.

---

57 Meaning 'new'.
58 Margaret Yaxley's signature is little more than a mark 'MY', in contrast with her firm signature of no. **22 [4074]**, written only a week before. Presumably she suffered from arthritis.

26. [4079] *Memorandum by Sir Nicholas Bacon I to Francis Boldero and George Nunn, 14 February 1567*

Instructions gyven to Frauncis Boldero and George Nune concerning Yaxleys marege 14 February 1566

Fyrst ye shall procede accordinge to the assurances at this tyme sent downe, which ar allowed of by Mr. Spencer and Mistres Yaxley as by thair letter appeare. And yf thay shall not agree to conclud in that sort, that than ymmediatly ye cause one to come up to certifye me by letter of the matters whereupon they sticke. And yf they shall proceade according to theise assurances than may ye promise them on my behalf that I am well content to assure the manner of Yaxley Hall to William Yaxley and to my doughter and to the heires of William paying for the *same* £600 and of that some to deducte £400 for the profittes of the wardes londes by me receyved besides all manner of allowaunces due unto me ~~and upon good~~ so as a good discharge is made unto me *for the same profyttes* upon such defalcation made to me, and assurance made from me of the said mannors. And ye may further say that ye have hard me dyverse tymes report that yf this mariege take as of good successe as I have hooped of that than I will *lett* them also have (upon a reasonable rekoning) the mannor of Melles. Ye may also asserteyn them that yf William Yaxley shall agree to mary with my brothers' doughter, that I meane in all poyntes to deale as well by hym as yf he maried myn own dowghter. And agayne yf thay shall refuse to procede in this mariege than ye may lett them understand that neyther do I meane to make any suche assurance of Yaxley Hall, nor of Melles nor ~~any suche~~ *so greate [*in Bacon's hand*]* defalcation ~~of~~ *for* the profittes by me receyved as is above remembred. And yet I am content upon the payment of 400 markes unto me betwene this and the fyrst day of Easter terme next, and upon a discharge of the said profittes, to make William Yaxley a clere discharge of his wardshipp and mariege. And as concerning the tendre of my brothers doughter[59] the cause of that was, ye may say (as occasion be offred) to make some assurance unto me of the value of his mariege untill suche *tyme* as these assurances might be concluded. Ye ar also to enforme them that I have talked with the yonge man for some joynture to be made to my doughter in possession which he hath graunted unto in hope whereof I am the rather wone to this conclusion.

The office was found *quindecimo Aprilis* and *primo Elizabethe*; he was of thage of 13 yeres and twoo moneth at the fyndinge of the office.

In Boldero's hand, with correction by Bacon. Endorsed in Sir Nicholas Bacon I's hand: 17 Febr. 1566.[60] Instructiones for Yaxleys maryage
2 ff.

27. [4080] *Sir Nicholas Bacon I to Miles Spencer and Margaret Yaxley, 15 February 1567*

After my hartie comendations. Theise be to signifie unto you that I have receyved your letter dated the 15 of January last according to the contentes whereof ye shall receyve assurances with all manner of thinges mete and convenyent for

---

59 Anne, daughter of James Bacon, the Lord Keeper's younger brother; she eventually married John Rivett of Brandeston. His elder brother Thomas had no children (*1561 visitation*, ed. Corder, p. 158).

60 Bacon's endorsement of 17 February appears to be a mistake, as the date of the memorandum is quite clear as 14 February, and it must relate to the following letter.

the perfictinge of them, agreaing as I trust unt to our own meaninges and to the contentation of us all. Wherein yf any thinge shall be mystaken by reason of the multitude of my busynes as I hoope there is not, I am contented yt shall be reformed according to reason. And therefore what soever this bearer my servaunt Frauncis Boldero *and George [*sic: Nunn omitted*]* shall doo in this matter I shall be contented to stond to it. And further I have thought good according to the desier conteyned in your letter to lett you understand by this bearer *my said servauntes* whome I have instructed at good length how liberally I meane to deale with the warde concerning the profittes of his londes that I have receyved over and besides suche allowaunces as of reason be due to me and also what I m and how well I meane to deale with hym concerning Yaxley Hall and otherwise so as this mariege betwene hym and my dowghter doo take place with both thair contentation. And for the better furtheraunce thereof I have appoynted the ward to come down with this bearer and my dowghter also. Thus hoopinge that God shall send good successe in this cause I bed you both right hartely fare well. 15 Febr. 1566

[*Postscript added down left margin*] I have also for all other matters betwen you and me concerning this mariage instructed this bearer my said servauntes to whome I pray you gyve credyt.

Draft in Boldero's hand, with date added by Bacon. Endorsed in Sir Nicholas Bacon I's hand: 15 Febr. 1566. The copy of my letter to Mr Spencer and Mistres Yaxley

1 f.

28. [4081] *Miles Spencer and Margaret Yaxley to Sir Nicholas Bacon I, 26 February 1567*

Right honorable our bounden dewty remembred, we have receyved your L. letters of the 15 day of February by your L. servantes Frances Bolderowe and George Nunne and have accomplysshed all the actes and demandes as they requyred of us or of eyther of us; and yf there be any thyng omytted concerninge the better assurans of our landes we shalbe all tymes redy at your L. comaundement and plesure to reforme the same. And we do also perceyve by your L. seid servantes in what sort your L. wo wylle dele concernyng the profettes of them the yonge mannys landes that your L. hath receyved, also howe your L. meaneth to dele with hym as concerninge Yaxley Halle. We have declared unto your L. seid sarvantes for howe many yerys your L. hath receyved the profett of his landes and to what somme yt dyd amount unto yerly. Trustynge that your L. wyll both honorably and lyberally dele with hym therin, partly for the good wylle that his pore father bore unto your L. in his lyffe tyme and also for that hereafter he shalbe a pore neybor of your L. sonne and especyally yf this marryage betwen your L. dowter and hym take place, as we trust and most hartely desyre yt may, so do your L. lyberalyte shall extend aswell to her as to hym. Thus sessyng to troble your L. comyttynge the rest to God and to your good L. with our dayly preyer for the preservacyon of your L. honor long to indure, at Norwich the 26 day of of February your L. humble orators 1566

Signed: Miles Spencer M Y[61] *Autograph.*

---

[61] Margaret Yaxley's initials are more clearly written than in no. **25 [4078]**.

Addressed: To the right honorable and ther synguler good lord Sir Nycholas Bacon knyght L Keper of the Gret Seale of Inglond
Endorsed in Sir Nicholas Bacon I's hand: 26 Febr. 1566 Mr Spencer and Mistres Yaxley
2 ff.; traces of seal.

29. [4082] *Francis Boldero and George Nunn to Sir Nicholas Bacon I, 29 February 1567*

Our dueties moost humbly remembred, yt may lyke your honour to understand that wee went ymmediatly to Norwiche where wee found Mr Spencer and Mrs Yaxley very well willing and ready to procede accordinge to the assurraunces sent down but wee could not in all ~~get~~ *this* tyme gett Sir Thomas Woodhouse and Mr Thorneton[62] togither for the one was riden unto Waxham and thother was ryding on to Cambrigshire. Notwithstanding *Mr. Thorneton* was contented to stay his journey and to retorne to Norwiche and dyd take the knowleges accordingly as by the same which wee send unto you by this bearer may appere. And afterward Sir Thomas Woodhouse dyd ~~the~~ ratifie the same and putting to his hand and seale. Wee have thought good *to signifie* the order of the doinge of the same, to thintent that yf there be any imperfection therein, that than they may be redressed as your L. shall thinke good, for wee could not have gotten them togither ~~before the~~ untill after the next assises. And wee have promised for your L., under our handes (for so Doctor Spencer required yt) that ye should assure Yaxley Hall according to your instructions. And for the £400 *whiche your L.* meane to allow thay seme to make a greater rekoning of the profittes of the wardes londes than so, nevertheles thay said thay would referre them selves to your honor therein. And for the rest of your instructions mete and requisite to be opened unto them wee have done yt accordingly. And towchinge the bargayne with Garsington, yt is concluded and possession taken according to the booke ye sent down.[63] And thus moost humbly wee take our leave. From Bury the 29 of February 1566.

Signed: Your L. moost bounden servauntes Fraunces Boldero George Nunne.
Holograph in Boldero's hand, with Nunn's autograph.
Postscript: Mistres Woodhouse have written unto your honor towching hir jugement of Mr Yaxleys disposition.

[*verso*] It may like your honour I have travayled for the gettyng of your arrerages wherof I have receyved fewe yett, but I trust at my comyng up to answer them all except Lynges wherof I trust your L is well answered and *except* Prestons who requyreth some deyes for the payment and offreth bondes to be made to Mr Nycholas Bacon, which I intend to receyve

Signed: Your obedyent servaunt George Nunne. *Holograph in Nunn's hand.*
Addressed: To the right honorable and thair singlar good L. and Master the L. Keaper of the Great Seale of Inglond

---

62 Probably William Thornton, JP in the Isle of Ely in the 1560s; his inquisition post mortem was held in Norfolk in 13 Elizabeth. He does not appear as a feoffee in any Bacon transaction.
63 *Bacon handlist*, no. **2549**: bargain and sale by William Garsington of Baconsthorpe (Nf.) to Nicholas Bacon I of the White Hart in Botesdale for £100 (31 January 1567); *ibid*. no. **2949**: bond by Garsington to Bacon to perform covenants (22 February 1567); *ibid*. no. **2551**: fine by Bacon to William Garsington and Isabella Garsington widow (16 April 1567).

Endorsed in Sir Nicholas Bacon I's hand: 29 Febr. 1566 Boldero and Nuns answere towching Yaxley maryage
2 ff.; traces of seal impression.

30.   [4083] *Sir Nicholas Bacon I to Nicholas Bacon II, 18 June 1567*

Sonne, I sende you by this bearer, the presentation I gave to Skarlet, to the beny-fice Eccles, which nowe is in my disposion agayne. I send you also two bills of reconinges, whereby it shall appire to you, what reparation hath ben done there, if the bills be true. Ye shall do well to examyn the troth of them and to certifye me in what case the parsonage standes for repration. Yt hath ben taken for a good bene-fyce, and a hansome mansion house, and therfore I would be glad some honest man that wold be residen, and worthye it, might have it. From my house at Charing Chrosse the 18 of June 1567

Signed: Your Father N. Bacon C.S. *Autograph.*
Addressed: To my sonne Nicholas Bacon
1 f.; seal impression.

31.   [4084] *Miles Spencer and Margaret Yaxley to Sir Nicholas Bacon I, 20 October 1567*

Our humble duties remembred to your good Lordshippe; it may please the same to be advertised that we undrestand by William Yaxley that at the tyme of his late awaytinge on your lordshippe he declared his mynd how he was inclined towchinge the matche which we and other his frendes had often perswaded with him and hertelie wisshed and hoped that hit might take place, aswell in respecte of his owne profitte and commodite as of our counfort and quyet of mynde, who otherwise wold never have entred the bondes we dyd for the payment of such a great summe of money, the one half whereof we never loke to receyve agayne at the handes of any gentleman of worshippe, considering the smale value of his owne landes charged with two ioynturs and also the ruyne of his howse voide of all furnyture. But now the case standinge as hit dothe and otherwise then our expectation was and desire is, we humblie beseche your lordshippe that we may undrestand what money remayneth in your lordshippes handes of the revenew of his landes duringe his nonage, wherby we may know our charge and so the soner make shifft for the rest which we shall not be hable to do without our great hinderaunce and loss and that wil turne to his smale profett hereafter. For he may well assure him self that neither his mother nor I wilbe willinge to make the like ioyntor of those landes to any other in so ample maner as we have done to your lordshippe. And because we are unhable to venter so great a travell as to London, and for that also the yonge man is both thought of us and likewise perswadith him self to be unapte to considre of the accompte which we undrestand your lord-shippe hath appoynted to be there made, therefore we humblie beseche your good lordshippe that you will admitte therunto a nighe kynsman of his, Maister Grym-ston,[64] who is a wise gentleman and one whose travell we have desyred in this behalf. This [*sic*] we will cease to trouble your lordshippe, nothinge dowtinge but like as we have dealt symplie and playnly with your lordshippe in all our doinges and reposed great confidence in your Honor, even so we shalbe used accordinglie.

---

[64]   Edward Grimston the elder of Ipswich: see no. **32 [4086]**.

And thus we pray almightie God to contynew your Lordshippe in longe life and incres of honor. Yeven at Norwich this 20 of Oct. 1567.

Signed: Your most humble and dailie orators Miles Spencer Marget Yaxlee[65] *Autograph.*
Addressed: To the right honorable and our singler good lord Sir Nicholas Bacon Lord Keper of the Great Seale of England
2 ff.; traces of seal.

32.   [4086] *Miles Spencer to Edward Grimston [Dec. 1567 «» Jan. 1568]*

Fyrst that yt will please my lord to acquyte or sett over unto William Yaxlee his wardshipe and mariage for that his mother and I neyther intend nor will have anye thinge to do with the same and the said William shall acquyte my Lord his servauntes and assygnes of all profyghtes receyved of his landes.

Item that yt will lykewyse please my L. to take a newe bonde for the 200 markes remeyninge to be paid at the feast of St John Baptyst and to cancell the recognisance and delyver all manner of indenturs bondes deedes fynes and other assurances made by the said Myles and Margrett for eyther of them concerninge the mariage of the said William, and all other evidences and wryghtinges by anye weyes or meanes belongynge to the said William, and yf yt shall not lyke my Lord to take a newe bond for the said 200 markes remeyninge and to cancell the said recognisance, then to geve a suffycyent dyschargde for the 800 markes alredye receyved.

Item that yt will please the said Lord Keper to covenaunt that he and Elizabethe Bacon one of the daughters of the said Lord at all tymes from tyme to tyme within five years nowe next ensewenge and also her husband (yf she the said Elizabethe before the end of the said fyve yeares shall chance to be maryed) shall do all suche acte and actes uppon request to be made by the said Myles Margrett and William or anye of them as shall be reasonablye devised or advysed by the said Myles Margrett and William or anye of them or there consell lerned in the lawe at the costes and chardges in the lawe of the said Myles Margrett and William for the cleare undoynge and extinguyshement of all suche interest and estate as she the said Elizabethe hathe or maye clayme in anye the landes tenementes or heredytamentes of the said Myles and Margrett or anye of them be yt by fyne to be levyed, decre to be made in the Chancerye, by the said Lordes apparance in a wrytte of ryght as garden to his said daughter, and therein to joyne the myse[66] and departe in dyspyght of court or otherwyse.[67]

Item that the said William shall stand unto suche ende as yow and Mr. Bolderowe shall make for the copyhold landes.

Copy in secretary's hand.
Addressed: To the wurshipfull Edward Grympston esquier at Ippiswiche
Endorsed: Concernyng Mr Yaxleys wardship
1 f.; traces of seal.

---

65 Margaret Yaxley's signature is restored once more as in no. **22 [4074]**.
66 That is, to accept the issue in the writ of right.
67 Departure in despite of court is the formal act of non-appearance in a collusive action, in order to obtain the desired judgement from the court.

33. [4085] *Sir Nicholas Bacon I to Nicholas Bacon II, 20 December 1567*

Sonne, I send you herin inclosed a letter to my L. of Elye,[68] which when you have read and perused, I wold you should cause to be sealyd, and delyvere it to my L. your owne handes, [*sic*] and with all I wold you shoulde advertise me what aunswere you do receyve, and there upon you shall understande what course is beste to be taken for the recovery of such thinges as be dewe by the patent.[69] When you come to my L. have good regard that your behaviour and wordes be altogether comly and modest: letting him nevertheles to understand, that if ye had not had this patent ye should have had a better thing in place of it. And if my L. will paye unto you that that is dewe unto you for your fee in readye moneye, and promyse to take reasonable order with you for the rest, by some convenyent tyme, then you shall do well to receyve the moneye, and lett the rest hang in question till some order maye be taken for the recovery of it. Ye writt nothing unto me howe my daughter your wief dothe, nor her mother, wherin you do not well. Commend me to them bothe, and tell them if they want any thinge this Christmas the fault is theirs and not myn, for they might have had it by a word of their mouthe or by writting. And thus fare you well. From my house besydes Charing Crosse the 20 of December 1567.

Signed: Your father N. Bacon C.S. *Autograph.*
Addressed: To my sonne Nicholas Bacon
1 f.; seal impression.

34. [4087] *Miles Spencer to Sir Nicholas Bacon I, January 1568*

My humble dewetye remembred to your good lordshipe, whearas I desyred Mr. Grympston to deale wythe your L. in matters towchynge the wardshippe of my nephewe Yaxlee, which ar in questyon; sythens his retorne I receyved certeyne articles agreed uppon betwene yow, whereby I perceyve your L. is contented to allowe £400 of the profyghtes of my nephewes socage landes towardes the payment of the thowsand markes, and the other 400 markes I shalbe contented to paye accordynge to the articles, trustynge the pryncipall matter that most towchythe his mother and me maye be dyschardged which is the incombrance of our landes, and therefore consyderinge that neyther my meaninge nor your L. demande ever was that your doughter should have anye other estate but condycyonall yf the maryage should passe betwene hir and my nephewe, which bothe his mother and I were most willinge to do uppon the greate desyre we hadd the maryage myght take effecte (and so I would God should helpe me at my most nede as I was will-inge yt myght have taken place) but nowe my trust is that yt will please your L. accordynge to honor and conscyence to take suche order as our landes maye be dyschardged thereof. And for that yt is a matter which hathe not a lytle troubled me in this my age, I have conferred with them that be lerned howe our landes maye be dyschardged of such troubles. Theye have made me suche devyses for the same as I send your L. herewith wherein I shall eftsons beseche your L. to deale

---

68 Richard Cox, Bishop of Ely 1559–81. For tension with Cox in 1572, see below, no. **62 [4116]**, and for his similar quarrels with the East Anglian magnate Lord North, an associate of the Bacons, see E.J. Bourgeois II, 'The queen, a bishop, and a peer: a clash for power in mid-Elizabethan Cambridgeshire', *Sixteenth Century Journal* 26 (1995), 3–15.

69 No doubt his patent as constable of the bishop of Ely's castle of Wisbech; he is mentioned as constable in 1568 (*CPR Elizabeth I, 1566–69*, no. 2386). I have not been able to trace the patent itself.

accordinglye and so shall I thinke my selfe moche bownden to your L. and unbur-
thened of that great care I am nowe in. Yt maye lyke your L. I have yett kept this
matter frome my nece, knowinge yf she should understand yt she would exclayme
uppon me in whome she reposed hir trust and become suche an importune sutor
to your L. as I thinke yow would not well lyke. Whearas I understand your L.
would gladlye have parte of the ~~maryage~~ monye, which is to be paid at mydsomer,
I have sent yow by this bearer 200 markes in gold and the other 200 markes shall
be paid at or on this syde the feast of St John Baptyst, besechinge your Lordshipe
that as I am redye to performe the articles apperteyninge to my covenaunt so yt
maye please your L. accordynge to honor and conscyence to geve me suffycyent
dyschardge for the same and also for the other 600 markes by your L. allowed and
that I maye receyve suche comfortable answere as my good meanynge towardes
your L. hathe deserved. And thus besechinge the holye gost longe to contynewe
your good L. in honor and healthe I humblye take my leave frome Norwiche, this
[*blank*] of Januarye 67

Signed: Your lordships humble oratour Miles Spencer. *Autograph.*
Addressed: To the ryght honorable and his singuler good lorde Sir Nycholas
Bacon knyght Lorde Keper of the Great Seale of England
Endorsed by Bacon: From Mr Spencer in Jan. 1567
2 ff.; traces of seal.

35. [4088] *Sir Nicholas Bacon I to Miles Spencer, February 1568*
After my hartie commendations. Theis be to signyfie to you that I finde by your last
advertisement that it is thought there shoulde be some further assuraunce made to
my doughter by the writinges that have passed bytwene you, Mistres Yaxley and
me concerning the marrage intended by us bytwene William Yaxley and my said
daughter, then was by us ment. For answer whereof and declaration of my true
meaning, theis be to lett you understand that if any suche thing have passed, it hath
as yt semes to me uppon consyderatyon of the wrytynges cheffly growen by the
execution of estates made by the counsaill of you and Mistres Yaxley according to
certen deedes sent unto me from you and her, never demaunded by me, nor ment
by me ever to have ben made. For had thassuraunce rested as I ment yt shoulde
upon the fynes knowledged, and upon the indenture that ledde the use of the said
fynes, whiche indenture declareth that the saide fynes were knowledged only in
consideration of the said mariage to be had to be hadde [*sic*], this doubte in myn
opynyon ~~had never happened~~ *shuld not have growne so grette*, besides if in
the indenture whereby the use of the said fynes were directed any falt were ~~(as I
thinke) there is not,~~ yet was there no blame in me for that, considering it was sent
down drawen in papyr to be consydered of by youre counsaill with a letter of myn
signyfieng ~~that~~ *that thinges myght be mystaken in the myltytuyd of busynes and
therefose [*sic for* therefore?]* if any thing were a mysse therein, I was content
that yt shoulde be reformed according to reason. And thus muche I have thought
good to wright unto yow for the declaration of my playn meaning and dealing in
this matter, and with all to let you understand that if any thing hath happened in
this proceding other wise then we, that were parties, ment, that in my iudgement it
were mete that, that trowble that shoulde growe thereby, shoulde light upon them
that have sought by any meanes to disapoincte that intention that was well ment
by us all. And if some man had the matter in handling, I think it woulde be used
to that ende. Neverthelesse I for my parte am content to ronne an other course and

so to use this matter as any man may repe the frutes of my labors *to there look that so do*. And therefor for your satisfaction and Mistres Yaxleys *who have ever delt well with me* I am content to declare and certifie you by this letter, that seing the marrage taketh not according as you ment it, that my meaning is not, nor never was that my doughter shoulde receyve any commoditie or profitt by any assuraunce or writing that have passed bytwene us concerning the land, either of you, or Mistres Yaxley*s* or William Yaxleys, and with all am hereby content also to promyse *agre* to do all maner of thinges that is mete for a father to do to his doughter to cause her *at hir full age* to discharge any interest that is thus by chaunce growen unto her by any of theis assuraunces, and in token thereof I send unto yow all thassuraunces, bondes and writinges remayning with me concerning those matters, to be cancelled or other wise used by you, as your selves shall thinke mete. *And allso an instrument under my hand and seale agreyng with the contentes of thys letter.*

Draft in secretary's hand, with insertions in Bacon's hand.
Endorsed by secretary: My L. letter to Mr D. Spencer. Februar. 1567
2 ff.

36. [4089] *Sir Nicholas Bacon I to Nicholas Bacon II, 27 July 1568*

Sonne, I send you hereinclosed a letter directyd to to [sic] Mr Asshefeild[70] to whome I fynd by his letter, which I send you also, you are muche beholden. This letter of myn to hym which I wold you should read, and then seale and delyver, it shall gyve you to understand what goodwill he hath to the bestowing of your brother Nathaneell with Mr Copledickes daughter.[71] If this might come to passe in forme as Mr Asshefeild writteth, the mayd being to be lyked, I could allowe aswell of it, as the former that I have made you pryvie to. You shall do well as occasion shall serve to lett Mr Asshefeild knowe that you fynd by me, howe much you are beholden to hym for his goodwill. And you are to take knowledge of this matter conteyned in his letter concerning Mr Copledickes daughter, as yourself shall think meete when you shall meete together. Mary of yourself to enter into it I lyke not, but if he shall make you acquaynted with it or aske you any question concerning it, then I wold you should lett hym knowe that I have made you privie to it. Besydes my meaning is that fewe should be acquaynted with it till I knowe what will come of it. Send me aunswere with speed particulerly by this bearer to the remembraunces I delyvered you, and therin lett me understand howe the ryver goeth forward, and of all the circumstances concerning it. And howe farefourth my sesterne house is in redynes, for it will not be long, or[72] my plomer and my fountayne maker wilbe with you. I meane not that this bearer shall tarrye aunswere from Mr. Asshefeild. Comend me to your mother, and to your wief. And so fare you well. From Gorhambury the 27 of July 1568.
Your father.

Signed: N. Bacon C.S. *Autograph.*

---

70 Robert Ashfield of Stowlangtoft.
71 Either Francis Copledike of Horham, who had six daughters, or more probably his brother John of Kirby Cane (Nf.), who had one daughter, Thomasine, as sole heir (*1561 visitation,* ed. Corder, pp. 143–4). This proposed marriage to Nathaniel did not take place. See also no. **41 [4094]** below.
72 Meaning 'ere'.

Postscript: I loke also to have from you or Boldro advertisement of Mr Russhes[73] aunswere concerning my wardes.

Addressed: To my sonne Nicholas Bacon at Redgrave

2 ff.; remains of seal.

37.   [4090] *Sir Nicholas Bacon I to Nicholas Bacon II, 24 August 1568*

Sonne, I have desyered my frend Mr Wythepowle[74] to come to Redgrave, to see my newe ryver whom I have enformed howe I wold have that parte of the ryver mad over the which my bridge shall go. And thearfore loke what order soever he taketh in that matter, in any wise lett it be performed. My desyer is that the bridg may stand iuste in the mydest betwene bothe the heedes of that parte of the ryver that the bridg doothe go over, and so shall the mydest of my water be iuste agaynst the mydest of my house, as the bridge is. And if it be otherwise wroght alredye, it [*sic*] I meane to have it reformed according to this order. From my house at Gorhambury the 24 of August 1568.

Signed: Your Father N. Bacon C.S. *Autograph.*

Addressed: To my sonne Nicholas Bacon at Redgrave

1 f.; seal impression.

38.   [4091] *Sir Nicholas Bacon I to Nicholas Bacon II, 13 September 1568*

Sonne I have appointed that this bearer Cure whoe is the workman that made my fowntayn and is nowe come downe to set it up and his servauntes should be lodged and borded with you. I thinke he woll end it in a fortnight or thre wekes at the furdest. And the two masons which have laid the steppes for the fowntayne I wold ye should will them immediatlie their worke being ended to come to me hether to Gorhamburye. Comend me to your mother and to your wife and kepe a reconinge of the charges of theis worke men because ye may have allowance for it. From Gorhambury the 12 of Septembre, 1568

Suche iron worke as Cure shall require to be made for the fowntayne, let James cawse the smithe to worke it for hyme that amendes my mouldes.

Signed: Your Father N. Bacon C.S. *Autograph.*

Addressed: To my sonne Nicholas Bacon

1 f.; traces of seal.

39.   [4092] *Sir Nicholas Bacon I to Nicholas Bacon II, 9 December 1568*

9 die decembris 1568.

Sone I fynde dyverse allowaunces demaunded whereof I have great mislikinge bycause thay be done with owt warraunte from me. And therefor I have gyven charge to G. Nune and James Vale to disburse no money withowt my warrunte in writinge. And therefor ye shall do well whan there is any thinge necessa[r]y to be done, to writte to me for my warraunte; yt is no great thinge so to do, and other-wise to do I canne have no likinge of yt.

---

[73] Probably Anthony Rush of Sudbourne, who married Eleanor, daughter of Nicholas Cutler of Eye and widow of Francis Ernley and John Wiseman (*1561 visitation*, ed. Corder, p. 136).

[74] Edward Withipoll of Christchurch House, Ipswich; he was celebrated for his skill with ornamental waterworks, and in the course of a dispute with the borough of Ipswich he was accused of releasing water from his ponds at Christchurch to wreak havoc in the streets of the town (TNA (PRO), STA C 5 J4/7, interrogatories).

Besides you shall do well ones or twise a weeke to looke to my woodes at Rikinghall and Hyndercley bycause I understand, speciallie those at Rikinghall be moche spoiled with cattall, and therefor Bucke must looke better to them or elles some other man must take yt *in* charge. And as to Heskew Wood in Hindercley I dowbt how Catton will performe his covenauntes except ye looke well to hym, the better theise thinges be done the better for yourself.

And beinge enformed that the vicarege of Mettingham is void ye shall do well to provide some honest man to be vicar there as shortly as may be which yf ye can not do than my meaning is that Odyan[75] shall provide one for I will not have the cure remayne unserved. And when ye go to Norwiche speake with my L. Busshope from me to spare from taking advantage by lappes.[76]

I would also that ye should here the matters in varyaunce Є between Corbold, Mr Waller and Chitting and se if ye can make a good end betwen them.[77]

I have also assented that there shalbe a bricke kylne made, and for the discharging of the charge that shall growe thereby that mony shalbe disbursed by G.N.[78] of my arrerages and my lyvinge there. And so fare ye well. From my house nighe Charing Crosse the 9 of Decembre 1568.

Signed: Your Father N. Bacon C.S. *Autograph.*
Addressed: To my sonne Nicholas Bacon at Redgrave
2 ff., torn; remains of seal.

40.   [4093] *Sir Nicholas Bacon I to Nicholas Bacon II, 18 December 1568*

Sonne I have considered how of Sir Wylliam Buttes letter and like very well the contentes of it and would be glad the purpose might be broughte to passe. I have caused the partie that remaynes here to be broken withall by a frende of his in the mater as of hymself and not from me. And both parties have seene one another. What wilbe the end I knowe not, but I trust somtyme the next tearme to understande more. I would be glad it might take good effect. Commend me to your mother and your wief to whom I wisshe as to my self. I am not yet determyned whether they shall come downe or no. I thinke rather nay. From the Courte this 18 of December 1568

Signed: Your Father N. Bacon C.S. *Autograph.*
Addressed: To my sonne Nycholas Bacon
1 f.; seal impression.

41.   [4094] *Sir Nicholas Bacon I to Nicholas Bacon II, 7 April 1569*

Sonne I send you herein inclosed the copie of a letter wherof one is sent to Sir Ambrose Germyn and a nother to Mr. Ashefeld.[79] This I have done because I proceade you should be acquainted howe I proceade in that matter. I se nowe it wilbe after midsomer or I shall come downe, and what tyme then I can not tell,

---

75 Gregory Odierne, the Bacon estate bailiff at Shipmeadow: see no. **57 [4111]** below.
76 On Bishop Parkhurst's presentations by lapse and his close working relationship with the Lord Keeper in appointments, see *The Letter Book of John Parkhurst Bishop of Norwich compiled during the years 1571–5*, ed. R.A. Houlbrooke (Norfolk Record Society 53, 1974/5), pp. 35–7.
77 William Corbold of Brockdish (Nf.), George Waller of Wortham and George Chitting of Wortham; Corbold and Chitting, servants of Bacon, were close relatives, while Waller was a close relative of the Yaxleys and associated with other religious conservatives among the Suffolk gentry.
78 George Nunn.
79 Robert Ashfield of Stowlangtoft, long-serving JP in Suffolk.

this gowte dothe soe ofte resorte unto me. If I find at my coming downe that ether these maides be unmaryed it is lyke that then I will se what good I can doe for yor brother in that matter. But mye meaninge is not to have anie staie made for that purpose. I wold be glad to here howe Sir Thomas Woodhowse my sone Woodhowse[80] and his wief and the whole howse at Redgrave and my godsonne dothe as shortlie as maye be. And whether the mowthe of the old wattering be not within the second water or noe. If it be not it muste be, for otherwise I feare yowr fishe wilbe leane. Thus with my hartie commendations to your mother[81] and your wife with Godes blessinge to my god sone I bid you farewell. From Goramburie the 7 of Aprill 1569

Signed: Your Father N. Bacon C.S. *Autograph.*
Addressed: To my sonne Nicholas Bacon at Redgrave.
2 ff.; seal impression.

42.   [4095] *Sir Nicholas Bacon I to Nicholas Bacon II, 16 April 1569*
I finde by your letters that Hunt[82] hathe ben with you. I trust he hathe performed the survey of Rickingall, if he have not, send to hyme to doe it. And as to the wateringe, leave it alone till I come to see it.

Albeit I misliked the pryce that my men have made of Lyns land, yet am I contented to give hyme fowre hundreth markes for it according as I have w̶ written to Boldero and Georg Nun. And looke what ye can make of it, above twentie marke a yeare, I am content you shall receave to h̶i̶s̶ your owne use. I ame glad *to hear* that your mother, your wief and my godsonne do well, and to your mother and your [*sic with 'wife' omitted?*] yow h̶ must have me hartely commended, and to my godsonne I send Godes blessing and myne. From my howse at Gorambury, the 16 of Aprill 1569

Signed: Your Father N. Bacon C.S. *Autograph.*
Addressed: To my sonne Nicholas Bacon.
1 f.; traces of seal.

43.   [4096] *Sir Nicholas Bacon I to Nicholas Bacon II, 22 May 1569*
Sonne, understanding that certeyne goodes of a fellone within the Oner of Eye hath ben taken and dryven a waye by an under officer of the Fraunces of St. A̶u̶d̶e̶r̶y̶e̶s̶ *Tawdryes*,[83] whereby that that is due and ought to be aunswered to the Quenes Majestie in the right of the Oner of Eye is lyke to be un-aunswered; therefor I have thought good to will you not to fayle but to be at the Court of the Oner which is to be holden as I understand the Wedensdaye in Wydsoneweek[84] next. Where my meaning is that this maner of taking of goodes out of the Oner should be examyned and enquyered, and that that which shalbe found to be done to the prejudice of the liberties should be presentid and recorded. And for your

---

80 Henry Woodhouse, married to the Lord Keeper's daughter Anne.
81 The younger Nicholas Bacon's mother-in-law, Anne Butts.
82 Probably John Le Hunt of Little Bradley, a civil lawyer and servant of Bacon's.
83 This is the only interlineation in a carefully written letter, and was clearly demanded by Bacon. May it be a derogatory play on words? The pejorative meaning of the word 'tawdry' is recorded in usages no earlier than the seventeenth century by the *Oxford English Dictionary*, but it is possible that we are here seeing a small piece of bitter humour from the Lord Keeper.
84 'Whitsunweek': Wednesday 1 June 1569.

better enformation howe to procead in this, I have desyered my very frend Mr Grymstone to be present with you, for your assistaunce, and besydes ye shall herewith receyve a letter to Mr Thurston to desyer him to be theare also, which ye must see delyvered unto him in tyme. From my house besydes Charing Crosse the 22 of Maye 1569,[85]

Signed: Your Father N. Bacon C.S. *Autograph.*
Addressed: To my sonne Nicholas Bacon.
1 f.; seal impression.

44.   [4097] *Sir Nicholas Bacon I to Nicholas Bacon II, 17 June 1569*

Sonne, the sonner I here aunswer of those thinges I commyttyd unto ye, the better. Therefor ye shall do well to be carefull and dilygent to send me as shortly as ye can aunswer of those matters, and that particulerly, and at large, so as I maye understand the matter the better. Besydes I wold Sir Clement Higham should be served of a bucke, or a brace of buckes, when he woll have them out of Redgrave.[86] Writen the 17 of June 1569.

Signed: Your Father N. Bacon C.S. *Autograph.*
Addressed: To my sonne Nicholas Bacon.
1 f.; seal impression.

45.   [4098] *Sir Nicholas Bacon I to Nicholas Bacon II, 4 October 1569*

I have receyved your letter, for aunswere wher ye shall understand that at my being in the country Boldro moved me that a man of his might suplye George Sowters office if he dyed (as he saied he was lyke). Yf my remembraunce fayle me not, I dyd graunt that his man should have it. George Nonne can best tell my aunswere for hee was bye. But if my graunt be past me, then ye shall do well to speak to Boldro for your meneye[87] who I think will not stick with ye. That Mistres Buttes, your wief and my godsonne dothe well I am glad of it. And so fare ye well. From the Courte the 4 of October 1569[88]

Signed: Your Father N. Bacon C.S. *Autograph.*
Holograph postscript: Comend me to my dowghter.
Addressed: To my sonne Nicholas Bacon.
1 f.; seal impression.

---

85 This letter follows closely on the grant of 18 February 1569 to the younger Nicholas of the stewardship of all former liberties purchased by Henry VIII from Charles Duke of Suffolk (which included the Honour of Eye): *CPR Elizabeth I, 1566–69*, no. 2575. This complemented the round-up of most other Suffolk royal stewardships for the Lord Keeper and his son in survivorship in 1562: *CPR Elizabeth I, 1560–63*, p. 256. The Lord Keeper displays a touchingly loyal solicitude for the queen's rights over those of the Dean and Chapter of Ely in St Audrey's liberty, not unconnected with the financial benefit for his family.

86 Sir Clement Higham was *Custos Rotulorum* for Suffolk, which may have something to do with this gift in the middle of a developing lawsuit over the rights of the Honour of Eye.

87 'Meinie' meaning 'household' – so by transference, member of the younger Bacon's household?

88 Notable in this letter is the lack of a sense of crisis at court. The duke of Norfolk had been arrested the day before for his flight from court, but the rebellion of the Catholic northern earls which dominated English politics during autumn 1569 had not yet broken out.

46. **[4099]** *Sir Nicholas Bacon I to Nicholas Bacon II, 9 November 1569*
Sonne, I send ye herein enclosed a letter directyd to Mr. Wyndham, which when ye have read, and well considered, I wold ye should close it and cause it to be delyvered; the soner that he repayereth up hether, and ye with him, the better, for I cannot see howe this matter can any further be well proc[ee]dyd in before his and your cumming to me.[89] And yeat this hast may not seeme to be procured by me, but rather that some busynes of yours ~~req~~ here with me requyers your jorney hether with speed. Ye writt for my letter in favour of one to be undershireve and ye tell me not his name, whereby I must writt for one that I knowe not, which I use not to do. Commend me to your wief her mother and the boye whom God blesse. From the Court the 9 of Novembre 1569

Signed: Your Father N. Bacon C.S. *Autograph.*
Addressed: To my sonne Nicholas Bacon.
1 f.; seal impression.

47. **[4101]** *Sir Nicholas Bacon I to Nicholas Bacon II [?December 1569][90]*
Sonne, I have as yet hard nothing of my provision of wheat. Ye shall do well to call upon it and to cause letters to be sent with it with them that bring it. I have appoynted Phillips to receyve it. You may tell my sonne Woodhouse[91] that I have spoken with Mr Myldmay for the stey of the parsonage of Lyngwood, according to the tenour of his letter which he hath promysed to see done.[92] I wold be glad to here howe my daughter Besses busynes goeth forward,[93] and whether my daughter Woodhouse[94] be brought a bedd or no, and howe my godsonne dothe,

Signed: N. Bacon C.S. *Autograph.*
Addressed: To my sonne Nicholas Bacon.
1 f.; traces of seal.

48. **[4100]** *Sir Nicholas Bacon I to William Phillips and to Richard Yaxley, 24 December 1569*
Phillips, there is to be receyved of Mr Yaxley the some of fyve hundred markes ~~in full payment~~ due to be payed to me nowe at Christmas. And bycause I cannot dischardge this debte due unto me by delyvery ~~and dischardging~~ of the bounde wherin he standeth bound unto me, therefore I have sent ye a quyttaunce for his discharge witnessing the receyt *of the same and dischardging him of his bound for the payment* of the same money. If he shall myslyke this maner of dischardge *by this acquyttaunce* then you are to lett him understand that I am not hable being here otherwise to dischardge his bond which I wolde gladly do, if I were

---

[89] Marriage negotiations between Francis Wyndham of Felbrigg and Elizabeth Bacon the younger: see nos. **47, 49 [4101, 4102]** below.

[90] The letter is dated by the reference to the Wyndham marriage, as noted below, and references to the business of supplying grain in no. **49 [4102]** below (which is apparently a reply to a reply to this letter).

[91] Henry Woodhouse.

[92] The rectory of Lingwood (Nf.) was leased by the Crown to a consortium headed by Thomas Ormesby on 26 June 1568, and on 23 May 1573 again to Robert Power, equerry of the stable: *CPR Elizabeth I, 1572–75*, no. 82(32). Mildmay was probably Sir Walter Mildmay, chancellor and under-treasurer of the Exchequer.

[93] Elizabeth Bacon the younger married Francis Wyndham in 1570: *1561 visitation*, ed. Corder, p. 159.

[94] Anne Bacon, who married Henry Woodhouse.

at London, and will not fayle to do it so sone as I maye come thether. And if he will come hether for that he myslyke the acquytaunce which I send you to be his suffycient dischardge (which my thinketh he should not) then will I make him here some other dischardg ~~to his contentation~~ *such as ought to content him*. I take Christmas daye to be the daye he should paye his money, and at my house nere Charing Crosse. Wherefore it behoveth you to be there, with some ~~bodye~~ testimony with you an hower afore the sonne going downe and half an hower after ~~with some to witnesse the same testyf~~ which maye beare witness that ye are redy to receyve the money.

~~If christ~~ As concerning the dagges[95] that ye writt of I doubt nothing but the rebelles ~~being~~ disparsed in the North as they be but that I shalbe provyded at easyer pryces and of good also. And therefore deale no further in that matter till ye heare further from me. And as to the Northen staves if you have receyved them they must be payed for otherwise lett them alone. From the Court the 24 of December 1569.

Post/ Phillips I send ye hereinclosed Mr Yaxleys letter which when you have read and perceyved it, ye maye ~~inclose~~ *seale* it and gyve it him.

[*Enclosure A*]
This bill ~~mad the xxvth of December 1569~~ witnesseth that I Sir Nicholas Bacon Knight Lord Keper of the Greate Seale of England have receyved and had the day of the date hereof of Richard Yaxley Esquyer, the somme of fyve houndred markes of good and lawfull money of England to me due the daye of the date hereof of which said some I *the said Sir Nicholas* clearly acquyt and dischardg the said Richard his heires executors and admynistrators by this presentes, in witnes whearof etc.

[*Enclosure B*]
Mr Yaxley, this is to signifye unto you that I have sent unto Phillips my servaunt, an acquytaunce for your dischardg of the fyve houndred markes which you are to paye me, bycause being here, I cannot make no nother dischardg but by acquyttaunce, but I meane ~~I~~ to do further at my cummming to London any thing that ye in reason maye requyer. And if ye shall desyer to have aquyttaunce of any other forme, then this that I have sent unto Phillips my servaunt for the receyt of your money, ye shall upon your cumming hether, and bringing with ye the copye of your bonde, receyve of me such a on under my hand and seale ~~such~~ as in reason ought to content ye. And so etc.

Draft in secretary's hand.
Endorsed in Bacon's hand: A copye of Yaxleys acyittaunce and letter.
2 ff.

49. [4102] *Sir Nicholas Bacon I to Nicholas Bacon II, 6 January 1570*

Sonne, I have receyved your letter, for aunswere whereof, this is to lett you under-stand that so sone as I shall learne that my corne is come to London, which in deed should have ben there you knowe, moch before this tyme, so sone shall you have aunswere of the fraight which I truste will not be long. If I forgitt thus to do, lett me be remembred of it. And as to the matter concerning my daughter Elizabeth,

---

95 Handguns. Sir Nicholas, with characteristic attention to financial detail, is determined to take advantage of the end of the northern rebellion, which for a while had seemed the most serious internal threat to survival which the Elizabethan regime had yet faced.

as I am glad to heare of his resort and lyking so am I sorye to understand that he persysteth in the intayling *his* land to the heire mayle. Neyther can I see howe my presyse aunswer made to him therin can agree with his proceading, except he thought that I wold cum further on, then my wordes then perported, but he shall fynde execept [*sic*] he will come to some reasonable porcion to be leefte to the heire generall which maye come of my daughter, I shall hardely be brought to yeld to so great a chardge as he requyers. Mye trust is bothe in that, and in other thinges to fynd him conformable to reason. And bycause in the begynning of the next tearme it was agreed that we should talke further of that matter, I think he will move you to come up with him for the performing thereof which I wold you should agree unto, for I meane not without you to make an ende. That your mother hath ben sick I am sory, and am glade of her amendement. That my daughter your wief and my daughter Woodhouse, and their children also do well, I am glad, and wishe it longe to contynue. From the Court the sixt of January 1569,

Signed: Your Father N. Bacon C.S. *Autograph.*
Addressed: To my sonne Nicholas Bacon.
2 ff.; traces of seal.

50.   [4103] *Sir Nicholas Bacon I to Nicholas Bacon II, 28 February 1570*

Sonne, Because your letters came to my handes at the Courte I am not able to geve such aunswere to the matter concernyng yong Mr. Coote as you desire to have untill such tyme as I have spoken with my brother, which I think will not be afore the next Tearme. And I make the lesse hast, because he offreth but fortie poundes presentlie a yeare withe his sonne, and but a hundreth poundes after his death for fyve hundreth markes to be geven in marryage, which offer (methinkes) hath no reason in it.[96]

Mr Wyndham and I ar gone through, and it is agreed that the marryage shalbe afore whytsontide. It semed unto me that he could be content to have the marriage at my howse at London, but having thought of that, I think it altogether unmete for dyvers respectes. And so ye shall do well to lett hym understand, when ye occasion shall serve you next to speake with hym.

I have taken order with James[97] for the proceding in my workes at Redgrave. Ye shall do well to speake to George Nun that he may have money according to such warrauntes as he hath or shall have of myne. And if he want warraunt, upon advertisement I will not fayle to sende hym sufficient.

I have not yet receyved my whole bargayne of wheate by twentie quarters. And so ye may lett my sone Woodhouse understand. From the Court the 28 of Februarye 1569.[98]

Signed: Your Father N. Bacon C.S. *Autograph.*
Addressed: To my sonne Nycholas Bacon.
1 f., torn; traces of seal.

---

[96]   This must be a marriage proposal between Nicholas Coote and Anne daughter of James Bacon, brother of the Lord Keeper; she did not marry Coote, very soon afterwards marrying John Rivett of Brandeston, with whom a marriage settlement was finalised on 13 June 1570 (*CPR Elizabeth I, 1569–72*, no. 1256; *1561 visitation*, ed. Corder, p. 158). Coote nevertheless sold Culford Hall to Nicholas Bacon II in 1585: TNA (PRO), C 66/1278, m. 2.

[97]   James Vale.

[98]   Address and date in a rougher hand, not the secretary's or Bacon's; same hand as endorsed address.

51. **[4104]** *Sir Nicholas Bacon I to Nicholas Bacon II, 13 July 1570*

Sonne, upon the recept of your letter, I dyd lette Mr Cowte to understand that albeit I have refused to all men to deale in such suytes as his is, it[99] upon your letter I was contented to writt to Mr Secretary in his favour for that matter, and so I have done.

And as touching the ward that ye writt of, on till such tyme that I maye knowe what her name is, and whether she be ward to Mr Crane in Suff. or to Mr Crane in the Court,[100] I cannot tell howe to writt nor to whom, but apon advertisement from you, I will not fayle to deale to the best and with the best speed I can. And therefore the soner ye advertise the better.

And as to my buyldinges, two thinges are to be considered. One is that the maker of my vayght[101] be not payed his hole somme till you see whether the vayght will hold after the earth be taken awaye. The second is that my steers do not drowne the light that is in the entry that leadeth to the galary chamber and withall, that all my instructions concerning the same steers, and the wyndowes perteyning to it be performed.

As touching a warraunt for more money ye do not writt for howe moche ye wold have warraunt, nor for howe moche I have alredy graunted warraunt. And therefore I am to seke what to do in it, and will do it upon your next advertisement. Commend me to your mother and your wief, and to my god sonne I wishe Godes blessing and myn. From Gorhambury the 13 of Julye 1570.

Signed: Your Father N. Bacon C.S. *Autograph.*
Addressed: To my sonne Nicholas Bacon.
1 f.; traces of seal.

52. **[4105]** *Sir Nicholas Bacon I to Nicholas Bacon II, 3 August 1570*

I have receyved your letter dated the first of August, for aunswere whereof this is to lett ye understand that I have delyvered to this bearer a presentation for the benefyce of Yaxley to be delyvered unto you. Besydes this bearer hath obteyned of me a graunt of a presentation to the benefice of Aldam to thuse of Phillip Thomson upon condicion that Wylkenson put in bound to you that the hole profittes of this benefice shalbe imployed to thuse of this Phillip; the chardge of the cure, and other ordynary chardges concerning the same deducted.[102]

And as touching the warraunt ye writte of for money, I meane to graunt no such warraunt untill I be advertised from you howe the same shalbe imployed, which maye easely be done bycause the bargaynes be made of great, with the breck layer and the freemason, the rest of the chardge consyste in wages of laborers, and in chardge of carryage, ~~which~~ whereof an estimation maye be made, and so these maye of the chardge of the glasse irne and lead *and carpentry worke*. And therefor ye shall do well to send unto ['*me*' omitted] such an advertisement, and therupon I will send you a warraunt, for somoch money as the chardges shall requyer.

I marvell that your wayneskottes should not be good, for they were chosen out

---

99   Apparently a form of 'yet'. Cf. no. **135 [4183]** below.
100   Probably respectively Robert Crane of Chilton, and Henry Crane his son.
101   That is, 'vault'.
102   The Crown presented Giles Poley to the vicarage of Yaxley on 3 August 1570 (the grant was dated from Bacon's house at Gorhambury), and Philip Thompson to Aldham on 15 November 1570: *CPR Elizabeth I, 1569–72*, nos. 376, 419.

of a great nomber. It cannot be but that he that chose them dyd deceyve me, onels [*sic*] he that telleth you so is deceyved. The chardge of this worke perteyning to the joyner you must certefye me also among the rest, and that maye ye easely do by thadvise of the ioyner, whether he worke it by the yard or he worke it by the daye. You should by your letters writt more particulerly howe my work goeth forward, and of such thinges as your letter concerne. Commend [*'me' omitted*] to your mother, your wief and to my godsonne to whom I wishe Godes blesshing and myn. From my house at Gorhambury the 3 of August 1570

Signed: Your Father N. Bacon C.S. *Autograph.*
Addressed: To my sonne Nicholas Bacon.
2 ff.; seal impression.

53. **[4106–7]** *Sir Nicholas Bacon I to Sir Thomas Cornwallis, Sir Clement Higham, Sir Ambrose Jermyn and Robert Ashfield, 20 «»23 October 1570*
After my hartie commendations. Wheare I ame enformed that Mr Robert Rooke-wood and my sonne this bearer hathe agreed to abide your order what shall be the pryce of the moytie of the mannor of Burgate and of all ~~his landes~~ Mr. Rooke-woodes landes and hereditamentes in the parishe of Burgate. This is to signifie unto ye that I for my parte doe lyke well and allowe of this their agreament. And withall I ame contented that what some of money soever shall be assessed bye you, as the iuste pryce of the premisses, I will see it trewly paide in soche sorte *and* at suche tyme as shalbe by you agreed, upon good assuraunce made unto me of the premysses. And besides I shall thinke my self moche beholden unto you for your travell and payne *to be* taken herein. Before this tyme a lyke offer was made by Mr Rookewood, but the sequele of it was suche that I might doubte what will be come of this. Nevertehelesse knowing you all as I doe I have thought good to mak a nother proof, assuringe you that what soever shalbe agreed upon by you according as is above written I will *do myn indevor to* see it performed ~~if it shall lye in my power~~, and besydes be glade and readie to doe asmoche for anie of you if it shall lye in my power. And[103]

Two unsigned copies in two different secretaries' hands; **[4106]**, *the earlier draft and a slightly fuller version, has been transcribed above.*
Endorsed by Bacon: **[4106]** The copye of my letter sent to the arbrytators [*sic*] for Burgate. *This copy further endorsed in another hand* vi[c] lx one acre d.[104] *and* **[4107]** *endorsed by Bacon:* The copye of the letter sent to Mr. Cornwalles and others
2 ff. **[4106]** *and 1f.* **[4107]**.

54. **[4108]** *Sir Thomas Cornwallis, Sir Clement Higham, Sir Ambrose Jermyn and Robert Ashfield to Sir Nicholas Bacon I, 23 October 1570*
Maye it please your good L. upon mocion made unto us by Mr Bacon your sonne and Mr Rookewoode for thorderinge of the price of Mr Rookewood his moytie of the manor of Burgate, we apoynted our meatinge at St Edmundes Bury the 23 of this instant, where then allso we rec. your L. letters signifienge your contentacion therin, and allso your promyse for the payment of suche price as shold be sett by us upon the same. Therupon we procedid to talke of the matier which at the first

---

103 No. **4107** ends 'And so etc'.
104 Presumably this is '661 and a half acres'.

we weare out of hoope to bringe to any good ende, aswell for that throughe want of conferringe and foresight of the parties we coulde not be instructed by them selves, or by any surveye, of the quantety of the grounde, and sundry natures and goodnes of the same, asalso for that we founde Mr Rookewoode in his demaunde, and your agentes in ther offers, so farre differinge. Neverthelesse knowynge your earnest desire to have the same (as your L. poore neyghbors and friendes) we dealt so earnestly in the matier that in thende we orderid it in such forme, as by the reporte of this bearer, and articles of agreament by him sent unto your L. from us it maye appeare. Your L. peradventur will thinke, we have *ben* somewhat bolde in stallinge so shorte dayes of payement, so we assure you Mr Rookewoode doth thinke we were more bolde with him, in defalkinge almost 400 markes which the land and woodes seamed to be worth, upon the particulare valuinge of the same. We therfore thought it better to streyne your L. with the quicker stalment of the paymentes, then to cherge you with such a somme of money more, or elles utterly to have broken of, and to have lefte the matier at large. We humbly desire your L. to take this our travell in goode parte, and to allowe of our friendly and earnest meanynge to pleasure your L. And it maye please you allso to stond good lorde hereafter *to Mr Rookwood* in all his reasonable sutes, which request he hath desired us most humbly on his behalf to make unto your L. And so with the remembrance of our humble and most hertye comendations unto your L. we take our leave, besechinge almighty God to continue your L. in good health and longe lief to his pleasure. At Bury the 23 of October,[105]

Signed: Your L. poore neyghbours humbly at commandement T. Cornwaleys Clement Heigham Ambros Jermyn Robert Ashefyld. *Autograph.*
Endorsed by Nicholas Bacon I: The letter from Mr Cornwall. and others
2 ff.

55. [4109] *Sir Nicholas Bacon I to Nicholas Bacon II, 27 November 1570*
Sonne, for aunswere of your letter this is to lett you understand, that I doo not myslyke your proceading with Mr Cornewallis. Mary if Rockwood come not up, and bring his evydence with him three or foure dayes befor the beginning of the next tearme it wilbe very hard to have the assuraunce betwene him and me made perfytt befor Candelmas, at which tyme the firste payment is to begyne, and therefor you shall do well to lett him knowe it. And as touching the smale pece of land lying in St Margaretes, I lyke well of the sale made thereof; for Tasboroughtes farme, my promyse was that he should have it for £700 exceipt I might have Shurlockes, and fayling of that I I [*sic*] am at libertie to sell it to the best, and so I meane to do.[106] And if I cannot sell it in grosse, then will I sell it by parcells as it shall lye meet for the byer, and as to the rest of the parcells ye shall do well to procure for them the best pryce ye can and to advertise me.

I had once concluded to sell the tythes of the parsonage of Walsham to two men in Walsham and I had gone thorowe with it (as Boldro can tell) saving that it was your wiefes ioynter, and so was the rent out of Parham which bothe I must have taken from her, and assigned a recompence, which then I could not, the rest of my land was so assured, but now seeing she maye have her recompence in Burgatt I

---

105 Cf. the formal agreement of 23 October about the bargain and sale, *Bacon handlist*, no. **2562**.
106 This must refer to Ilketshall rather than South Elmham St Margaret; Bacon owned the manor. 'Tasborought' is probably John Tasborough of South Elmham St Peter.

have thought it not amysse to parte with them, exceipt I maye sell the better my thinges about Mettingham. You shall do well to speake with Boldro about this, for there was a draught for the tythes of the parsonage which if Boldro hath not is lost, but I think Boldro can remembre the maner of the bargayne for to that bargayne I could be content to conclud, and I wold Boldroo should prove whether they that should have bought it will nowe have it, and if George Bacon[107] or any body els will bye the rent out of Parham for £500, thought I gyve the longer dayes, I am content to procede with that also. Ye shall do well to think of thies thinges, and whan Rockwood cometh up to come up with him. And commend [*me*] to your mother and to your wief, and God bleshe bothe your yonge children. From my house at Charinge Crosse the 27 of November 1570

Signed: Your Father N. Bacon C.S. *Autograph.*
Postscript: Tell George Nunne that I loke to see him here at the begyning of the next tearme with as moche money as he can gather up for me, his son is under-shiref ~~not~~ but not without much ado, I wold gladly see Boldroo there then also, if his helth will suffer.[108]
Addressed: To my sonne Nicholas Bacon.
2 ff., torn; traces of seal.

56.   [4110] *Sir Nicholas Bacon I to Nicholas Bacon II, 12 February 1571*
Sonne the bargayne betwene *mee* Mr Rookewoode and me is broken, both because I fynd by his evidence nowe last browght up unto me that all his land is entayled, and that he canne put in no bonde for the performaunce of his cove-nauntes, but by his deathe they wilbe in effecte voyde, and suertie ye will find none.[109] Bothe for this cause and other respectes the bargayne is disolved, where-uppon he prayed me that I would assente to some partition whereunto I agreed, uppon his sute, so as the land might be devided, in such sorte, as I maye have juste cause to thinke uppon the consideration of it by my selfe, I maye finde juste cause to thinke, [*sic*] I am not over straytelie dealt withall. And for the well bringinge this to passe I have thought good that he showlde devise suche a partition, as he in reason thinkethe mete and equall. And I would on the other parte that you, call-inge unto you Bolderoe and George Nunne, should make a partition suche as you thinke equall, wherein it behovethe you to take thadvise of those that knowe the goodnes of the growndes and the value of the woodes for I am sure thother partie shall not want good advise in that matter, ~~my~~

My meaninge is, that bothe theise partitions, thone made by him, and thother by you should be browght up to me in the begynninge of the nexte terme at which tyme I loke to see you Bolderoe and George Nunne here. And I dowte nothinge, but uppon the sight of theise partitions, we shall growe to good end, and make a perfite severaunce. And so fare you well. From the Courte this 12 of Februarie 1570.

Signed: Your Father N. Bacon C.S. *Autograph.*

---

107   Of Hessett, son of Thomas, a cousin of the Lord Keeper.
108   The Sheriff who had to be persuaded to take the younger Nunn as under-sheriff was Bacon's close friend Edmund Withipoll. Nunn must have been under-sheriff in Norfolk, since Henry Hannam is recorded for Suffolk in 1570–1: MacCulloch, *Suffolk*, p. 91, n. 126.
109   This refers to the draft agreement of January 1571: *Bacon handlist*, no. **2563**.

Postscript: Yf you shall find Mr Rookewod eyther slacke or untoward in this, then you shall do well to put in your cattell and fede in common.[110]
Addressed: To my sonne Nicholas Bacon at Redgrave.
2 ff.

57. [4111] *Sir Nicholas Bacon I to Nicholas Bacon II, 13 February 1571*

Sonne I send you herein enclosed, a bill of complaynte exhibited unto me, by one of my tenauntes of Shepmedowe, agaynste my servaunte Odierne. And for that his requeste is that you, and ane other whom I will appoynte should have the hearinge of the matter, and to end it, I would have you therefore, calle Bolderoe and George Nunne to you, and to examyne the cause on bothe sides, and thereuppon to make some end betwene them yf you canne, yf not, then to certyfie unto me, what you thinke of it, and in whom the faulte is. And so fare you well. From my howse nere Charinge Crosse this 13 of Februarie 1570

Signed: Your Father N. Bacon C.S. *Autograph.*
Addressed: To my sonne Nic[*holas*] Bacon at Redgrave.[111]
2 ff., torn; remains of seal.

58. [4112] *Sir Nicholas Bacon I to Nicholas Bacon II, 23 February 1571*

I have receyved your letter, for answere whereof you shall understond that yf the lond of George Dedham be worth fiftene pownd by yeare, over and above all charges, and will hold that value, then doe I like verie well of the bargayne and the price of £300, to be payd at suche dayes as is conteyned in your letter, and you shall do well, to let me understond by the next mesenger the particularities, that is howe manie acres of medowe, howe many of pasture, howe many of arable, bene conteyned within that bargayne. I have not forgotten my sonne Woodhowse, for 3 days *be*fore the receipte of your letter, I had my L. of Warwickes consent that he showld remayne in his office,[112] and I meane to se what I canne doe for you, but I mervayle muche, that I heare not from you, concerninge the letter which I wrote unto you towching Burgate, neyther what further you heare, or understond, from Thomas Buttes; at the leste you showld have written a parentizes[113] yf it be trewe that you have no further as yet to write unto me in those matters. Comend me unto my dawghter, God blesse your children. And so fare you well from my howse nere Charinge Crosse this 23 of Februarie 1570.

Signed: Your Father N. Bacon C.S. *Autograph.*
Addressed: To my sonne Nicholas Bacon at Redgrave.
1 f.

59. [4113] *Sir Nicholas Bacon I to Nicholas Bacon II, 13 April 1571*

For answere of your letter, this *is* to let you understond that I am glad to heare of the childes amendment. And as to the fynyshinge of my house, I would that James showld provide some able workeman for the goynge forward and fynisshinge of the same without taryeng for any that is to be sente from hence, ~~becau The~~

---

110 The agreement which resulted (8 April 1571) is Bacon handlist, no. 2564, and see acquittance for first payment for the moiety, ibid., no. 2565.
111 First six words of the letter appear, an abandoned first attempt, on the dorse of f. 1.
112 As Vice-Admiral of Norfolk and Suffolk.
113 'A parenthesis', i.e. a postscript.

because I meane to send none, the worke is so little that is to be done; the soner that this worke goethe in hand, towching my howse, the better it shall please me. And as towchinge the fowntayne, I would not have you meddle with it tyll you heare further from me. I dowte not but Bolderoe will come to you assone as he canne. Commend me to your wiefe and her mother. And so fare you well, from my howse nere Charinge Cros this 13 of Aprill 1571

Signed: Your Father N. Bacon C.S. *Autograph.*
Addressed: To my sonne Nicholas Bacon at Redgrave.
2 ff.; seal impression.

60.   [4114] *Sir Nicholas Bacon I to Nicholas Bacon II, 19 June 1571*
Sonne as towching lead, it appeares by former advertysementes that the halfe fooder which I sent dow[n]e with the lead which is to be fyned owt of the lead asshes remayninge at Redgrave, wherof I thinke no body makes rekenynge, would suffice for that, that I showld stond ~~iin~~ *in* neade of at this tyme. And to saye trewely it is to late to provide any from hence. And therfor yf there be nede in dede as I thinke there is not, some shifte muste be made there in the contry. And so fare you well from my howse nere Charing Crosse this 19 of June 1571,

Signed: Your Father N. Bacon C.S. *Autograph.*
Postscript: I am glad to here that my sonne Woodhowse takethe so good wayes with hym for his owne profite, and am very well contente that Bolderoe and George Nunne shall survey his mannors at such tyme as their leyser will serve them without hynderaunce to my busynes as at my comyng downe I will declare unto them, for the matter will aske a lenger tyme then you thinke. The benefice of Ingham I have alredy geven to Holte of Bury.[114] I beleve no man takes care to calle for the evydence of Burgate, and the cowrte rolles and the coppies of such evidence that concernes the land that I have bowght, and of other landes remayninge in Rookwoodes handes.
Addressed: To my sonne Nicholas Bacon at Redgrave.
2 ff.; seal impression.

61.   [4115] *Sir Nicholas Bacon I to Nicholas Bacon II, 15 July 1571*
Sonne, my determynation to come into Suffolk accordinge as I meant growethe very dowtfull to be performed partly dowting my healthe, but cheifly for other respectes wherof I thowght good to make you pryvie; nevertheles if it shalbe my chaunce, to fynd that I maye contynue my former determynation, you shall understond it in tyme. Commend me to your mother, and to my daughter your wief. And God blesse the infauntes. I would be glad to heare howe all theise folkes do, and howe my thinges go forward at Redgrave. And I dowte not but you and the rest takes care howe my landes of Burgate so deare bowght shalbe leatten at Myhelmes next, otherwise you forget me and yourself to. Ther would be a certyficate made unto me what they be that would hire those landes and at what prises; I hard of sondry that were suyters, but yf no body followe the matter yt will neyther be good for you nor for me. Yt would be notyfied (yf it be not done alredye) that the land is to be leaten, and therfor those that are to deale with it are to come and shewe in what sort they will take it, and what they will geve for arable, what for

---

114   I have not found this presentation on the patent rolls, but Robert Holte was instituted to Ingham in 1571: Freeman Bullen, 'Beneficed clergy, 1551–1631', p. 306.

pasture, what for meadowe which would be entered into wrighting, and that would be browght unto me by your selfe.[115] And for the better doyng of this, you are to calle unto you yf you thinke so good eyther Bolderoe or George Nunne. Mary in the handelinge of theis thinges you are to reserve as muche rent wheat as you maye to be delyvered at Redgrave as the thinge was necessary to your hows. The more dyligence you use in this matter the better for us both. You do not forget I am sure my remembraunces. And so fare you well, from Gorhamburie this 15 of July 1571

Signed: Your Father N. Bacon C.S. *Autograph.*
Postscript in Bacon's hand: Wryght at large and not scantly.
Addressed: To my sonne Nycholas Bacon at Redgrave.
2 ff.; seal impression.

62.   [4116] *Sir Nicholas Bacon I to Nicholas Bacon II, 16 February 1572*
Sonne, I send you herein enclosed, a letter sent to me from my L. of Ely, for answer of a letter that I sent to hym, the copie wherof you shall receyve herewith. When you have red them bothe, and considered of them, you shall do well to retorne them to me agayne, and withall to advertise me what be the faultes that my L. fyndes ~~of~~ *in* your deputies of the office of Constableshipp.[116] And yf they be not alredie understonded to you, you shall do well at your convenyent leisor to repayre to my L., and to understond them at his handes. And so fare you well. From the Court this 16 of Februarie 1571

Signed: Your father N. Bacon C.S. *Autograph.*
Postscript: Synce the wrighting of this letter I have receyved your letter dated the 17 of this monethe. For answere wherof I thinke it good, that Balam[117] be called up hether to me at suche tyme as you maye be here also, and for that purpose I send you a letter directed unto hym withowt date to be dated by you, at suche tyme as your leysor will serve you best to come up, and then to cause it to be delyvered unto hym. I thinke the tyme wilbe best the weke before the next terme, at which tyme I have appoynted my sonne Woodhows to be here. And as towching your brother Nathaniell, I canne send no answere because he is sicke of the smale pockes but it shall not be longe after his recoverye but you shall receyve answere from me.
1 f., second sheet torn off; traces of seal.

63.   [4117] *Sir Nicholas Bacon I to Nicholas Bacon II, 17 April 1572*
Sonne, the daye that you departed, I receyved a letter from the levetenaunte of the Tower,[118] which I send you by this bearer whereby you may perceyve his intention yf no promyse hath passed you before the receipte of this. I had rather this man joyned with you then any other for sondrie respectes. Neverthelesse yf your word

---

115 It would be interesting to know how and where this notification was to be done. It might have been done by proclamation or notice on market days, or possibly by networks of friends and friends of friends. Possibly scriveners' offices were a venue for enquiries, and one could compare the way in which parliamentary election campaigns used informal channels of communication.

116 The constableship of the bishop of Ely's castle at Wisbech: see above, no. 33 [4085].

117 Probably Robert Balam, a JP in the Isle of Ely in the 1560s; he died in 1573.

118 Sir Owen Hopton of Yoxford. This letter, together with the next, concerns the younger Bacon's proposal to stand for knight of the shire in the 1572 parliamentary election. For overall comment on the letters, see MacCulloch, *Suffolk*, pp. 33, 88–90, 94–5, 240–3.

Plate 3: *Letter 64 [4118]: Sir Nicholas Bacon I to Nicholas Bacon II, 24 April 1572. A rare example of a letter entirely in the Lord Keeper's hand, on a matter of the highest confidentiality: voting alliances in a county parliamentary election.*

be passed kepe it in any wise; except by concent you canne be delyvered of it. And so fare you well. From the Cowrt this 17 of Aprill 1572

Signed: Your Father N. Bacon C.S. *Autograph.*
Postscript: My answere to Mr Lyvetenauntes letter was that I could do nothing without hearing from you because I knewe not what promyse had passed you.
Addressed: To my sonne Nicholas Bacon at Redgrave.
2 ff.; remains of seal.

64. [4118] *Sir Nicholas Bacon I to Nicholas Bacon II, 24 April 1572*
Soon I have rec. your letter and for answere I meane not for a £100 *charge* and more you shuld take lackes in thys that you have entryd into,[119] albeit in dede I had no greate desyre to have you delt in yt at thys tyme but seyng you have gon so farr ~ye~ I wold not have you yeld for feare of charge. And yet *you* must take great

---
119 That is, 'that you should run short of money in the enterprise which you have begun'. 'Lacks' means 'deficiency'.

hede that my name be non otherwyse usyd then you have wreton. The Master of the Rolles[120] told me that all hys tenauntes shuld goo with you at the motion of Mr Walgrave.[121] The dyffyculte that you shall fynd wyll rest in thys, that yf the Sir R. Wyngfyld and yo the Master of the Requestes[122] doo joyne to gether ageynst you and non other joyne with you, then perchaunce the matter wyll be the harder, but yet yt may be you shall doo well i nowe. I You wryght nothyng of Homerston and Badbye who methynkes myght do sumwhat with the Esch. tenauntes[123] and what Hasset, Gaudye and Plater may do about Metyngham I knowe not.[124] I can sey no more but God send yt good speed. What so ever cums of yt, the inway[125] of T. Butes be not amysse. Wreton at 3 of the clock thys Thursday the 24 of Aprill 1571[126] the same instant I rec. your letter,

Signed: Your Father N. Bacon C.S. *Holograph.*
Addressed in hand of secretary: To my sonne Nicholas Bacon.
1 f.; remains of seal.

65.   [4119] *Sir Nicholas Bacon I to Nicholas Bacon II, 1 June 1572*
Sonne the soner you repayre up the better. I have receyved the survey of Mr Bosomes land who requyreth answers with spede, which I cannot make without you.[127] And so fare well. From my howse besides Charing Crosse this first of June 1572,

Signed: Your Father N. Bacon C.S. *Autograph.*
Addressed: To my sonne Nicholas Bacon at Redgrave.
1 f.; traces of seal.

66.   [4120] *Sir Nicholas Bacon I to Nicholas Bacon II, 1 July 1572*
Sonne, let me knowe, and have word from you assone as you may what becomes of the bargayne of Studdie. And so fare you well. From my house besides Charing Crosse this first of July 1572,

Signed: Your Father N. Bacon C.S. *Autograph.*
Addressed: To my sonne Nicholas Bacon at Redgrave
1 f.; traces of seal.

67.   [4121] *Sir Nicholas Bacon I to Francis Boldero, 16 July 1572*
I receyved your letter, dated the 8 of this moneth the 16 of the same. And so it is requyred that Hunt showld come downe for the ~~quantity~~ *measuring* of the

---

120   Sir William Cordell of Long Melford Hall.
121   William Waldegrave of Bures.
122   Sir Robert Wingfield of Letheringham and Thomas Seckford the younger of Woodbridge. Wingfield had been knight of the shire in 1563, and became second knight in this election, 'joined' in partnership with Bacon; Seckford had been knight of the shire in 1571.
123   'Exchequer tenants': William Humberston was Crown Surveyor in the county, and Thomas Badby was Crown Receiver of Suffolk and Cambridgeshire.
124   John Blennerhasset of Barsham, Bassingbourn Gawdy of Mendham and Thomas Playters of Sotterley were all based in the neighbourhood of the Bacon estates at Mettingham.
125   Apparently for 'envy'?. If so, this appears to be a dismissive remark about Thomas Butts.
126   The combination of day and date makes it certain that Bacon has made a slip, and the year is in fact 1572.
127   Bacon made payment to Robert Bozome of Stody for lands purchased in Norfolk (Nf.) in October 1572: *Bacon handlist*, no. 3506. See also the following letters, nos. **66–67, 69 [4120–1, 4122]**.

grownd before I receyved your letter. The Quenes highnes within theis 8 or 9 dayes will be at my howse, and before her highnes departure thence I cannot forbeare Hunt. But immediatelie after I will not fayle to send hym downe to go thorowge with theise thinges. I mervayle I receyved no letter from my sonne concernyng this matter, and concernyng Thomas Buttes also.[128] I do not se that it wilbe any great matter to Mr Bozome to forbeare a fortnyght, seynges I meane to go thorowgh, except thinges falle otherwise out then I have ~~bend~~ bene advertyzed. Yt shalbe well done that uppon Huntes comyng downe ~~so~~ and uppon conclusion of the assuraunce, order be taken for the leatting of the ~~land~~ *shepecowrse* with a stocke, and also for the leating of the land. Tell my sonne that I thinke it very straung that in a matter of this wayght he wrighteth nothing to me neyther doth he wright what he hath done towching the sale of the tythes in Walsham, and in the sale of Mannynges land, which I gave hym speciall chardge to loke unto. Theise be thinges I must have answere of, for otherwise, I knowe not howe to brynge theise matters well to passe. And therfor he shall do well to let me understond what maye be done in it. And so fare you well. From my howse at Gorhamburie this 16 of Julie 1572,

Signed: Your Master N. Bacon C.S. *Autograph.*
Addressed: To my servaunt Frauncis Boldero at Burie
2 ff.; traces of seal.

68.   [4121A] *Sir Nicholas Bacon I to Nicholas Bacon II, 18 July 1572*

Sonne, because the Quenes Majestie shalbe here with me the 26 of this moneth beyng Saturday, therfor I would you showld geve warnyng to 12 of my men, such as you shall thinke most mete and handsome to serve, to be here on Fryday night before, thone halfe of them to be gentlemen and the other halfe yeomen or nere there abowghtes. Se this done with spede. Fare you well. From Gorhamburie this 18 of Julie 1572,

Signed: Your Father N. Bacon C.S. *Autograph.*
Postscript: You must geve them warnyng to come in their lyveries.
Addressed: To my sonne Nicholas Bacon at Redgrave.
2 ff., torn; traces of seal.

69.   [4122] *Sir Nicholas Bacon I to Nicholas Bacon II, 23 August 1572*[129]

I receyved your letter at London whiles I was abowght the subsedie. For answer wherof because I understond that Mr Bozom still grateth uppon me in thinges not reasonable to be demaunded but as it showld seme he is perswaded that I will paye whatsoever ~~I~~ *he* will aske, therfor for answer you shall let hym understond as followethe.

First that his demaund was to have thone halfe of the money at Mich'as and the other halfe at our ladie daye, which because I could not provide so sone, I ded desire to have hallowemes, and one monethe after our Ladie daye, wherunto he assented, and so I was advertyzed from you and Boldero, and therfor the bargayne shall breake rather then I will chaunge the tyme. Trewe it is that Boldero told me,

---

[128]   This may refer to Butts' responsibility for collection of the first subsidy in the Norfolk hundreds of Gallow, Brothercross, Launditch and Smithdon in 1571: see *Bacon handlist*, no. **2953**.

[129]   A contemporary copy of this letter is printed in *Nathaniel Bacon papers* I, 28–31, but I have thought it worth reproducing the original here in full.

he ded desire to have £400 at Mich'as, but that was as a matter of favour wherunto I never assented. And albeit it were no matter to me to paye so muche at London, yet dealing so hardlie with me as I find he doethe, I meane not to graunt it. Marry, I gave lybertie to Hunte, yf he cowld fynd hym *to* deale well with me in the matters in controversie then to promyse it and otherwise not, but this dealing deserveth it not.

I fynd by Huntes certificate that besides the allowaunce that he demaundethe for hedges and dikes. And besides that he will nedis delyver his moore, and marshe, and firrey and braken growndes at 3s 4d the acre without gyvyng any maner of allowaunce as he owght because in dede more is no pasture. And besides also there is picked out of newe certen smale parcelles not before conteyned in the former surveyes, wherof one conteynes but 14 perches and another 1 rood and such like, wherby I se that there is not inche of grownd but I shall paye to dere for it. And besides that I must take his headlondes lieng abroad in the feildes for severall meadowe, and his copie land at the price of fre land. Besides all this I saye and besides such other like thinges, he demaundethe nowe a newe allowaunce for fower acres which liethe, neyther he nor his tenaunt canne tell where. And whersoever it liethe, open to a comon it liethe and so hath bene used, and this must I nedes take for severall (for so he sayethe) and I must offend all the comoners for using of it so. And besides it is certyfyed that he leateth it but for 20d, and I at the least must paye 4s for it. But I meane to pay neyther thone nor the other, except I may knowe where it liethe, and howe to hold it in severaltie as I buy it: this pece *as he sayethe* liethe in Gunthorp. There is another acre lieng in Hunworthe of the same nature called Brewerie which neyther ~~neyther~~ Mr Bozom nor his tenaunt canne tell where it liethe, and therfor is unmeasured as the rest is, and yet I must take it as measured and in valewe. But I meane not so to do.

Besides I was enformed and certyfyed from Mr Bosome by you and Boldero that I showld pay nothing for the woodes, and in the former surveyes they were not conteyned in dede. And nowe in this survey he valewethe a rowe in Studdie cont. 3 roodes at 3s 4d the acre. And at like price he valewethe an alder carre, in Brynton, cont. one acre 3 roodes, and thus by this meanes, I am to paye 24 yeres purchase for theise woodes, which I was promysed I showld not paye for in respect I pay so dere for the rest, but so I meane not to do.

Agayne he sekethe nowe to delyver me Brakes in valewe growyng uppon the comon in Burnyngham, which semethe straunge, and also one pece of grownd being in Whynnes Close not yet measured nor heretofore surveyed, and this he valeweth at 3s 4d by yere. But I meane not to take it so before I understond better of it.

There be sondry other thinges wherin his dealing is very hard but those I overpasse. Trewe it is, that yf the land laye not as it dothe, I would not geve so much for it by fyve hundred markes neyther is it so much worthe by that some. Yt is much a worse penyworthe then Rokewoodes bargayne which was yll enowghe. To be short, except Mr Bozome will yeld in this matter of 4s acres in Gunthorpe and for the one acre in Hunworthe and for the matter of the woodes and for his braky Revenewe, and for the lond in whinnes, I meane not to conclude with hym but that the bargayne shall breake. And agayne yf he be content to yeld in theise matter *which in ded be but tryfles* I am content he shall have his £300, yea £500, rather then fayle so I may pay it in London because I have no money in the contry as you knowe.

It is also very straunge to me that Boldero showld measure the close called Pasture Close, but for 33 acres where by Huntes measure it is 57 acres.

Besides where dryfte wayes be thorowghe the pastures and meadowes me thinkes there showld be allowaunce geven unto me for them; whether *there* be or not I knowe not.

He doethe demaund £26 for the shepes course but I will geve but £25 for so it was agreed.

This bargayne hath caused much posting up and downe more then it is worthe, and therfor let this bearer retorne unto me, and send you me answere at your leysor. I se still there groweth newe thinges which I am wearie of.

I retorne unto you Huntes survey paynfully and diligentlie done and the former also, and the particuler valewe delyvered by Mr Bozom.

His rentes of asise ar encreased above the former certyficate *signyfied by hymselfe* by 16d a yere. Belike it is growen newe by his capon and his two hennes. It were well done to have a particuler rentall both of the rentes of asise and also of the out rentes.

Whether the bargayne breake or not take let the wrightinges be reserved for therby shall it appere that the breache groweth not thorowghe my defawlte.

I heare nothing what profe hath bene made for the leating of it which were mete to be done, lest els I lose the best part of my next yeres rent to amend the bargayne withall, neyther do you certyfie me what you have done towching the sale of my landes and tythes that I appoynted you to sell. Besides I would be advertyzed whether the Manor of Thornham were abbey landes or Bisshopps landes or of what possessions it was.

If this bargayne take I am content my sonne Wyndham or Mr Bell, whether of them he will chose, shall drawe the wrightinges betwene us.[130] Comend me to my dawghter and her mother, and so fare you well. From my howse at Gorhamburie this 23 of August 1572.

Signed: Your Father N. Bacon C.S. *Autograph.*
Addressed: To my sonne Nicholas
2 ff.

70. [4123] *Francis Boldero and George Nunn to William Corbold, 26 September 1572*

Burgat/ After harty *comendations* thes are to lett you understand that my Lordes audytt is appoynted to be kept at Redgravehall the Weddensday before Symonde and Judes day beinge 22 daye of October next cominge for the recept of the rentes revenues and profittes of his manor of Burgat, wherfore thes are to require you to be than ther with your rentalles extractes and acquittances ready to yeld and to geve up an accompt and to make payment of all suche sommes of money as ye are to be charged withall by reason of your collection and baylywicke wherof fayle ye not. And so right hartely fare ye well. From Redgrave the 26 of September 1572

Signed: Your loving frend Fraunces Boldero George Nune
Addressed: To William Corbold bayliff of Burgat
1 f.

---

130 Francis Wyndham, or Robert Bell (of the Middle Temple and Outwell, Nf.).

71. [4123A] *Sir Nicholas Bacon I and Lady Anne Bacon to Nicholas Bacon II, Francis Boldero and George Nunn, 16 November 1572*

Complaynt is made unto me, by Buckes wief this bearer that the will of her former husbond Howlot is broken by my servaunt Howlot. Theise ar therfor to will you to calle before you Howlot my servaunt and this bearer and her husbond Buck my servaunt also as you knowe, and after the matter fully examyned to take such order as the justice of the cause shall requyre and yf you shall fynd eyther of the parties obstinate and not conformable to that that you shall thinke reasonable. Then to signifie unto me the state of the matter and in whom you shall fynd the default to thend I may deale therein as justice shall requyre.[131] And so fare you well. From my howse besides Charing Crosse this 16 of Novembre 1572

Signed: N. Bacon C.S. *Autograph.*
Postscript by Lady Bacon:

I pray *yow* sonne do that you may to healpe the owld mother to lyve in qwiett and comfort with her own childrine in her owld and few dayes by liklyodd and spare not to enforme ~~the~~ my Lord the truth. She sayth it greveth her ~~she sayth~~ to have her childern at variance, and she is very sori for her eldest sonne.

Your father is in the gowte at this present, but his payne now is tollerable God be thanked

Signed: Your Mother A. Bacon. *Holograph.*

Addressed: To my sonne Nicholas Bacon and to my servauntes Frauncis Boldero and Georg Nunne geve theise
2 ff.; traces of seal.

72. [4124] *Sir Nicholas Bacon I to Nicholas Bacon II, 5 December 1572*

Sonne, I have of late receyved a letter from my L. of Surrey[132] from Walden End very duetyfull to the Quenes Majestie and full of curtesie to me. And because I would be lothe that he showld thinke such a letter bestowed uppon a forgetfull man and the rather to encorag hym in this his well doyng I have thowght good to advise you sometyme, this Christmes, to repayre unto hym and to visite hym and to use towardes hym all poyntes of curtesie. Yf you showld come up at the tyme appoynted to be holden for the parlament, you might do it then. But because I am not certen of the contynewaunce of it, therfor I thinke it ~~best~~ were better you showld do it some tyme within the 12 dayes.[133] And seyng you shall retorne home agayne I thinke he will take it in the more thankfull part. And yet my meanynge

---

131 Punctuation of original as shown.
132 Philip Howard, son and heir of Thomas Duke of Norfolk (executed 2 June 1572), and then fifteen years old; he is here styled Earl of Surrey by courtesy title. Later he would succeed as Earl of Arundel but forfeited his honours by attainder for high treason, 1589. This proposed visit was of great diplomatic significance in the tense political atmosphere following the duke's execution.
133 The alternatives were (1) that the younger Bacon could kill two birds with one stone by visiting Howard on his way to Parliament, travelling down to London via the Cambridge main road which would take him near Audley End at Saffron Walden, Howard's home; (2) that he could make a special visit to Howard over the Christmas season. This is an important detail of national politics. The Lord Keeper was currently at the centre of tense negotiations with Queen Elizabeth about the fate of Mary Queen of Scots; proceedings against Mary would entail a recall of Parliament, already once prorogued to 1 November 1572 without result. Evidently he hoped at this stage that the queen would be persuaded to allow a speedy recall after Christmas. In the event, Elizabeth avoided a decision about Mary being pressed on her by postponing another meeting of Parlia-

is not that you showld make any more acquaynted with this jorney then of necessitie you must. My L. of Sussex who hath offered me to cary this letter and to se it delyvered, cometh to Attleborowghe.[134] And therfor you shall do well to waight uppon *hym*. Commend me to your mother and to your wife. And so fare you well. From ~~my howse~~ the Cowrt this 5 of Decembre 1572

Signed: Your Father N. Bacon C.S. *Autograph, with insertion in Bacon's hand.*
Addressed: To my sonne [Nicholas] Bacon a[t Redgrave][135]
2 ff.; traces of seal.

73. [4125] *Sir Nicholas Bacon I to Nicholas Bacon II, 18 March 1573*

Sonne, Sir Ambrose Germyn hath written unto me for a pardon to be obteyned for one Morris, who was at the last Assises condempned for invocation of spirites, as it semeth by his wrighting by somewhat to straight a proceading in lawe. And besides he wrighteth that the prisoner is become a very repentaunt and sorowfull man for his offence. Neverthelesse I have forborne and meane to forbeare to proceade in it, untill I heare agayne from you, whether the contry thinketh the man worthie death or no. And yf you had bene at the assises as you showld have bene, yf you had done well, you might have enformed me of this of your owne knowledg. But nowe ~~y~~ in defawlt therof you ar to speake with Mr Pooley who is best acquaynted in this matter or with Mr Ashefeild yf he were at the asises, or els with them both.[136] And theruppon to advertise me imediately, because this matter canne aske no longe tyme. I mervayle it is so long since I hard from you. In the begynnyng of the next tearme I loke to se you here for the fynysshing of thinges and to knowe what is done for the leatting of Studdie. Comend me to your wief and her mother. God blesse the children and so fare you well. From my howse besides Charing Crosse this 18th of Marche 1572[137]

Signed: Your Father N. Bacon C.S. *Autograph.*
Postscript in Lord Keeper Bacon's hand, erased: ~~If this man be of any wealthe as I heare he ys and yn[138] he sholde have his charge yf he canne gette his pardone.~~
Addressed: To my sonne Nicholas Bacon at Redgrave
2 ff.; traces of seal.

74. [4126] *Sir Nicholas Bacon I to Nicholas Bacon II, 22 March 1573*

Sonne, I send you a letter herein enclosed directed to Sir Ambrose Germyn which when you have read I would you showld seale it [an]d cause it to b[e] delyvered unto hym, and let [h]ym knowe that it came unto you with other letter[s] directed

---

ment until 1576. See J.E. Neale, *Elizabeth I and her parliaments 1559–1581* (London, 1953), pp. 305–14.

134 It is interesting that the earl of Sussex appears to have been co-operating with Bacon in this enterprise. Attleborough was the principal East Anglian residence of the Radcliffe earls of Sussex.

135 The removal of the seal-tag has taken away text.

136 All three JPs named were of the Bury area: Sir Ambrose Jermyn of Rushbrooke, Thomas Poley (probably then resident either at Icklingham or Mildenhall) and Robert Ashfield of Stowlangtoft. The younger Nicholas Bacon was only named as a JP sometime during 1572, and was already falling short of his father's high standards.

137 *Bacon handlist,* no. **3517** makes it clear that the Lord Keeper's interest in this case was not merely altruistic: this is an acquittance (21 November 1574) for money due from John Morice, felon, and claimed by Bacon, presumably as lessee of the Liberty of St Edmund. See also no. **84 [4134]** below.

138 For 'then'?

50

to you for busynes of myne, by a meseng[er] of my owne, or els let it be delyvered so as it be not knowen it came from your handes. Comend me to your wyfe and to her mother. God ~~bless~~ blesse the children. From my howse besides Charing Crosse this 22 of March 1572

Signed: Your Father N. Bacon C.S. *Autograph.*
Addressed: To my sonne Nicholas Bacon in Suff.
1 f., damaged; seal impression.

75.   [4127] *Sir Nicholas Bacon I to Nicholas Bacon II, 18 June 1573*
Sonne, I meane, yf my health will so suffer, to begynne my jorney towardes Suff. the morowe after Midsomer daye beyng Thursdaye. And that night to go to Sir Robert Chesters to my bed, and on Fryday following to goe from thense to my L. Northes, and on Saturday from my L. Northes to Redgrave to my bed, and there to remayne Sonday, and on Mondaye to go to Norwiche.[139] The rest of my jorney ~~tyll~~ *concernyng* my retorne, I have not yet determyned of. You shall do well to let my men have warnyng to mete me on the waye uppon Newe Market Heathe. I spake to my sone Woodhows that you showld cause James Wright to laye in a hoggeshed of claret wyne agaynst my comyng, and to foresee we waunte no bere. The rest that is to be provided I leave to your consideration. Comend me to your mother and to your wief, God blesse your children. Fare you well. From my house at Gorhamburie this 28 of June 1573

Signed: Your Father N. Bacon C.S. *Autograph.*
Addressed: To my sonne Nicholas Bacon at Redgrave
1 f.; seal impression.

76.   [4128] *Sir Nicholas Bacon I to Nicholas Bacon II, 10 July 1573*
Blackman hath sued unto me that he might retorne to prove what answer he showld have of wydowe Coke which I have graunted unto hym. His desire is that he might understond a determynate answer one waye or otherwise in his suyte, wherunto I would you showld geve such furtheraunce as you maye and therein to use all the good wayes and meanes that you convenyently canne. And so fare you well. From Chipenham[140] this 10 of July 1573

Signed: Your Father N. Bacon C.S. *Autograph.*
Addressed: To my sonne Nicholas Bacon at Redgrave
1 f.

77.   [4129] *Sir Nicholas Bacon I to Francis Boldero, 12 November 1573*
Boldero, as towching the evidence of Lynnes land I have none of them, but an indenture of bargayne and sale from Lynne to me. As to the rest it is to be knowen of Lynne to whom he delyvered them, and what he that receyved them hath done with them, for it were a very shrowde turne they showld be lost.

And as to the fencing of Burfold woode, I would be glad to understond the chardge of the doynge of it, and what men will take for the hedging diking and quycke settyng of a rodde, and theruppon, I will ~~resolv~~ resolve what shalbe done,

---

139   Sir Robert Chester lived at Royston (Herts.) and Lord North at Kirtling (Cambs.).
140   Home of Bacon's relative Thomas Rivett: see *1561 visitation*, ed. Corder, p. 272, and above, no. **26 [4079]**.

and the soner I be advertyzed the better. It was some fawlt in my sonne and James Vale that I was not advertysed of it before this tyme, and therfor let it nowe be done out of hand.

And as towching the taxe of Burgate, I for my opynyon and knowledg thinke that every man showld paye rate, and rate lyke, as the numbre of acres be that he holdethe, except the custome be to the contrary which is unknowen to me. This is trewe where the taxe is levied uppon landes and where it is levied uppon goodes and cattle, there it must be answered according acco to the rates of goodes and cattles that men possesse. Because you have not written to me in theise matters, therfor I am to seke in them. And as towching the arrerages, tyll Georg Nunne come I canne saye nothing. Fare you well. From my howse besides Charing Crosse this 12 of Novembre 1573

Signed: Your Master N. Bacon C.S. *Autograph.*
Postscript: I [*sic*] semeth to me that I showld perfect my reconynges by hym that you sent up with the bokes, which I do not allowe of, nor cannot end my reconynges but by your selfe, and therby am dryven *to defer* the fynysshing of them tyll the next tearme that you maye come, wherof I have no liking and yet sicknes must be borne withall.
Addressed: [To my] servaunt Francis [Bold]ero at Bury
1 f., damaged; remains of seal impression.

78. <**[4129A]** *Sir Nicholas Bacon I to Nathaniel Bacon, 30 November 1573: published in* **Nathaniel Bacon papers I, 98–9.** *Sends terrier of Stiffkey, to be copied for Francis Wyndham. Nathaniel to confer with Charles Calthorpe. Sir Nicholas recommends sale of Eccles lands in order to purchase manor of Netherhall*>

79. **[4130]** *Sir Nicholas Bacon I to Nicholas Bacon II, 22 June 1574*
Sonne, wheare I had a lease made by the Duchie Cowrt[141] in the begynnyng of the Quenes Majesties raigne of the warren of Myldenhall, yelding the rent yerely of £4, which lease I sold to Mr Bedingfeild shortly after for £40 which Mr Bedingfeyld sold the same over to one Hogge the bearer of this letter for 100 markes as Hogge tellethe me; now so it is that Hogge hath bene here with me, and hath browght with hym thold lease, and hath desired me to surrender the same, and to take a newe lease of the Duchie Cowrt, for 21 yeres, which I have done, whereuppon, Hogge this bearer suethe nowe to me that he might buy my interest in this newe lease, and he would geve me a convenyent fyne for the same. Trewe it is that I must graunt hym 7 yeres of my newe lease, yf it be trewe as he sayethe, that he hath yet 7 yeres to come of the old lease which he was content I showld surrendre. But he desirethe that he might have besides those 7, 13 yeres more which is the whole interest I have in this newe lease saving one yere, which is the last of the 21 yeres which he agreeth I showld reserve to my selfe as I ded in my bargayne to Mr Bedingfeild. Myne answer to hym *Hogge* in this suyte hathe bene that before I understond from you, howe my howse of Redgrave eyther is alredie, or hereafter maye be provided of conyes, I cannot growe to no certen conclusion with hym.

---

[141] The Court of the Duchy of Lancaster, of which Mildenhall formed a part. Proceedings of 1575 in which William Hogge of Barton Milles, lessee of the Mildenhall warren from Sir Nicholas Bacon, lays complaint against Edmund Bedingfield esquire, Thomas Geson and John Percyvall, are TNA (PRO), DL 1/100/H14.

And therfor I have told hym that eyther you must come and speake with me, or else you must at good lengthe advertise me, what the yerely valewe of this warrein is worthe. And for your better instruction what moved me thus to do I send you a letter herein enclosed wherein I am enformed that this warrein shoulde be worthe 100 markes by yere which is muche otherwyse then I thowght. And besidis that the stocke of conyes is worth £100. You shall do well diligently to examyne the trothe of this matter, and to take a tyme with this bearer to considre with your selfe whether your busynes will suffer you to come uppe, or else to wright to me your letter in this matter. And in that meane tyme you are to enforme your selfe of the whole trothe of the valewe of this thing, and that done eyther to geve hym answer, that you will come upp with hym, or els send your letter by hym. This matter will more towche you then me and therfor you are to take care of it. And so fare you well. Comend me to your wief and my sister her mother. God blesse the children. From my howse besides Charing Crosse this 22 of June 1574

Signed: Your Father N. Bacon C.S. *Autograph.*
Addressed: To my sonne Nicholas Bacon at Redgrave
2 ff.; seal impression.

80. [4131] *Sir Nicholas Bacon I to Nicholas Bacon II, 22 June 1574*

Sonne, uppon suyte made unto me by this bearer the scholemaster of Botesdale, I am content that he shalbe absent from the schole one monethe, accompting the tyme that he hath alredie bene absent, to be parte of that monethe, so as he doth substitute one behind hym, that shalbe sufficiently able to enstruct the children in this his absence. And because he shall commence Master of Arte at the next Comencement, I would you showld cause one bucke of this season to be dely-vered unto hym out of Redgrave Parke. And where he enformeth me, that he hathe planted the scholehows yard with crabbe stocke, and that for default of sufficient fencing, he cannot kepe that grownd severall, I am contented, that tymbre shalbe felled for the paling of the same, and that the same shalbe paled at my chardge, and that this letter shalbe a sufficient warraunte for the payment of that money. And so fare you well. From my howse besides Charing Crosse this 22 of June 1574[142]

Signed: Your Father N. Bacon C.S. *Autograph.*
Addressed: To my sonne Nicholas Bacon at Redgrave
2 ff.; remains of seal.

81. [4138] *William Dryver to his sister, 28 July 1574*

Wellbeloved sister after my hartie commendations unto yow, trustinge in god yow are in as good health with the reste of my brothers and sisters as I was at the wrightinge hereof etc. I am at this tyme bouldened to trowble *yow, * and more desyerus to heere from yow, for that I have sent yow thre or fower lettres and never as yet rec'd any answer, wherein I greatly wonder at your descourtisie shewed to me, as in refrayning from wrighting, but if their be any thing that I have mesused my self towardes yow I coulde gladly in any respect, or desoffended yow in any poynt, I woulde gladly with your reconfermation avoyed, and be very sorrofull for the desgratfulnes of me towars yow, but as for that I reffer it to your descrestion further more I am determyned and also perswaded of dyvers of my frendes to

---

[142] Botesdale School was founded by letters patent granted to Nicholas Bacon, 28 July 1561 (dated from Redgrave): *CPR Elizabeth I, 1560–63*, p. 104.

speacke with Mr Borrowe for the agrement of the howes at Lyme howes,[143] in the which I would gladly have your counsell, for now I am come to yeeres, and partely as yow doe knowe the howes and the land comes in to my handes tel suche tyme as my brothers comes to yeres, and then to tacke suche agrement as right and lawe will give us. Sence my comynge over I have learned at Stepney and in other places that Borrow is a marveylus suttell man, and seckes wayes he can devyes to defeact us of that small livinge that we have. Notwithstandinge with your good conselinge of me, and your favorable lettres to hym, we shall in suche wayes use the matter that it shalbe to ~~your~~ my great proffet, and also to your good contentation and wellickinge of. Thus bid I yow hartely farwel, comyttinge yow to the tuycyon of almightie god. From London le 28 July 1574

Signed: Your welbeloved brother Willyam Dryver. *Holograph.*[144]
Postscript: My aunt Dannet with my sister Moore hathe their commendations unto yow and woulde gladly here from yow if it were possible therefore if yow doe wright send your letters to the Crosse Keyes in Grassyous Treet[145] and their they shalbe saffly delyvered. Thus at their request I am the more bouldened to trowble yow.
1 f.

82.   [4132] *Sir Nicholas Bacon I to Nicholas Bacon II, 6 September 1574*
Sonne, I send you herewith a letter sent me by Boldero, wherin he remembreth me of thre severall men to serve in his place for keping of my cowrtes, wherof I like best of Androwes. But because he told me that he would remove his dwelling from Bury to Ely, therfor I cannot se howe he canne be fit for that purpose, and as to Hunt, I thinke he was never acquaynted with keping of cowrtes; and as to the third what for age, and what for sicknes, I dowbt howe he showld be able to go thorowghe withall.[146] I repose my selfe cheifly uppon Androwes because I knowe hym both just and honest, but yet I will not resolve therin till I speake with hym, and eyther heare from you, or speake with you. There be matters of surveyes that requyre great paynes and diligence, and so doth the taking of my accomptes requyre good skill and I dowbt whether Androwes hath bene acquaynted with those thinges. The man that you and I talked of whether he hath skill to take accomptes, or no, I dowbt of, nether do I knowe what interteignement he will aske. Theise matters would be well considered, for the well chosing of this man shall stond both you and me in very great stead. Agayne yf we shall agre uppon hym that we first talked of, then were it mete that he came uppe and you with hym to understond his chardg althowgh you taried but a day. Commend me to your mother and to my dawghter. God blesse the children. And so fare you well. From my howse at Gorhambury this 6 of Septembre 1574

Signed: Your Father N. Bacon C.S. *Autograph.*
Addressed: To my sonne Nicholas Bacon at Redgrave
2 ff.; seal impression.

---

143   Limehouse in east London.
144   Written in an accomplished hand, with italic signature, pompous vocabulary and exotic spellings, but with many small slips and insertions. It is not clear whether this letter has any original association with the Redgrave correspondence.
145   Gracious Street in London.
146   Thomas Andrewes of Bury St Edmunds was a JP in Suffolk and John Le Hunt of Little Bradley was about to become one, no doubt on the Lord Keeper's recommendation.

83. **[4133]** *Sir Nicholas Bacon I to Nicholas Bacon II, 10 October 1574*

Sonne, I have receyved your letter conteyning the comendation of Mr Lany[147] as a mete man to serve me in the office of Steward for keping of my cowrtes, and for the taking of my accomptes and according to your comendation, I am content to make profe of hym and he to make profe of me, and as eyther of us shall like other, wherof I dowbt little (fynding hym such a one as you wright) but that we shall contynewe together. Therfor you shall do well with his consent to geve warnyng for the keping of my cowrtes as shortly as may be. And as towching the keping of myne audicte, warnyng would be geven by your selfe or by Georg Nunne, that such a tyme be apoynted for the same, a littell befor the feast of all S'tes as Mr Lany, your selfe, and Georg Nunne shall thinke mete. I meant that Boldero showld enforme hym that showld take my accomptes *Mr Lany I meane* howe to do it, but that fayling, Georg Nunne must helpe to *enforme hym to* take ~~uppe~~ the same. And for their better instructions I send downe by this bearer the last yeres accompt and the last yeres viewe.

I dowbt nothing but you have sent to Nathaniell my letter for the £80 that he is to paye, and will calle uppon the receipt of the same according to our last agreement.

I dowbt not but you have kept your daye with Boldero for the receyving of my wrightinges according to his promyse.

After I receyve answer from Hunt for the survey of Burrowghe I will not fayle to retorne answer to my sonne Woodhows concernyng that matter, and you knowe that the fawlt is not myne that it hath not bene done alredie.

As towching Hogge, I like well that for the somme of £80 to be payd for a fyne according to the tenor of your letter and for 6 cupple of conyes to be answered for Redgrave according to the tenor of the same letter, I am contented he shall have a lease out of my lease for twenti yeres, so as one yere be reserved to my selfe and the orygynall lease to remayne with me according as you wright.[148] You are to send me answer of theise thinges by the next convenyent messenger as leysor will serve. From the Cowrt this 10 of Octobre 1574,

Signed: Your Father N. Bacon C.S. *Autograph.*
Addressed: To my sonne Nicholas Bacon at Redgrave
1 f.; traces of seal.

84. **[4134]** *Sir Nicholas Bacon I to Nicholas Bacon II, 21 November 1574*

Sonne, this bearer is content to paye to your handes as he enformeth me the some of £50, so as I would covenaunt to save hym harmeles agaynst the heyers executors or admynystrators of Moryce, for which purpose, I send you a wrighting herein enclosed which I would you showld delyver to hym as my dede, so that he pay the fyftie powndes unto you, and so as you receyve *of* hym the counterpane of this wryghting sealed and subscribed by hym. And besides this beyng done, I would also you showld speake to Mr Higham for the *delyvery of the oblygation concernyng the* payment of the seid fiftie powndes unto hym.[149]

This bearer also sueth unto me for a newe lease of his fearme in Tymworth

---

[147] Probably John Lany or Laney of Ipswich: see *History of Parliament 1558–1603* II, 437.

[148] Probably a sub-lease for the warren at Mildenhall: see above, no. **79 [4130]**.

[149] The 'wrighting' to which this refers is *Bacon handlist*, no. **3517**, a receipt by Bacon from William Spalding of Timworth, yeoman, for £100 due by bond to John Morice, felon, claimed by Sir Nicholas: also 21 November 1574. See also no. **73 [4125]** above.

late Talbottes. My answer hath bene to hym that before I heare howe many acres of grownd there is of every kinde belonging to the fearme and howe he hath performed the conditions conteyned in his former lease, I meane not to make any newe lease, and therfor I pray you cause Georg Nonne to survey it, and yf you ded se it your selfe it were the better. And so fare you well. From my howse besides Charing Crosse this 21 of Novembre 1574,

Signed: Your Father N. Bacon C.S. *Autograph.*
Addressed: To my sonne Nicholas Bacon at Redgrave
2 ff.; remains of seal.

85.   [4135] *Sir Nicholas Bacon I to Nicholas Bacon II, 27 November 1574*

Sonne, I send unto you herein enclosed a bille of complaynt exhibited unto me by my tenauntes of Burgate and Botesdale agaynst Wylkinson parson of Burgat conteynyng many extremyties offered unto them by hym. I would therfor that you ~~shouwld~~ showld calle Wilkynson before you, and such and so many of them as shall seme good unto you, and to examyne the trewth of the matter. And theruppon to take such order with Wylkynson, that he may lyve orderly and quyetly amongest his neyghbowrs, as becometh hym to do, which yf you cannot bryng to passe, then I would have you advertise me what you shall fynd in the matter to thend I maye take such further order therin as the justice and equytie of the cause shall requyre. And so fare you well. From my howse besides Charing Crosse this 27 of Novembre 1574

Signed: Your Father N. Bacon C.S. *Autograph.*
Addressed: To my sonne Nicholas Bacon at Redgrave
2 ff.; seal impression.

86.   [4136] *Sir Nicholas Bacon I to Nicholas Bacon II, 20 December 1574*

Sonne, I have receyved your letter and the cast of spare hawkes that you sent me, and so have I Mr Wigmores letter, for answer of which letter you shall do well to tell Mr Wigmore from me that I never gave allowaunce to my fearmor for buylding of newe howses, without he had first a warraunt from me willing hym to buyld the same, neyther do I thinke that any man else doth so. And as to Fynchams land, I do not meane to deale with it except I may have it *at* a reasonable pryce. I have learned alredy to my chardg what it is to buy a thing that lyeth comodyously, but I meane never to do so agayne, uppon no mans credite or report. I mervaile very muche that Georg Nonne wrighteth nothing to me towching my revennewe. Yf those that he putteth in trust do not kepe tutche, then is my present money become a debt which I utterly myslike. I mervayle I hard not from you howe my cowrtes keping and myne audict ~~hath~~ have proceaded and what liking or mysliking is to be had of the newe officer. Comende me to your wief and to Mistres Buttes. God blesse the children. And so fare you well. From the Court this 20 of December 1574

Signed: Your Father N. Bacon C.S. *Autograph.*
Addressed: [To my] sonne ~~M.L.~~ *Nicholas Bacon* at Redgrave
2 ff., torn; remains of seal.

87. [4137] *Sir Nicholas Bacon I to Nicholas Bacon II, 28 December 1574*
Sonne, I heare nothing of Georg Nonne. You shall do well to send to hym, and to cause hym as shortlie as he canne, to come uppe, and yf he bring any money with hym besides that which he sayeth he hath delyvered to the Clothiers, he shall do well to come uppe well accompayned because I heare of sondry robberies comytted by the highe waye. And so fare you well. From my howse besides Charing Crosse this Childermes daye 1574

Signed: Your Father N. Bacon C.S. *Autograph.*
Addressed: To my sonne Nicholas Bacon at Redgrave
2 ff., torn; remains of seal.

88. [4139] *Sir Nicholas Bacon I to Edmund Bacon, 17 August 1575*
After my hartie comendations. This is to signifie unto you, that as I remember I wrote a lettre in Trynyty Tearme which was delyvered to your handes to be delyvered to such persons as I had good hope of would have made an end of the controversies betwene those that pretend to be parsons of Heggesset *and the parisshioners there*. And because I heare that those troubles be not well ended (as I wishe they were) neyther have I any answer of my seid lettre wherof I mervayle very much. Therfor I have thowght good hereby to requyre you, yf the causes and controversies cannot be compownded by your meane, that then you procure an answer from those to whom I wrote by your assent signyfyeng whose defawlt it is that theis troubles do not growe to an end, because I may therby constrayn those in whom the default is to performe that which justice requyreth to be done. And so fare you well. From my howse at Gorhambury this 17 of August 1575

Signed: N. Bacon C.S. *Autograph.*
Addressed: To my cosyn Edmond Bacon esquyer
2 ff.; seal impression.

89. <[4139A] *Nathaniel Bacon to Sir Nicholas Bacon I, 12 August 1576: published in* **Nathaniel Bacon papers** *I, 200–201, and see note 335,* **ibid.,** *p. 305. Spanish pirates on the Norfolk coast, under Captains Carew and Hubbert. Building work at Stiffkey.>*

90. <[4139B] *Sir Nicholas Bacon I to Nathaniel Bacon, 21 June 1578: published in* **Nathaniel Bacon papers** *II, 12–13. Business regarding a decree in the Court of Wards.>*

91. [4140] *Lady Anne Bacon to Sir Nicholas Bacon II [?May–July 1579]*
Syr, as yow sent me worde by Osborn, as soone as I understood of my Lorde Treasurer[150] comming from the Coort *this* afternoone I lett him know what yow sayd of Nathanaelles lett of comming. That the lett shulde be trew which is named *I am* sorye, for it is a great pain, but to be playn, as I can not now change, when I fyrst harde his wyffe was comme and not he, I looked not for him. My Lord Tresurer hath appointed to morow at 2 of the clock in the afternoone *to heare the matter* and so wylled to certefye yow. I pray God worke in your hart as *reachyng* a dispotion [sic] to end *well* as I at the fyrst by his grace gate a

---

150 William Cecil, Lord Burghley, Lady Anne's brother-in-law. Osborn was probably John Osborn, secretary to the late Lord Keeper: see *Nathaniel Bacon papers* I, 272.

very rare example to beginn well immediatly upon your fatheres death, of a most faythfull hart ever to him, and the lyke desyre to confyrm your goode will still. Yf eny yll cownsell, as the world is full of subtiltee, go abowt to alter your own nature which hetherto I have taken to be well enclyned, I pray *yow* good Syr Nicolas Bacon lett it do no hurt betwyxt us where there hath ben so long a continuance of more then common amytee. Yow being the sonne, and I the wyff, and now the weedoe of the same *good* father and husband. So I byd yow hartely fare well and shalbe very glad when wee many mete together frendely. From Shudloes Howse this Monday.[151]

Signed: Your well wyller alweyes A. Bacon. *Holograph.*
Addressed: To Sir Nicholas Bakon
2 ff.; traces of seal.

92.   <[4140a] *Lady Elizabeth Neville to Nathaniel Bacon, 10 March 1580/1 «»1584: published* **Nathaniel Bacon papers II, 179–180.** *Has abandoned hope of coming to Norfolk with Sir Henry Neville: do not write to him to request their visit. Partiality of William Ayloff the Assize Judge.>*

93.   [4141] *Sir Henry Woodhouse to Sir Nicholas Bacon II [?1583]*
Brothar, if the munny be cum to Norwytch I pray cawse Felgate to delivar £20 to this bearar Jhon Lacoke and I shall allowe it to you in my recconing. You are wysshed here at Waxham and thus I leve you

Signed: Your loving brothar Henry Woodhowse. *Holograph.*
Addressed: To the right worshippfull his loving brothar Sir Nicolas Bacon knight
1 f.; traces of seal.

94.   [4142] *Sir Henry Woodhouse to Sir Nicholas Bacon II [?1583]*
Brothar, my besenes faleth owght [?so] here at Waxham as I cannot well be at Norwitch this day as I did appointe with my self, I have thearefore thawght good to wright unto you consarning the speche you delivered to me for the reconenges by twixt us. I have for the parformanse ther of sent you here inclosed an acquittanse for the full resaite of all suche sums of munny as wer due unto me from you for the purchas of Ingham and allso a bille of my hande of £15 which I have resaived more then was due unto me. With this I am to requiar from yow a note undar your hande to this effecket: that wheare I do stand bownd with you for the paiment of sartaine summs of munny namlye to Mr Calthrope and Mr Pecke and Jhon Taylar, that you doo acknowledge the same debtes to be yours only, and to discharge me of them, as I remembar this was the affecke of the speche consarning this mattar at my being with you. If thear be in your considerasion anny *thing* for my securite nedfull for you to add to the writing, I pray do it, and what shall *be* requiset for my parte to you you shall find me ever redie to parfore it and to conclud I wishe Ingham all yours and then I wowlde saie more then now I will write. Thus good brothar fare well

Signed: Your all wais to cumaund Henry Woodhowse. *Holograph.*

---

[151] This letter probably concerns the dispute between Nicholas and Nathaniel Bacon about their father's will: see especially Nicholas's and Nathaniel's letters to the Lord Treasurer, *Nathaniel Bacon papers* II, 77–9, 81–2, and Burghley's letter of reproof, *ibid.*, 93–5. See also *ibid.*, 100–7. The dispute seems to have been solved by winter 1580: *ibid.*, 119–20.

Addressed: To the right worshippfull his loving brothar Sir Nycolas Bacon knight
Endorsed: Sir Henry Woodhouse lettre for the purchase of the Moyitie of the Manor of Ingham
1 f., text very faded by damp; seal impression.

95. [4143] *Edward Clinton alias Fiennes, Earl of Lincoln to Sir Nicholas Bacon II, 20 April 1583*

Whereas the offices of Clarkeshipp or Regestership and Submarshalshipp for the Admiraltie withein the counties of Norfolk and Suffolk withe the proffites of the same be uppon the deathe of Anthony Stile thelder the late exersiser of the saide offices lawfully vested in Anthony Style the younger, sonne of the foresaide Anthony the elder, as by severall grauntes and patentes therof made by me may at large appeare; I have therefore thought good to requyer you to suffer the saide Anthony Stile the younger quietly and peaseablie to use and excercise the saide offices as hathe byn accustomed, witheout any your contradiccion or impediment. And that from hensforthe you accepte and take him for lawfull Clark or Regester and Submarshall in the Counties aforesaide according to the severall tenors of the patentes made in this behalf. And so fare you well. From the Courte at Grenewiche this 20 of Aprill 1583

Signed: E. Lyncoln. *Autograph.*
Addressed: [T]o my lovinge frende the Viceadmirall of Suffolk or his deputie
Endorsed: L. Admyrall for the admytting of yonge Anthony Style to the ~~deputie-shipe~~ Clerkship of the Viceadmirall
2 ff., torn; remains of seal.

96. [4144] *Richard Arkenstall to Sir Nicholas Bacon II, 13 November 1585*

Right worshipfull I signifyed unto your servaunt when he was with me that according to the warrant which he shewed me from the Right Honorable the Lord Treasuror I wold paye your fees accordingly and so towld him that if it pleased you to send to me abowte the ende of the audit which wold be imediatly after Hallomas last that then it shold be ready, I mean the arrerages which were dewe at Christmas last.[152] And for that as yet I heare nothing from you I thought good to wright unto your worshipp hereof, the rather for that I have ben allwayes furthering you herein, and least you shold send in vayne not fynding me at home I thought good also to sett downe a certen day when (if it please God) I will not fayle to be at Ely, viz. the second of December next, at which tyme I do hymbly require my Lordes letter for my warrant together with a sufficient acquitance for the receipte of that fowerscoore powndes of arrerages. And for that which may growe dewe at Christmas next, I am to intrete you most hartely that you spare to send unto me untill I may speke with you or sume from you at Candelmas terme next. And so nothing dowbting of your worshipps good favour I am ready at your commandement in any thinges I can. And so with my dewty remembred I humbly take my leave, and besech almightye God to have you alwayes in his blessed keping. At Ely this 13 of November 1585

---

152   The fee at issue must be for Bacon's constableship of Wisbech castle, then in the hands of the Crown because of the vacancy of the diocese of Ely; hence the involvement of the Lord Treasurer, Lord Burghley.

Signed: Your worshipps at commaundement Richard Arkenstall. *Holograph.*
Postscript: Post scriptum. I was gretely troubled when you sent to me for mony for which I was bownd and had sent and payd ~~to~~ but nowe I hope you have receyved the same for that since I receyved my bond. I shalbe also at my howse at Wilberton[153] which your servaunt knoweth, until the 22 of November next if it please you to send.

Addressed: To the right worshipfull Sir Nicholas Bacon knight at his howse at Burry or elswhere
2 ff.; traces of seal.

97.   [4145] *Robert Rogers to Margaret Matson, 22 April 1586*
With right hartye comendations etc. For asmoche as I am informed that my olde good worshipfull master and yours is into Suffolk whom I wold gladly have wayted uppon if he had been at home and ~~wl~~ wold gladly sene youe myne old acquayntaunce and very gode frynde but that I kepe a court at Welles this day for Mr Doyle whiche is my lotte etc. Thease are to put you nowe in remembraunce of the fyftye pound of *hoppys* whiche I sent you the last yere and ar yet on payed fore whiche came to 16s 8d after 4d the pound. That ye wold send me the money by the goodman Dey, the bringer herof. I will thing [*sic*] my self beholden onto you as knoweth the lyving god who preseve and kepe you in heth to his pleasure. Scribled at ~~Warth~~ Warham this 22 of Aprile Anno 1586

Signed: by your assured frynde Robert Rogers. *Holograph.*
Addressed: To his very frynd Margaret Matson servaunte to the right worshipfull Thomas Buttes Esquire delyver these at Littell Walsingham
1 f.; traces of seal.

98.   [4147] *William Cecil, Lord Burghley to Sir Nicholas Bacon II, 18 June 1586*
After my verie hartie commendations: wheareas I understand that notwith-standing the nowe seaven years since order was geven for the felling of certaine trees within the parke of Eye for repair of the pales thereof, theare hath nothing been thearein done by reason as it is pretended of sum services which her Majes-ties tenauntes within that Honor refuse to doo, which of duetye theie are bownd unto, I hartelie praie you being steward of the honnor to informe your self hereof, so that sum speedie order maie be taken for amendment of the pale, according to such direction as formerlie hath been directed thearein. Soe fare you well. From Westminster this 18 of June 1586

Signed: Your verie loving frend W. Burghley. *Autograph.*
Addressed: To the R. worshipfull my verie loving frend Sir Nicholas Bacon knight
2 ff; seal impression.

---

153   Wilburton in Cambridgeshire.

99. [4156] *Sir Nicholas Bacon II to Privy Council, beginning of July [1586]*[154]

Mi humble dutye remembred to yower good L., I ame to be an humble sutor unto yower ~~L~~ honors to stande my good Lordes that in the servyce of her Majestyes the actyons beinge so ~~lewde~~ *many and untolerable* agaynst me ~~and so many~~ *and takynge ordynarye cowrse of justice and honesty as I have done* I maye not be thus used by hys brother not onelye to my ~~great~~ *utter* dyscredyte but also *to the* greate dyscoragemente ~~to~~ *of* both to my selfe and other* justyces of peace havynge any occatyon to deale in the lyke actyon or any other servyce of her Majestye and therefore good my Lordes seinge I have ~~bor~~ taken the ordynarye cowrse of justyce ~~and refused~~ *and forbourne thys chalenge* in respecte of yower honorable favors ~~and~~ the peace and quyet of my cowntrye *to stande my good L.* (which other wyse I protest before the lyvinge God I wolde never have pute yt uppe)[155] ~~[H]~~ *~~to stande my good Lordes~~* humblye ~~desyer yow~~ *referreynge my selfe and my cause* with all dutye as dothe becomme me to yower grave consyderatyons I dutyfullye take my leave. From London the [*blank*] of ~~June~~ Julye

Unsigned: draft.
2 ff.

100. [4148] *Sir Nicholas Bacon II to John Monford, 24 August [1586]*[156]

Monford, I have letten unto Mr. Daye the bearer herof my fearme at Ryboroughe for tenn yeares for the which he shall paye fowre scoore and £6 a yeare, and he shall have everye yeare into his bargayne 2 acres of wood. And if he lycke any of the arrable grounde which lyeth next the sheeps corse that my cosyne Blackman[157] doe occupye, than I am contented that he shall have that, at such rate as thay be nowe letten ~~to him for~~, to my cosen Blackman. And so I byd you farwell. From Culford this 24 of August.

Signed: Your master Nycholas Bacon. *Autograph.*
Postscript: Yt is also agred that he shall paye no fearme untyll Mighelmas com twelfemonth and than he shall paye the whole fearme
Addressed: To my servante John Monford at Egmer
Endorsed with notes: John Freman servant to Sir William Buttes and balif of the husbandry there abought 60 yeres *and more* last paste can testyfye that the shepe of Fytt and those whose estate Fytt nowe hath have alweys from tyme to tyme been beyghted and chased of and ~~never~~ *not* suffered to feade there. And further he canne saye that the weye called Dalling Wey or Dallingate lieth on the north parte of the ground that Fytt claymeth feade with his shepe in.

Robert Pownser sheperd to Sir William Buttes abought ~~23~~ 28 yeres last paste and for vi yeres then next following testefyeth ut supra.

---

[154] This draft is dateable by reference to Smith, *County and court*, pp. 183–5, describing the major feud between on the one hand Bacon and Bassingbourn Gawdy and on the other Thomas Lovell of Harling (Nf.); it seems to relate in date and subject matter to the challenge to a duel by Lovell on 1 July 1586 (note its reference to Bacon forbearing 'thys chalenge').

[155] That is, refused the challenge to a duel, or tolerated the insult.

[156] This can be dated by reference to *Bacon handlist*, nos. 4425–34.

[157] Robert Blackman married Anne the sister of Lord Keeper Sir Nicholas Bacon and had children Robert and Jane.

sub pena pro Thoma Bacon
>pro Johanne Freman
>pro Thoma Mann

Robertus Barker *shepherd to Sir William Buttes* abought 16 yeres sithens past and for 8 yeres then following dyd ~~alweys~~ diverse tymes at his comandement dryve and chase the shepe of Fytt of the ground in questyon somtyme 3 tymes in one daye with his dogge and old Fytt being present ~~dyd~~ many tymes did ~~never~~ *not* saye any thing to him for the same.

Thomas Man ~~abought~~ sheperd to Sir William Buttes aboute 23 yeres last past for one yere then next following dyd dyverse yeres aswell of when Thornage flock were not there as otherwyse chase ~~be~~ and beyte of with his dogges Fittes shepe uppon the grounde in questyon.

John Wylson abought ~~16~~ *15th of 16 yeres and 7 yeres ~~before that~~ after* yeres past being sheperd to Fytte of the foldcours that Fytt claymeth to have feade with in Thornage Heathe seythe that at diverse tymes within the same term as well when the lordes flock of Thornage were there feading as otherwyse ~~were~~ the shepe of the sayde Fytt were by Sir William Buttes his servants beyted and dryven of and not suffered to feade on the southe part of the wey nere ~~leving~~ Saxlingham Heathe and once he was beaten by Sir Williams servauntes.[158]
1 f.

101.   [4146] *Edward Coke to Sir Nicholas Bacon II, 30 April [?1587]*[159]
Sir Nicholas, I have indifferently and safely for you drawen and perfected a dede indented of feffment, I trust according to your meaninge, saving that I knewe not the copihold rent, for no more but the copihold rent canne be reserved, for if the free rent should be ~~payd~~ reserved out of this land then should he be driven to pay the fre rent twise which I knowe is not your meaninge. I pray you let your servant serch in some of your particuler accountes and therwithall peruse his copyes and the ~~rent~~ copihold rent will soone appeare but I durst not my selfe apporcion the rent for feare I should preiudice your right, for want of instruction. The rent must be sett down before you seale and deliver these bookes, wherof I pray you have care. There is no other thing nedfull for you to be remembred but to take bonde for the residewe of your money if any remayne which I knowe I neede not remember you of. And thus commending me humbly to you and my good lady, I humbly take my leave and betake you to God. From Huntingfeld Hall this last of Aprill

Signed: Your w. at commandment Edward Coke. *Holograph.*
Postscript: The partyes could not seale and deliver the counterpayne to your use because the rent is not yet settled, but after the rent ~~p~~ be putt in let Welles seale and deliver his part and the rest shall do the like at my returne.
Addressed: To the right worshippfull Sir Nicholas Bacon knight at Redgrave
Endorsed, early seventeenth-century hand: Sir Edward Cokes letter to Sir Nicholas Bacon. *Also in Bacon's hand* Item my rente hennes
Item bande for my mony d. at Mychelltyde.

---

158   These depositions may relate to the dispute about a foldcourse on Thornage Heath mentioned below, no. **99 [4156]**.
159   This can probably be dated by reference to *Bacon handlist*, no. **2615**, a lease from Bacon to John Wells of Beccles, yeoman, of lands in Shipmeadow and elsewhere, 1 May 1587. The feoffees include Edward Bouthe and Robert Carre of Huntingfield, probably servants or tenants of Coke's.

Item the rec. for the lande last purchased by Welles
1 f.; traces of seal.

102.   [4149] *Edward Bacon to Sir Nicholas Bacon II, 27 October 1587*

Brother Bacon, Mr Alderman Marsam is answered according to apointment five
hundred pounds, the interest therof amonteth to £16, the monnie was all answered
him by the tenthe of October accordinge to his owne accompte. I have your
statute cancelled, he is content to forbeare for thinterest untill your comynge upp,
I offered him my bill for thinterest but he said he would retaine yours without your
further prejudice. I will se what I can do towchinge the severinge of the Queenes
rent of Brampfeilde from Mettingham, and howe I shall get yt doune I will signifie
hereafter unto you. Thus with hartie comendations to my sister and Mistres Butts,
I leave prayinge God all good to you and yours, from London this 27 of October
1587

Signed: Your loving brother Edward Bacon. *Autograph.*
Addressed: To the right worshippfull and his lovinge brother Sir Nicholas Bacon
knight at Redgrave Hall
Endorsed: Mr Edward Bacons letter concerning Mr Aldermans mony
1 f.; seal impression.

103.   [4150] *Sir John Higham, Sir Robert Jermyn, Sir Philip Parker and Sir Robert Wingfield, Deputy Lieutenants of Suffolk, to Sir Nicholas Bacon II, 19 June 1588*

After our hartye commendations. Forsomuch as we fynd by conference of
warantes dyrected to the high Constables of the Hundred of Hoxon that contra-
ryety hath arisen touching the devison of men and furnyture in that Hundred,
wherof many inconvenyences may ensue which we are desyerous to prevent, we
have thought *good* hereby to put you in memory what certifycate we have heretofore *in November last* sent to the LLs. of the Cownsele, havyng warraunt for
the same from yow and Sir William Spryng, towchyng the sortyng of men and
armor in that Hundred of Hoxon which we hope and so we desyer may acordyngly
contynew betwen yow and Mr Forth,[160] who is apoynted to that charge which Sir
William Spryng had. Towchyng your number of 400 men allotted to your conduc-
tion, thus yt ys set downe for the part of Hoxon Hundred, viz. in the part therof
under your charg able men 300, of them taken into your band 70, which nombers
are expressed thus to be furnished, viz. corseletes 10, alman ryvetes 20, calyvers
20, long bowes 20. In the resydew therof then under the charge of Sir Wylliam
Spryng, able men 320, of them taken into his band 116, which are mentyoned thus
to be furnished viz. corseletes 20, alman ryvetes 10, calyvers 52, long bowes 34.
The supply of the rest of your 400 men are certified to be in the Hundred of Harts-
mere, in which the able men be in nomber 924. This devision heretofore assented
unto and certified as yow se, in which ther be sufficient nombers of men to supply
both our bandes, we praye you very hartely may styll be continewed. Our contrye
hath for manye yeares caryed great credyt for the good agrement emongest the
gent. and lamentable yt were that so small a cause shold be the begynnyng of any
disagrement. We therfore wishe that we maye so farre prevayle with you herin,
as by our order a fynall determynation may herof be made, without appelyng to

---

160   Robert Forth of Butley priory.

higher authoryty. And thus wishyng the same and expectyng your answer, we do very hartelye bydd yow farewell. From Ipswych this 19 of June 1588[161]

Signed: Your very lovyng fryndes Robert Wyngfeld, Phillip Parker, Roberte Jermyn, John Heigham. *Autograph.*

Addressed: To the right worshipfull and our very good frynd Sir Nycholas Bacon knight

Endorsed in italic hand: A lettre from the Leiftenauntes touchinge the devission of Hoxton Hundred

2 ff.; seal impressions.

104. [4150A] *Sir Francis Walsingham to Sir Nicholas Bacon II, 2 August 1588*

Sir, I understand aswell by your lettres as the bearer therof the great forwardness yow have shewed in providing the two geldinges fitt for service, that I wrott for, for the which I can not butt think my self much beeholding to yow. And whereas yow finde the Tenantes of the Duchie[162] theraboutes verie unwilling to perfourme that my request, I can not butt take it in verie ill parte, considering I have not any waie done it in respect of any pr[iva]te benefitt, butt only for the advancing of the publick service in this time of so imminent daunger. Wherfore theie shall finde mee if (as occasion shall heerafter bee proferd) to thinck of them accordingly. And so I bidd you right hartilie farewell. From the Courte at St James the second of August 1588

Signed: Your verie loving frind Francis Walsingham. *Autograph.*

Addressed: To the right worshipfull my verie loving frind Sir Nicholas Bacon knight

Endorsed in italic hand: The last lettre. Sir Francis Walsinghams lettre for the patrenels.

2 ff.; seal impression.

105. [4151] *Robert Cotton to Sir Nicholas Bacon II, 2 December 1588*

Sir, I should have bin most glad to have fownd you att Culpher[163] according to my expectation. My evell hap lykwise to cum thether to short of m[y] Ladye your wyffe. I am presently to go unto Lond[on] and for thatt happely I may see the gentlema[n] of Kent with whom I delt dealte for the mariag[e] of his daughters before my goinge over, and do nott knowe since whatt hathe proceded. I wou[ld] have bin glad att this tyme to have understandinge off your determination so as yff now myselfe may do any servyce herin I desire you will commande me, and wyll do my best indevore with all diligence.

I most hartely pray you to deliver unto my servaunt this bearer, fyvetene pownnds for thatt in th truthe I am now to pay att London fyvetye pownndes which I tooke up in Germany upon my travell. And herein you may helpe to furnyshe me: assuringe my selfe upo[n] the redinesse of your assistance herein. Allth[ow] I have

---

[161] This letter was written as the Spanish Armada was setting out from its bases in Portugal and Spain.

[162] That is, the Duchy of Lancaster; Sir Francis was chancellor of the duchy and was evidently trying to use this rather desperate revival of feudalism as one expedient for defence in the Armada crisis.

[163] Probably Culford Hall, which Sir Nicholas Bacon had bought in 1585 before himself rebuilding it.

nott here your bond to send unto y[ou] I pray you to bare with me for the same and the which att my cumminge from London shall [be] deliverd unto you. In the meane tyme [I] have sent you by my servaunt my accquitta[nce] for the receyte off fyvetene powndes which I pray accepte of and lett him receyve the monye which att this tyme may greatly pleasure me. Thus my most harty commendacions unto you and my good lady your bedfellowe, I take my leave. Culpher, this munday the 2 of December 1588

Signed: Yours assuredly to dispose and commande Robert Cotton.[164] *Holograph.*
Addressed: To the right worshipfull Sir Nycholas Bacon knighte att his house att Redgrave
Endorsed in italic hand: Mr Cotton his lettre and acquittanc for £15.
1 f., torn; traces of seal.

106.   [4152] *Henry, Lord Hunsdon to Sir Nicholas Bacon II, 9 April 1589*[165]
After my hartie commendations. Wheras her Majestie upon good deliberation, and dewe advisement of my L. Th'er and the rest of her heighnes privie Councell, did grant unto my sonne John Carie and Sir Arthur Henningham a commission for the repayring of Chrismas Lane, which in like mannor the whole universitie of Cambridg confirmed to be a peece of work verie necessarie and needfull to be taken in hand. Forasmuch as I understand that allbeyt most of the better sort in thoes cownties are verie well affected towardes the proceeding thereof, yow alone have undertaken to oppose your selfe agaynst yt, first at Burie, and then at Thetford in Norfolk, wher yow have nothing to doe, wherat I greatlie marvell, that yow should goe about to alienate the peoples myndes from this action, consydering that yowrselfe have a commission (which as yt seemes) is in a worse measure of greevance then this.[166] I have therfore thought good heereby to advise yow to surceaze from diswading the same, so that yt may take such good effecte as her Majesties meaning was in the graunting thereof, otherwise assure your selfe that the discredyt of this commission shall bring smale credyt to your owne, for yow cannot crosse this so greatlie, but yow shall fynd that other of yours well encowntered. And so wishing yow to have dew regard heereof I commit yow to the Allmightie. At the Court at Whitehall this 9 of Aprill 1589

Signed: Your loving frende Hounsdon. *Autograph.*
Addressed: To the right worshipfull my loving frend, Sir Nicholas Bacon knighte
Endorsed by Bacon: 9 of Aprill 1589. My L. of Hunsdons lettre concernyng Cristmas Lane browght to me on Frydaye after supper beyng the 11 of Aprill 1589
2 ff.; seal impression.

---

164   He cannot be the famous antiquary Sir Robert Bruce Cotton, but is probably the son of Thomas Cotton of Landwade (Cambs.).

165   For the major East Anglian dispute about the repair of Christmas Lane in Metfield, involving Lord Hunsdon as Lord Lieutenant, for which this and the next letter provide major evidence, see Smith, *County and court*, pp. 230–34, and MacCulloch, *Suffolk*, pp. 260–7, especially pp. 263–4.

166   I have not been able to identify the commission which provoked this sarcasm. Bacon was on a multitude of military and civil commissions.

107. [4153] *Sir Nicholas Bacon II to Henry, Lord Hunsdon, 12 April 1589*
My humble duetie remembred to your good L. I have receyved your L. lettre
dated the 9 of Aprill the 11 of the same monthe wherein I do fynde your honour
the dothe charge me that I have bene thonely dealer agaynst the comyssion of
Christmas Lane, and that most of the better sorte are very willing in the furtheraunce of the same and this to be done at Burie *and* Thetford. So it is my very
good L. that that which was done at Burie was done not onely by the consentes
of all the Justices there, by a letter directed to your L. and the rest of my LL., but
also by bothe the great enquestes of our countrie or at the least by the most parte
of them by a supplication delyvered publiquelie delyvered to our justice of Assise
whereunto I was no waye pryvie before the delyverie of it, humblie desiring hym
to use some good meanes for the staye of it consideringe the great charges that the
countrie of late had bene at, and were likelie still to be, so that (with your honorable favour be it spoken) they have done me great wronge that thus have enformed
your L. agaynst me. But I wishe it might please your L. to enter into the state of
our countrie and generally to enquyre whether men be willinge or not, and howe
harde it is for pore men to come by mony at this tyme, and what other inconvenyences maye ensue of this, and then I have no dowbte but your honorable wysdome
shall fynde that we the Justices of our countrie had great nede to doe that which
we ded, hoping that your L. above all the rest beyinge our Lieutenaunte uppon
whom next under her Majestie, we doe onely depend, would seke all good meanes
to ease us of so great a burden as this is. And whereas your L. dothe wright that I
have a comyssion in a worse nature of grevaunce then this is, I protest unto your
L. I doe not knowe your meanynge, and therfore I must crave pardon of your L. in
not answering of the same. I am also to be an humble suytor unto your L. that it
would please you to conceave that honorable opynyon of me, as of one, that in all
duetie dothe honour you and yours and would be glad in any thinge that conserns
my selfe to do you that honorable service which I confesse in duetie is due unto
you. And so I humblie take my leave praying God that you had the-[*two words
illegible below heavy erasure*] From Redgrave this 12 of Aprill 1589

Signed: NB. *Draft in clerk's hand.*
Endorsed: A copie of my lettre to the L. Chamberleyne concerning Christmes
Lane
1 f.

108. [4154] *Sir Robert Drury to Robert Mawe, 8 June 1590*[167]
Mr Mawe I pray you to sende the mony *me* by this bearer the reste of the monny
due to me, by Sir Nicholas Bacon, which by your account and myne this other
nyght, as I remember came to thir twenty three pownde. If Sir Nicholas Bacon
require any backe againe I wil repaye so muche backe to you as he requireth.
Written this 8 of June 1590

Signed: R. Drury. *Autograph.*
1 f.

---

[167] This is the first surviving evidence of the Drury connection which will become so important in
the collection: see Introduction, p. 000.

Plate 4: *Letter 109 [4157]: Robert Mawe to Sir Nicholas Bacon II, 20 June [?1590]. An illustration of how impenetrable the handwriting of an Elizabethan lawyer could be.*

109. [4157] *Robert Mawe to Sir Nicholas Bacon II, 20 June [?1590]*

Sir since the beginninge of this terme I had some speache with Mr Attorney towchinge the sute in the Exchecker and informed him (as I do certeynelie knowe by vewe of matter under my Lord your fathers hand) that by the sur payment of the £100 a yeare that yowe are nowe sued for, the Quenes Majestie saved yearlie ~~£267~~ £277 7s 7d and therfore praid him that he would not be to earnest in callinge for an answer, but that we might have some reasonable tyme to fynde out what matter we have to satisfye her Majestie in lawe; and have gotten yowe daie untyll the next terme to put in yowre answer. He told Mr Warner and me since that upon sundaie last he movd her Majestie to weyinge[168] this and suche like sutes and told her that if her old servauntes weare called in question for suryety may [sic] ~~so longe after the~~ it wold be a meane to abat ther loves toward her, and that she answered againe that yf the matter in lawe should fall out aganst yowe yet she wold deale gratiouslye with yow. And thus muche I thought to signify unto yow and wilbe redy to deale with Mr Kempe and Mr Patten according as your lettres and warrant purport and in the meane space humbly take my leave this 20 of June 1590[169]

Signed: Your worshippes ever at your commaundement Robert Mawe. *Holograph.*
Addressed: To the right worshipfull Sir Nicholas Bacon knighte at Redgrave
2 ff.

110. [4155] *Thomas Higham to Sir Nicholas Bacon II, 14 October 1590*

Sir so sone as occation is offered, I shall not fayle (God willing) to see performed, as carefully as I can, the effecte of your letter delivered to me, but in the meane time I am to advertise you, that this present day, the fourtene of October, thear cam Mr Thomas Croftes, who kepeth at Sir William Heydons, Robert Jervis gent. and Robert Hind yeman, Sir Williams men, with Richard Lawsone *clarke* parson of Laverinset,[170] and James Leman laborer of Hoult Market, with two others whose names as yet I can not learne but by his instrument was a mesurer of ground *and his servant*. Theas men mesured one pease of ground on Thornage Heath butteling on the north part to Laverinset, and is the pease whear they have used usurpingly to com, and allso ane other part of Thornage Heath toward the east, with two peases of coppy hould lond in the tenner and occupation of Henry Bacon of Thornage afore sayd *houlden of this maner* thear unto adioyning, without the privite eyther of you, my La. or the tenant, liyng farre distant from the pease of the north part, as also from all the lond, or liberty of sheapes course, of the sayd Sir William. Even as they wear finishing this last parsell cam John Knightes my La. servant, who asked them what they ded measuring thear, to whom the stranger whom he know not, answered for no harme, which licke a found man he was satisfised [sic] with, and so they all departed. What may be done in this case I besheche your wor. consider with your counsell, that this untemperate dealing of him and his, may be so qualefied, as my La. may enioy hur living with quiet, and your inheritance no way empeched, by thear sinister practises, and over bould attemtes. Thus referring all to your graver consideration I sease to trouble you.

---

168 This reading is uncertain.
169 *Bacon handlist* reads this as 1591: the reading is difficult, and even 1598 is possible. The most likely interpretation is 1590.
170 Letheringsett (Nf.).

Remembering my La. harty commendations to you and my La. and my sister with my owne I commit ye to thalmighty. Thornag 1590

Signed: Your ~~nephew~~ uncle and frind to be commanded Thomas Heigham. *Holograph.*

Postcript:

Sir if this contrary cours of his will broche a new the cause late in controversy, my La. sendeth you terrers and other writinges with the pleding at this last triall. If it will not be suffitient to bring the matter in question, yet I dought not but you may by proses call them severally to London to answear what they have done. God grant you good succes in this and all the reast of your good causes and so in hast I leave to trouble you. TH.

Bocons Land mesured by them is 12 ac. the reast of heath thearto adioyning ~~and~~ thear which mesured I account 3 ac. or thear abought.

The pease one the north part I estme abought ~~30 ac.~~ 40 ac.[171]

Addressed: To the right worshipfull and his assuered good nephew Sir Nicolas Bacon knight at Culford

2 ff.

111. [4158] *Sir Nicholas Bacon II to Sir Robert Jermyn, 6 May 1592*[172]

Good Sir Robert, I thanke you hartely for your letter and for your good newes. I also understande by the same that ther showld be payd unto Sir Jhon Scott on hundred powndes at our Lady day last. Surly if I be ryghtly informed, ther is as ~~myche~~ *muche* more dewe from Sir Jhon Scott then that, which I do thinke will very hardly be come by with owt sut, and ther fore untyll I se howe that shalbe awnswerd, it were very hard for me to enter into the payment of it: for if I showld, I were lyke inowghe to awnser it my self which I knowe is fare from your menynge. As it showld seme ther is also dwe from my Lady Scott in dette for blackes, for the funarall of hir husband taken upe by hir selfe in hir wedowhoode, a matter that dothe nothinge concern Sir Robert Drury neyther the will of Sir ~~Whi~~ Wyllyam Drury, and for my Lady to have all the goodes that were valuede at suche reasonable pryses as she had them and to be no wayes chargable with the debttes, but to thurst [*sic*] everye charge upon the heyer, I can not se howe this can be awnswerd owt of so small a porcyon as Sir Robert Drury hath consydering the dette of the Quens Maj'st. And therfor good Sir Robert tyll thinges be waied in deferently and consyder the weake estat of the poor jentellman, which if his ablyty [*sic*] served hym hath a mynd to paye every man. I do fear thes ar but devyses of Sir Jhon Scotte to shorten his own reckonynges with alle: but lett Sir Jhon shewe his accomtt and se our demandes, and then it will easley appere where the falt is. In the mene tyme I pray you satysfye Sir Willyam Waldgrave and your self. Sir Robert is very willinge to paye his fathers debttes according to his poor estate which is very well known unto you. Thus with my very harty commendations to your selfe and the good ladys I pray God blesse us and them. Redgrave the 6 of May[173]

---

171 See also above, no. **101 [4148]**.
172 Bulk of text printed in Bald, *Donne and the Drurys*, p. 24.
173 Sir William Drury's widow had remarried Sir John Scott.

Endorsed in italic hand: The copy of Mr Baons [*sic*] letter to Sir Robert Jermyn the 6 of May 1592
2 ff.

112. [4159] *Henry Knyvett*[174] *to Lady Bacon, 30 March 1595*

Good Madame, I am sory that my wante of skill hathe hindered me from doeing yow that sarvice whiche I desired, but if yow mislyke of any thinge which is bought if yow please to returne them, I will see them changed with speede. I can not think that there is an other fassion for a cheayne, then that of goulde and perle suche as was bought for my La. Drurye, or ells a chayne of a playne lynke beynge fyne goulde. The parte There is not any of goulde and perle redy made to be had for any mony that is worthe the buyinge, neyther can I fynde a chayne with a playne lynke of good goulde, but I have bespoken one of eyther sorte whiche will be redy within six dayes. In the meane tyme I beseche yow to sende me worde whiche fassion will beste like yow, but in my opynion that of goulde and perle dothe make the best shewe. There is but one border in all Chepeside of so good a fassion as I think will contente yow, and that is like that whiche was bought for my La. Drwry, but the price is £24 bycawse it is more massyve in goulde then the other was. I woolde have sent your La. that border and a chayne of goulde and perle (the beste that I can fynde redy made) but not halfe so well wroughte as my La. Drurye's was, together with a chayne of a playne lynke if I coulde have had them uppon lykinge, I offered to leave there owne prises in mony untell I returnd them agayne, but they *the gouldsmithes* were lothe to hassarde the losse of the sale of them whiche they expecte daylie. There is an other border latelie shewed me of goulde and perle, the worke cutte oute and the amell[175] blacke, but this I thinke to be to auncient for neis D. Bacon.[176] Your man hathe lefte thre skore poundes with me which I was in hope sholde have byn bestowed before his goinge from London, but this Lent hathe is not the best tyme to fynde choyse of good workmanshippe amonge the gouldesmithes, the neerer towards Ester the better choyese. I can nott make any gouldsmith understande your meaninge tutching the litle buttons to be laced with with rubyes to be laced with perle for a necklace, but they say your La. mente litle pillers with rubies to be laced with perle. Goode Madam satisfie me herein as shortly as yow may, and what your pleasure is tutchinge the chayne and borders. I have sente your La. the braceletes mended, the workmanshippe and the gould whiche was wantynge reforme 15s, which I have recayved of your man. If any thinge contaynde in the note here inclosed doe mislyke yow upon the retorne of them with knowledge of the faultes yow shall have them changed. Thus with the remembrance of my best duty to your La. and to good Sir Nicholas Bacon I humbly take my leeve this 30 of Marche 1595

Signed: Your La. to be commanded in all I am able Henry Knyvett. *Holograph.*
Postscript: Your La. shall receave your braclets by this berer your sarvaunt.
Addressed: To the right worshipfull my singuler good Ladie the La. Bacon at Culforde
2 ff.; seal impression.

---

174 Henry Knyvett was brother to Sir Thomas Knyvett of Ashwellthorpe, whose son married Elizabeth the daughter and coheir of Nathaniel Bacon.
175 For 'enamel'.
176 'Niece Dame Bacon' or 'nice Dame Bacon'?

113. [4160] *Henry Knyvett to Lady Bacon, 17 April 1595*
Good Madame, I have done my beste to have suche thinges *provided* as it pleased yow to wrighte for, althoughe my busynes was suche that I was constrayned to ryde into Norffolke. I have therefore sente yow by Mr Gawdies man a chayne of goulde and perle and a border cutte throwe and inameled with black, the prises yow shall ~~knowe b~~ perceave by the goldesmythes note whiche is packt uppe in one of the boxes. The fyve pillers ar in my conceapte the hardest peniworthe, but if yow mislyke them it maye please yow to sende them unto me agayne before the beginning of the nexte terme and the price whiche I have paide for them shall be retorned agayne. All the reste of the thinges which your La. did wrighte for were provided and sente downe by Mr Gawdies man. The prises of the chayne boorders and pillers amounteth to fyftye nyne poundes, so is there lefte of the £60 dely-vered to me by your man Hill 20s, which I have sente your La. hereinclosed. And so restinge at your Ladiships commaundment I committ yow to the protection of our good God. Fletestrete in greate hast this 17 of Aprill 1595,

Signed: Your La. well assured poore frende Henry Knyvett. *Holograph.*
Addressed: To the right worshipfull my singuler good Ladie the Bacon [*sic*] at Culforde
Endorsed with memorandum: Left of Dolls £200 besydes the apparill £24 11s.
2 ff.; remains of seal.

114. [4162] *Cover-sheet for lost letter to the authorities in Milan [?1596]*[177]
Endorsed: Al conde di Selbes. del cons'o de su Mag'r su castellano de Mylan. Milan
1 f.; seal impression.

115. [4161] *Robert Devereux, Earl of Essex, to the Grand Duke of Tuscany,*[178] *from the English Court, 1 March 1596. Letter of introduction for the bearer, travelling in Italy to benefit from the change of air and to consult the most eminent physicians there about his health after an illness acquired in the Low Countries: he is a gentleman of good family, much favoured at Court and by the Earl. It would much oblige the Earl if the Grand Duke would show him favour and protection.*[179]
Serenissimo Gran Duca
Il presentator di questa venendo costa in fermo d'una debolezza presa nelli Paesi bassi con speranza dit[ ]uorne remedio nella mutatione dell'aria et col consiglio di quei e[minen]tissimi medici d'Italia: non ho potuto mancar di raccomandargli al[la] Serenita Vostra essendo gentilhuomo di buona casa, et ben visto et rispettato in questa corte et a me molto caro per particulari rispetti et pe[r] il suo valore et meriti. Cosi la Serenita Vostra rede come io piglio liberta in ogni occurrenza di valermi delli suoi favori senza sapi[ ] modo di disobligarmene se non con l'offerta di quella poca servitu che Vostra Serenita puo hauer di me; la quale sara sempre molto pronta [*one word missing*] affezzionata. Non voglio ora darla piu lungo fastidio ma supplicando instantissimamente alla medesima di fare il sudetto

---

[177] This is likely to have been the cover-sheet for a similar letter of introduction to no. **115 [4161]**.
[178] Ferdinando I de' Medici (1587–1609).
[179] This letter was probably intended for the use of Sir Robert Drury on a projected expedition to Italy, but he did not use it, joining Essex's expedition to raid Cadiz instead: Bald, *Donne and the Drurys*, p. 35.

G[en]tilhuomo degno delle sue grazie et protettione le bacio con devotiss[ ] affezzione le mani. Di Corte allo primo di Marzo 1595

Signed: Della Serenita Vostra, affezzionatissimo per servirla Essex. *Autograph.*
Addressed: All Serenissimo Gran Duca di Toscana
2 ff.; 2 fine seal impressions.

116.   [4163] *Robert Mawe to Sir Nicholas Bacon II, 12 May 1597*
Sir, I have paide to Mr Flecher the tailor this 12 of Maie 1597 upon your letters fowerscore poundes fyve shillinges seaven pence, and have taken a note of his hand for it. But he tells me he made a note of it before his comyng ~~of~~ *from* Culford and dd. it to Robert Felgat. The rest I shalbe redy to dispose of as it shall please yowe to appoynt. And so with the remembraunce of my very humble dutie to your good self and my good lady humbly I take my leave. At Lincolns Inne this 12 of Maie 1597,

Signed: Your worshippes ever assuredly to be comaunded Robert Mawe.
Endorsed in another hand: A discharge of fower skore pownds five shillings 7 pence payed to Fletcher in May anno 1597
1 f.

117.   [4164] *Sir Nicholas Bacon II to Sir John Townshend [before 22 June 1599], and receipt by Myles Lookes to Sir John Townshend, 22 June 1599*
My verye good nephewe I praye yow paye to Loockes £17 of the money yow have promysed to paye me verye shortelye, and thys shall be a warrante for yower dyscharge of so mutche,

Signed: Yowers in all love and frendeshype N. Bacon. *Holograph.*
Addressed: To my verye lovynge nephewe Sir Jhone Towensendes

Memorandum on same sheet: Receyved the 22 of June 1599 of Sir John Townshend knight the sum of seventene poundis dew to Myles Lookes of Gyest[180] miller from Sir Nicholas Bacon Knight. Simon Lookes. *Autograph.*
2 ff.

118.   [4165] *Humphrey Fowler to Robert Felgate, 24 October 1599*
Good Mr Felgatte afoord mee yf not this fryndshippe, yet this equitie, concerninge the litle Conninglye. Lett me not paie two rentes for one yeare: in good truethe, I had paid the one halfe yeares rente, before that you or any creature in the world acquaincted mee with any heyghninge of any rente. It ys an unreasonable heyghninge of yt to heyghen yt from 18s to above 40s yearelie. When I took yt, it is well knowen that noe man would geve 2s an acre for yt; I must paie for myne owne cost bestowed on yt. I am well contented to do yt for the time to come, because therebie I shall bwye my quiett occupiynge of myne owne gleabe liynge beyonde it. Yf that were not, I would not geve god a mercie for the penyworth, or yf yt wyll please them to allowe mee a waie (flye to yt I cannot) I wyll not so greatelie desyre yt. I am not to word at the Audite or at Redgrave for the matter, I must not, I wyll not, thoughe I lose yt, or whatsoever els. I praie you therefore lett mee use your

---

180   Guist (Nf.).

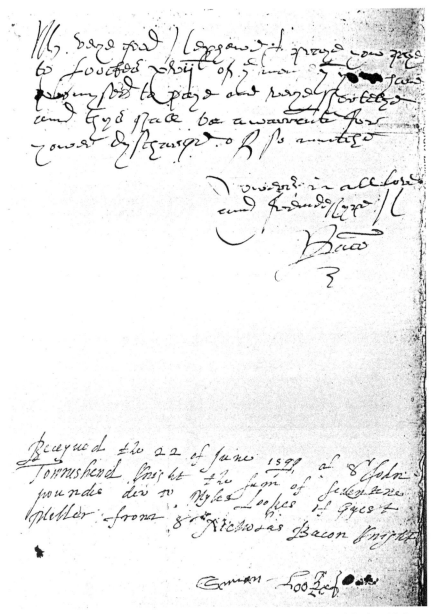

Plate 5: *Letter 117 [4164]: Sir Nicholas Bacon II to Sir John Townshend [before 22 June 1599], and receipt by Myles Lookes to Sir John Townshend, 22 June 1599. An example rare in this collection of the handwriting of the first Baronet.*

favour and helpe in yt. I wyll thinke mee selfe beholden to you for my quiett in yt.
So I commend you to God, who keepe you. 24 Octobris 1599.

Signed: Your poore frynd Humphrey Fowler. *Holograph.*
Addressed: To my verie good frynd Mr Robert Felghatte Steward at Redgrave
Hall
1 f.

119.   [4166] *James Taverner to Sir Nicholas Bacon II, 28 October 1599*

My humble duetie to your good worshipp and my good ladye alweys remembred.
I am herby so bowld as to remember you of your worshipfull favour in the behalf
of this bearer Robert Payn my sone in lawe, of whose duetyfull servyce and good
behavour both to your self and my said good ladye I make no dowbt of but that
he woll imploye himself with all good will and dylygance as apperteyneth. And
Sir Nicholas you were so busye at Styffkye when I brought hether my bookes of
rentalles towching the rentes and dueties of hir Majesties manor *of Wighton*
issuyng out of your manor of ~~Wighton~~ Egmer as that you cowld have no good
convenyent tyme to peruse the said rentalles, wherfore I have *thought* good
herbye to certyfye you of the severall parcelles of the same, viz.

> *Pro duabus sectis et intracione earundem 2s 4d. Egmer pro Letefee[181] ibidem*
> *2s 9d ob. Pro dimidia secta et intracione eiusdem pro terris in Giges 7d. Et pro*
> *redditis vocatis Warepownd[182] 3d. Summa per annum 5s 11d ob.*

And there be now this last mychelmas three yeres behynd unpaid which cometh
to the somme of 17s 10d ob. And syns that I am nowe levyng of myn unprofytable
offyce here of this hir Majesties collection and ageyne your worshipps, having at
hand your auditor your baylyes and farmer here, I praye that they nowe at laste
maye agree and determyn suche good order herin as that I maye be paid the arrerages aforsaid, for as I take yt yt is tyme, syns that now also therewithall *I* gyve
over this my elvyshe[183] offyce which I hope in God shall never happ ageyne to me
for any tenur of myn duryng my lef tyme. And so I praying to the Almightie for
the increas of your good worshipp do take my leave for this tyme at Wighton this
28 of October 1599

Signed: Your Worshipps alweys to commaund James Taverner. *Holograph.*
Addressed: To the right worshippfull Sir Nycholas Bacon knight
Endorsed: 28 Octobre 1599 James Tavernor for suyte fynes out of Egmere. Answer
was sent that the Q.[184] Lettres Patentes had discharged them.
1 f.; seal impression.

120.   [4167] *Lady Anne Bacon to Sir Nicholas Bacon II, 3 March 1600*

Sir Nicholas Bacon, I commende me unto yow, and to your ladye hopinge of your
good health. I thancke God myn owne health ys not verye good, but I beare yt with
pacience. And I thincke myselfe beholdinge to yow for havinge care of payenge

---

[181] The Leet Fee: presumably a fee for presiding in the Leet.
[182] Perhaps for a rent due from a geldable unit of land ('wara'); or possibly a variant on 'wardpenny':
    a fee paid in lieu of military service.
[183] 'Elvish': i.e. troublesome, mischievous.
[184] This letter is not clearly written, but is most plausibly 'Q' for 'Queen's'; it could be 'K' for
    'King's'.

me myne anuytie in good tyme for I have neede of yt alwayes before yt commeth to my handes. At this tyme yow have written to one Mr Cooke to paye me a hundered poundes at the Ladye daye next, of whome I shalbe verye well content to receave yt yf he paye yt to me then, but if he dothe fayle me and yow then, at the daye, I hope yow will have care of me, to see me payed. And so with prayer to God for this tyme I leave yow to his protection. From my lodinge [*sic*] in Fleete Streete this third of Marche 1599,

Signed: Your Lo. mother in the Lord very frind A. Bacon Χηρα[185] *Autograph, Lady Anne's hand beginning at 'in the Lord'.*
Addressed: To my lovinge sonne Sir Nicholas Bacon at Colford
2 ff.

121.   [4170] *Sir Nicholas Bacon II to Robert Mawe, 27 May 1600*

After my hartie comendations, I have sent you herinclosed an acquittanc from my mother for threskoor poundes which was due unto hir for hir thirdes of the manor of Thornham. I have likwise sent you herin closed a bill of Mr Atturneys[186] hande for fyfty poundes wherof £20 I have receyved at his chamber in London; the other £30 remaynethe due still. I praye shewe Mr Atturney the bill because that by that bill he may see what is due ~~from~~ to my mother. I have likwyse takne order with my brother for to send upp £33 6s 8d presentlye which is the third part of a £100 ~~who~~ which he should pay for his part. And soe if these sommes be allowed unto you I praye bringe downe the remaynder with you. Thus desyringe you to geve Mr Atturney hartie thankes for his paynes in this cause I committe you to God. Redgrave the 27 of May 1600

Signed: Yower lovynge freinde N. Bacon. *Autograph.*
Holograph postscript: I praye you remember the release to be drawen and shewed to Sir Edward Stafforde[187] and Sir Thomas Scotte of my sonne Drewryes causes.
Addressed: To my very loveinge frinde Mr Robert Mawe at his chamber at Lincons Inn
Endorsed by Mawe: Sir Nicholas Bacons lettres for payment to Mr Attorny for discharge of the informat.
2 ff.; traces of seal.

122.   [4169] *Lady Anne Drury to Sir Nicholas Bacon II [c. 1601]*

Sir I receved a letter from myne uncle Parker[188] which I have sent you, hoping that itt shall not be any way prejudiciall unto you to satisfy his desyre, and Mr Mawe I know wilbe very carefull to retorne them back unto you; I am very loth to be thus

---

185 'Chera' or 'widow'. Lady Anne, Lord Keeper Bacon's widow, was one of the famously well-educated daughters of Sir Anthony Cooke. She has often been accused of eccentricity or even, in her last years, senility, largely on the strength of the old *Dictionary of National Biography*'s statement that 'her mind gave way during the later years of her protracted life' (*op. cit., s.v.* Bacon, Anne). However, it is clear that even at this late stage in her life, she had not forgotten her Greek.

186 The Attorney General was Sir Edward Coke. See also no. **126 [4173]** below.

187 Brother to Lady Scott, the widow of Sir William Drury and Sir Robert Drury's mother.

188 George Parker of Whepstead, 'this sprite', was one of the executors of Sir William Drury, and was the last of the executors to give Sir Nicholas Bacon an acquittance for receipts of estate revenues, in 1601 (Bacon Collection MS no. **3817**), which suggests a possible date for this letter. Parker had married one of Sir William's sisters, hence he was Lady Drury's uncle. See Bald, *Donne and the Drurys*, pp. 29–30, 59.

troblesome unto you but that I assu[re] my selfe, this sprite waches all occasions to doo no good betweene your selfe and my husband which I am still driven to cross and pray for prevention. So humbly craving your dayly blessing I remayne

Signed: Your most dutyfull loving daughter Anne Drury. *Holograph.*
Addressed: To the right worshipfull my dearely beloved father Sir Nicholas Bacon knight at Redgrave
1 f.; fine seal impression.

123. [4168] *Sir John Popham to Sir Nicholas Bacon II, 4 February 1601*[189]
With my verie hartie comendations. For the endinge of the controversies betweene yow and Sir Robert Drury, I finde him vearie readie and willinge to conforme himselfe to any good order. For asmuche as it will be bothe a tedious and cumbersome course to procure the Queenes hande to a privie seale for your discharge, the matter beinge of noe more momente then a bonde of twoe hundred markes, I doe wishe that yow wolde be content to take assurance from him to your likinge for your indempnitie in that behalfe. And for ~~your~~ his sisters porcions he is contented at his now beinge in the countrey to assigne over soe muche ~~rentes~~ *rente* for five yeeres as maie equall or surmounte the yeerelie paimentes of twoe hundred poundes, or better, which I holde in my opinion to be a fitt course. For thereby his sisters may be well assured of their due, and Sir Robert finde himselfe verie favorablie dealt withall at your handes. And eaven soe assuringe my selfe yow will take due consideration herof, for this present I bid yow hartelie farewell. Att Sergeants Inne this fourth of Februarie 1600

Signed: Your verie assured frend John Popham. *Autograph.*
Postscript: Touchinge the matter of the ordinarie to be kept at thassises, everie justice to beare his owne particuler of it, and the Sheriff to be charged but for himselfe.[190]
Addressed: To the right w'll my verie good frende Sir Nicholas Bacon knight
2 ff.; traces of seal.

124. [4172] *Henry Glemham to Sir Nicholas Bacon II, 3 October, [1601 «» 1624]*[191]
Sir I cam to Berry to have sene yow but heard yow were gone to London, but about this time to returne. I have sent to know your pleasure about the musters where in uppon your answer I shall be ready to obey your directyon. Yf yow please to bestow a hound of me for the fox, I shall account my selfe much behoulding to yow. Yf yow have none yow know will hunt the chase, your fastest will go nere to fitt me, or yff yow will not bestow one of me, what yow lend I will safely kepe, and willingly restore at your pleasure. Thus with the remembrance of my servis to my lady and your selfe ~~with~~ I rest
October the third/

Signed: Ever your assured frend and servant Henrie Glemham. *Holograph.*
1 f., torn.

---

[189] Text printed in Bald, *Donne and the Drurys*, pp. 31–2.
[190] Popham was the senior assize judge on the Eastern Circuit at the time. The 'ordinary' was the formal dinner held for judges, sheriff and JPs during a session of the assizes. Disputes about how to pay for it were not uncommon.
[191] This must be after 1601, when Sir Henry became a muster commissioner for Suffolk.

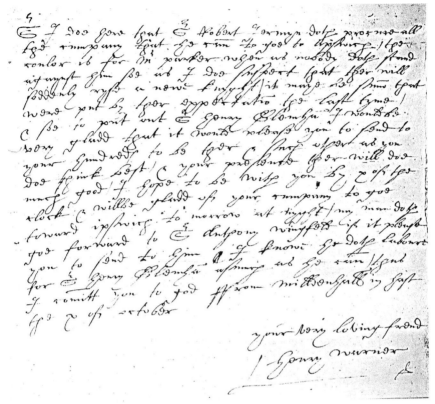

Plate 6: *Letter 125: [4171] Henry Warner to Sir Nicholas Bacon II, 10 October 1601.*
Another important witness to a contest at a county parliamentary election which would
otherwise be unknown to us.

125. [4171] *Henry Warner to Sir Nicholas Bacon II, 10 October 1601*

Sir I doe here that Sir Robert Jermyn doth procure all the cumpany that he cann
to goe to Ipswich. The coulor is for Mr Parker when as nobody doth stand agaynst
him, soe as I doe suspect that ther will soddenly ryse a newe knyght. It maye be
summe that were put by ther expectation the last tyme, and soe to put out Sir
Henry Glemham. I would be very gladd that it would please you to send to your
hundredes to be ther, and your presence ther will doe much good. I hope to be with
you by 10 of the clock and willbe gladd of your cumpany to goe toward Ipswich to
morrow at nyght. My man doth goe forward to Sir Anthony Wingfeld if it please
you to send to him. I knowe he doth laboure for Sir Henry Glemham asmuch as he
cann. Thus I committ you to God. From Mildenhall in hast the 10 of October[192]

Signed: Your very loving frend Henry Warner. *Holograph.*
Addressed: To the ryght worshipfull Sir Nicholas Bacon knyght
2 ff.; seal impression.

---

[192] This can be dated by the circumstances and result of the 1601 county election to Parliament.
Glemham was elected as knight of the shire, with Calthorpe Parker, eldest son of the county
magnate Sir Philip. For discussion, see MacCulloch, *Suffolk*, pp. 335–6.

126. **[4173]** *Denis Fisher to John Hill, 2 February 1602*

Mr Hill, I moste hertelye recomend me unto you not for getynge my dutye to your good knighte to whom I owe my moste boundente dutye. Syr I have receaved your leter wherin I perceave you have not r. all my rente but I praye good Mr Hill yf yt be posyble gete yt all for me and brynge yt with you, for I have extreordenarye ocasyon to use yt which mackes me staye in London oneley for that and I praye of all kyndnes brynge with you the £33 that Syr Nycolas Baken your good knyghte and myne hath receaved of Mr Wrenham by the apoyntmente of Mr Atorney[193] for the burnynge of my barne in Budesdale and this my leter shalbe your syffysyente warrante. And at your comynge to London, I hope by your good meanes to tacke soche order for my howse that I shall not have ocasyon to come ther in manye yeares, and so expecktynge your comynge I most hartelye tacke my leave. London the 2 daye of Februarye 1601

Signed: Your asuered frynd to comaund Denis Fysher. *Holograph.*
Note in another hand: M. dd. to my fellowe Hill the 13th daie of Februariie 1601 £32 which I rece. of Mr. Warners man for burnynge of a barne at the White Horse *at Bodsdale* by the salte peter men[194]
Addressed: To his verye good frynd Mr Hill atendante one the right worshipfull Syr Nycolas Bacon knyght at Redgrave
2 ff.; traces of seal.

127. **[4174]** *Sir Nicholas Bacon II to Robert Mawe, 21 October 1602*

Mr Maugh wheras my tennantes of Walsham have taken ordere with me for the stayinge of the sute bettwen us, therfor I praye you deliver out ther bondes unto them for ther discharge therin, and soe I commit you to God, from Redgrave this 21 of October 1602

Signed: Your lovinge frinde N. Bacon. *Autograph.*
Addressed: To my lovinge frinde Mr Maugh at Bury
Endorsed by Mawe: Mich. 44 *et* 45.[195] Sir Nicholas Bacons lettres for staie of the sute againte the tenauntes of Walsham
2 ff.; seal impression.

128. **[4175]** *William Felgate to Lady Bacon, 11 July 1603*

Right Worshipfull maye it pleas you to understand I rec. from you fyften poundes the which I hav payde to Mistres Ryppyn according to your direxsion and I hav sent to you hearin inclosed the agrement my uncle made with hur, with hyr recytt f in full dich charge for the mony. It pleaseth God to contineu his visitasion upon us every daye more and more.[196] I hav sent yow a just note and treu bref not of them that dyed this least wek with in the lybertyes of the cyty and in the cyty I and I doe very belev thear dyed as many without the lybertis. I praye God to be mercyfull to us. The reiche men as all for the most *part are* fled the cytye. Thus being very bould in trubling your I worship I comitt you to the Lord. London this 11th of July

---

193 The Attorney General was Sir Edward Coke. See also no. **121 [4170]** above.
194 Royal collectors of saltpetre for the manufacture of gunpowder were notoriously unpopular, even when they were not burning down barns.
195 Michaelmas Term, 44 and 45 Elizabeth.
196 This refers to a major outbreak of plague in London.

Signed: ~~Your shipes in all dutye to~~ Your worshipes in all duty to command William Felgate. *Holograph.*[197]

Addressed: To the right worshipfull and very ~~good Lady~~ good Lady Bacon at Redgrav Hoall

2 ff.

129.   [4176] *Thomas Sackville, Lord Buckhurst to Sir Nicholas Bacon II, 15 February 1604*

After my hartie commendations. Whereas by vertue of your office of the Steward-ship of parte of the Honor of Clare in the County of Norfolk you have heretofore from tyme to tyme graunted estates of the copiehold or customarye landes and tenements within the said Honor as they continuallie have happened or fallen. Forasmuch as the Kinge Majestyes pleasure is otherwise to dispose of the same lands and tenements; these are therefore in his Majestyes name to will and require you from henceforth to forbeare to graunte any estate or admit any tenaunt to the copie hold or customarye landes of the said Honor *whereof the tax is arbitrable* untill his Majestyes pleasure be by me further signifyed unto you. And that forth-with you send up a true certificat of the ~~the~~ totall summe of the yerelie rentes of all the copiehold lands of the said Honor, and whether the Tenauntes there have estates of inheritaunce or for terme of lief or lives or at will and what fyne herriet or other proffit is due to the King upon everye alteration discent or graunte. And a true estimate what an acre of meadowe an acre of pasture and an acre of arable land there is worth upon improvement by common reputation, and what store of woodes underwoodes and tymber trees are upon the same copiehold premisses. And whether there be any myne or mynes of mettall cole or other thinge on them or any of them or any other matter of proffit what soever apperteyning to the King's Majestye and withall to certifie unto me the name or names of all and everye the justices of peace dwelling within or nere the said Honor. Of all which I doubt not you will have especiall regard as you tender his Majestyes service. And so do wish you hartily well. At the Court this 15 of Februarye 1603

Signed: Your loving freind T. Buckhurst. *Autograph.*

Addressed: To my lovinge frende Sir Nicholas Bacon knighte steward of parte of the Kinges Majestyes Honor of Clare in the countye of Norfolk or to anye other steward of the said mannor [*sic*]

2 ff.; fine seal impression. With summary of contents accurately itemised in seven sections, in hand of Bacon's secretary: 1 f. **[4177]**.

130.   [4178] *Thomas Daynes to Lady Anne Drury, 20 August 1604*[198]

Vertuous ladie, in the plentie of soe fitt messengers I would not be silent for head-ache, neither would I have yowre Ladieshipp thinke that I pryvent imputation by writeing, but am glad of the opportunitie since I sawe yow and that within few dayes after it pleased God to humble me by sicknes even to the dore of the grave, but hath in mercie given *me* hope that yet he will lende me a few dayes to suffer with my brethren, that must indure, and to testife my love and indiffer-ency to them that shall not soe suffer and yet in there faithfull course shall not

---

197   The hand is competent, but the letter shows signs of difficulty in composition, with its eccentric spelling and erasures.

198   Extracts printed in Bald, *Donne and the Drurys*, p. 51.

want crosse thinges. I heare that Mr Beadle[199] hath lately handled the point of these indifferent thinges and set downe his iudgment what he thinkes. But (right Christian Ladie) he is but one and the cause is ~~ould~~ elder then he and I. I hope he used warie caveates and all little enough in a matter of this difficultie. But if I had bene of his counsell in meditation he should have drowned those thoughtes in a sea of silence. It is carried and I feare miscarried also. It came to me inlarged beyonde Mr Halles report[200] who tould the particulars which he hearde of the hearing (for he was not an hearer) and they sounde harsh in the eares of the best. I confesse it had bene fitt for a Clerum in Cambridge or synode in the countrie, but how fitt for a pulpitt or Bury pulpitt I knowe not.[201] Good Madame I besech ye communicate with hym in this poynt that we may be certifyed of his wordes and meaning. Least an unfitt tyme or place of uttering, or not soe advised hearing turne unhappiely our ioynt consultations for comon good into distracted exposi-tions of mens persons and speaches. My kinswoman, daughter to my cousin, still importunes me to put yowre Ladie shippe in mynde of her desire and myne for her to be in the chamber with yow where Mr Beadles kinswoman is, if she or yow or both dislike continuance. I thanke yowre Ladieshippe much that ~~are~~ still yow are the good Ladie Drury. Indede love is not houlden by indenture of dayes and places nor with respect of persons, but the true love of God is to love where God loveth. And in this one thinge especiallie (as in many *other* thinges also) yow seme to me to resemble our heavenly father and to be his beloved daughter, who is not onely good, but constant also which maketh the good so much more good, though not in hym who is absolute and for ever, yet to us pore wormes that tast his cup and fede daily at his table. It gladed my soule (he knoweth that made and searcheth it) when I sawe yowre Ladieshippes face, but much more tenfould when by passage of speach I founde the good Ladie Anne Drury to be still the same to the despised number of Christes most honorable armie. And if I could adde any thinge to my Christian and due reverence and that high respect in which ever since I knew yow I have honored yow in the highest seate of my best thoughtes, I would not be wanting to let yowre ladieshippe knowe yt. I much more admire the constancie of good, then the good ~~alone~~ it selfe. Yowre Ladieshippe seeth that somewhat droppes out of my heade to my penn till my paper invirone[202] and border[203] my speach but my due regarde of yowre Ladieshippes *vertues* will indure no streites, least of all will my thoughte be withoulden when I consider how graciously God hath dealt with yow to make ye love his voyce from heaven, ~~and when he~~ *And when he* had taught yow the necessity of preching to send yow soe able and honest a voice which is no doubt the Lordes, that the Lorde may be yowres. Soe God hath dealt with you as not more with the most, yet scarce a few have this favour in these degrees, an hart so to honour the temple of God

---

[199] William Bedell, future bishop of Kilmore, who succeeded the celebrated preacher George Eastey as rector of St Mary's Bury St Edmunds in 1602. The issue at stake was conformity to the eccle-siastical canons of 1604, which had aroused fury among the less conciliatory Puritan clergy; they faced deprivation, and Daynes is expressing his sympathy with these suffering 'brethren' against Bedell's commendation of acceptance of matters indifferent.

[200] The first mention of Joseph Hall, by now rector of Hawstead on Sir Robert Drury's presenta-tion.

[201] Meaning that Bedell could have expressed his opinions in an academic or clerical gathering, but not in front of the laity.

[202] Meaning 'turn round' or 'obscure'.

[203] For 'broider', i.e. embroider.

and the God of the temple that the promise is yowre. The Lorde blesse yow good Madame. In the bowels of Christ I do most hartily wish yowre precedeing in the way of life, that when we shall forgoe these shadowes as life and present peace, we may enioy the durable habitations where is roume enough for all the faythfull Amen. Come Lord Jesus Amen. The grace of our Lord Jesus Christe be with our spirites Amen. Bongay August 20 1604[204]

Signed: Your Ladieshippes humble and faithfull servant and pore welwisher in the truth Thomas Daynes. *Holograph.*
Addressed: To the right worshipfull and vertuous Ladie the Ladie Anne Drury Hawstead
Endorsed: From Mr Danes
2 ff.; traces of seal.

131. [4179] *Thomas Daynes to Lady Anne Drury [undated]* [205]
Blessed Ladie, the remembrance of yower late letters [?so fr]yndly written and faythfully delivered, ~~dwelle~~ dwelleth [ ]ner on my thoughtes as a debt to be payde. I have made up the summe at last even the summe of acknow[l]edgment of my most humble and christian dutie and love for the truthes sake and have sent it here-inclosed in this paper. I hope yowre Ladieshippe, yea I am assured, yow will not be curious thowgh a crackt groate or two come in payment. If yow please to take such as we can *give*, yow shall have it the oftener and willinger. I ned not teach yowre Ladieshippe being daily and often so well instructed I speake even my very hart, but while yow shall be in this tabernacle and my selfe can conveniently, I will be bould to put yow in remembrance to continue in that most holy faith which yow have imbrased, knoweing that [n]o honour or rewarde made of earth is like the glory and fruite of a good conscience and sownde profession. And good Madame, without suspicion of flattery [le]t me speake my judgment and thowghtes. I doe often [?in] my gladsome thoughtes of yowre Ladieshippes [v]ertue and truth to God and his, solace myselfe and doe bowe my knees to the throne of grace for yowre godly beginninges and procedeinges, the end whereof let it be perfect peace to yowre soule for ever. Heare oh Lord in heaven and confirme the worde ~~of~~ and desier of thy pore servant. Good Madame give me leave still as hitherto to cloth my selfe with the ~~ornamen~~ ornament of yowre favour among those that love us all for his sake that hath loved us [?ever]. And vouchsafe me yowre Ladieshippes prayers and favors at the least though the sunne of [? two words] shall looke upon us and disfigure our countenance in the bleareyed sight of worldly ~~sences~~ senses [word illegible] seeth [? two words]an neither yet do his servantes [? one word] by sa[?two words]th
we desire yowre Ladie[shipe ....]
and conscionable preceden[...]
yowre ment[..]n the [...]
children of afflict[ion ...]
at last in the me[...]
shall pittie[...]
that shall [...]

---

204 Daynes was incumbent of Flixton St Mary near Bungay in 1588: Freeman Bullen, 'Beneficed clergy, 1551–1631', p. 301.
205 This letter, which cannot precisely be dated, is placed here simply in relation to the previous item. The text is badly damaged.

them new thoughtes which gr[...]
mercy I end good Madame [...]
eve [...] that peculiar peace which [...]
[?canne neve]r take away, that it [...]
preserve our soules and bodies blamele[s] [...]
comeng of our Lord Jesus Christ [...]
The grace of our Lord Jesus Ch[rist] [...]
spirits Amen.

Signed: Yower La[dieshippes humble and faithfull] servant [*words missing*] Thom[as Daynes]. *Holograph.*
Addressed: To the right worshippfull and Christian Ladie the Ladie Anne Drury Hawstead Hall
2 ff., torn.

132. **[4181]** *Robert Felgate to Sir Nicholas Bacon II [14 September 1604]*[206]
Sir these ar to let you understand ~~that~~ that I fynn Mr Crane and Mr Stranman hoe is to have Chelton and other landes till Mr Cran com to age verye wellinge to doe any thinge for the maytenige of her righte and for Mr Fostecues estate. For his goodes at his deathe, I have down my best to reache in to the vallue ther of and fynndinge noe plate [*word erased*] above two or three peces and then ~~all thair~~ the most part of the stuff beinge ould Mr Cranes I thyncke the holl stocke ~~will~~ of that he have at Chyldeton will not com to above £500 at the uttermost and ther is such crynge out by servantes for wages and recknions yt would petye one to hear them. Sir Jo. befor I came yester daye, was gonn to Blutes hall[207] wheare Mr Fostecue cut of his lyfe and I sent one to hym with your letter and he wrot to me ~~that one Mr~~ by one Mr Thourtone ho marred an nece of his that he should componde, so we have bynn in speche about cowposesion. And I thyncke £100 is the most I shall get and I would I had good assurance for that, and foe the concludinge I and Mr Thontone ame ~~cuming a~~ goinge towardes ~~Sudburye~~ Burye and ther before Sir Jo. Higham and D. Mawe I hoppe we shall conclud. And staned[208] seasinge of any goodes till lat yestere *night* and this morninge in hopp I should have componded othewise and I woud yt wear past, for I heare Camptyn[209] Fostecue and Mr Henry Waldegrave is gonn up to gett the wardshippe ~~of the goodes~~ and the goodes as in the oners[210] right etc. So I dought mouche troble ~~I can~~ So for wounte of tym I end in hast this present Frydaye at Chylton about 10 of the clocke

---

206 For a brief account of Dudley Fortescue, which however does not mention his suicide which is the subject of this and the following letters, see *History of Parliament 1558–1603*, II, 145. The suicide of Fortescue is described by Adam Winthrop in *Winthrop papers*, ed. J. Winthrop (Massachusetts Historical Society, 1929), I, 86: he 'did hange him selfe at Mrs Turnours his wives mothers house nere Cambridge shire videlicet at Bluntes Hall in litle Wrattinge'. Suicide was a *felo de se*, meriting confiscation of goods and also necessitating the wardship of the deceased's children, and so triggered an unseemly scramble between rival jurisdictions. This letter can be precisely dated because of the timing between Fortescue's suicide, dated by Winthrop to Sunday 9 September 1604, and the mention in no. **134 [4182]** of a Privy Council letter written on Monday 17 September; the only available Friday is 14 September.

207 Blunt's Hall in Little Wratting: see *Winthrop Papers* I, 86.

208 Apparently for 'stayed'.

209 Apparently for 'Captain'?

210 Apparently for 'Honour's'. In other words, they were trying to obtain the wardship and goods in right of the Honour of Clare, exempt from the jurisdictions either of the Sheriff or Bacon's Liberty of St Edmund.

Signed: Your w's sarvante Robert Felgat. *Holograph.*
Addressed: To the right worshipfull Sir Nicholas Bacon knight
Endorsed by Felgate: I sent one with a letter to Mr Mawe ~~to~~ yesterday to com to me with all convent spead to Chelton but I neaver heare of hym I was never so wear of any besnes in my lyfe ~~I~~ [*word illegible erased*]
2 ff.; remains of seal.

133. [4180] *Privy Council to Sir Nicholas Bacon II, 17 September 1604*

After our hartie commendations; whereas the Kinges Majestie being informed of the unhappie ende of Dudley Fortescu Esqr. of Chillton in the Countie of Suffolke (who is saied to have wickedly hanged himself) hathe upon humble suite graunted the goods of the saide Fortescu (being forfeited unto his highnes by that desperate and wicked acte) unto Mistres Margaret Hartseye of the Queenes Majesties Bedd Chamber; although wee suppose that of your owne accorde, and as apperteyneth to the duetie of your office, either yow have taken order alreadie, or will take order for seisure to be made of the said goodes to his Majesties use, in suche sorte as there may be no fraude committed by embezeling, or any unlawfull conveyance of them; nevertheles to moove yow unto the more dilligence therein, wee do heereby lett yow know his Majesties pleasure, that especiall care *and order* be used and taken for the enquirie and seazure of all the goodes of the said Fortescu, to the ende that his graunt unto the aforesaid gentlewoman may be the more effectuall and beneficiall as it is by his Majestie intended. And therefore wee do in his Majesties name require yow to cause dilligent and speedie enquirie to be made by all due meanes of the saide goodes that are to be founde in that Countie of Suffolke; and to take care, that they may be seazed on to his Majesties use; and kept safelie untill farther order shalbe given for the disposing of them *either in whole or in parte from the children* according to his Majesties pleasure. Which not doubting but yow will see performed by your selfe and suche officers and ministers under yow, to whome it may appertaine, wee bidd yow hartelie farewell. From the Court at Windsor the 17th of September 1604.
High Sheriff of the County of Suffolk/

Signed: Your loving freendes Northumberland Lenox Suffolke Cranborne W. Knollys J. Balmerino J. Stanhope. *Autograph.*
Addressed: To our verie loving freend Sir Nicholas Bacon knight, highe Sheriffe of the Countie of Suffolke.
2 ff.; traces of seal.

134. [4182] *Sir Nicholas Bacon II to Privy Council [?19 September 1604]*

Maye it please your Lo. to be advertised that I have receyved a letter from your honnors dated the seaventene daye of September the neintenth of the same month concering [*sic*] a seacer to be made to the Kinges Majesties use of the goodes and chattells late Dudly Fortescue esquier who hanged hime selfe. So it is if it may please your honours that those goodes which weare within the Frances of Bury ~~wher his house stoode~~ doe of right appertaine unto me as parcell of mine inheritance in the right of my libertis graunted by letters pattentes from Edward the sixt to my Lo. Darcye and so sould to my father and allowd me in the Exchequer in a coranto uppon a judgment by speciall wordes *of* ~~by~~ felo de se and so sould by me to the widdoe of Dudly Fortescue since the tyme of his death for one hundred poundes to the use of his children and payment of certaine debtes due unto his servauntes which bargaine and sale I have shewed unto this bearrer and lickwise my coranto for his better satisfaction and therfor I humbly desyre your honnors favors that the Kinges Majestie maye be *made* acquainted withall for avoydinge of further truble. What goodes he hade in in other places I knowe not. If I cane inquire of anye out of the Francis I shalbe readye to make ceaser *of them* according to your Ho. pleasures. I doe knowe of my owne knowled wher he ought eight hundred poundes and payed interest for it at the tyme of his death, and therfor his goodes not so great as *I heare* the information hath bine given unto your Lo. And the rather because the most of his platte and much of his housold stuffe are the goodes of Mr Cranne who is now a ward *to the Kinges Majestie* given him by his Grandfather at the tyme of his death *and to be delivered unto him at the age of* *to the kinges Majestie given him by his grandfather at the time of his death and to be delivered unto him at the age of one and twentye **years** as I am informed*[211] which if it had binne otherwise I would never have sould them for an hundred poundes And so in all dutye I humbly take my leave

Draft in secretary's hand.
Addressed: To the right honorable the Lo. of hir [*sic*] Majesties Privie Counsell
2 ff.

135.   [4183] *William Rockitt to Thomas Rockitt, 9 April 1606*
Brother my hartie commendations to you, my sister your wyfe my cossens, your childeren and other my brother and sisters not forgotten. I understand that your towne of Bury is somwhat vysetted with the sickenes, by the which I am very sorie.[212] I have receyved your letters dated the 14 of February last for which I hartelye thanke you for your grett paines and now boulde to trouble you agayne. I understande by your letters that Sir Nicholas Bacon knoweth that he shoulde have lande in Redborne[213] which in dede lyeth by my lande which is 8 acres or thar aboute in tow parcells, 6 acres errable in one closse and 2 acres of meddowes in a comon meddowe or ther aboute of litle valewe becawse they be out of harte. No cost ~~besto~~ cost bestowed of them, by reason therof they be lesse worth in yerelie valewe and partely no man aboute us knoweth who owe them, but I my self only, and so they goe under the name of Sir Francys Bacon his land. Wherfore my earnest desyer is now that you wolde parle with your frende to Sir Nicholas Bacon that I might hyre yt of him att such yerelie rent as yt shall please him to leate yt. Yet is not worth above 3s 4d the acre by yere, but yt[214] I wolde have yt att what yerelie rent yt shall please him to leate yt before any other; I wolde have yt for 3 or 4 yeres. I wolde have gladlie a bought yt but becawse yt lieth betwen Sir Nicholas and Sir Francys in title I would be very loth to breade my self troble. And in the meane tyme Sir Nicholas Bacon may be fullie certefied both of the quantitie and quallitie of the lande, and yf ther be any more of that houlde I can learne yt out for him. Yf ~~yt~~ therfore yt may please him that I may be his tenaunte for yt, I will do my best to seeke out for eny other lande of his ther aboute. I am loth to deale with the purchase till I see ther title cleare. Whefore I pray deale to hyre yt for me. And thus expectinge your answere herein writinge directinge yt to my cossen

---

211   I have repositioned this passage, rewritten for clarity below the main text.
212   This was the well-known major 1606 epidemic of plague at Bury St Edmunds.
213   In Hertfordshire.
214   For 'yet'? Cf. no. **51 [4104]** above.

Henry Rockitt, I hartelie betake you and your to the protection of thallmightie. St Albans this 9 of Aprill 1606

Signed: Your very lovinge brother William Rockitt. *Holograph.*
Addressed: To his very lovinge brother Mr Thomas Rockitt in Cookrowe in Bury St Edmunde
1 f.; seal impression.

136.   [4184] *Thomas Keighley to Sir Robert Drury, 15 January 1607*

Sir according unto promise I have provided for you one man to be a groome of the stable, one who is a very honest mann, a very sufficient to fellowe [*sic*] to discharge the place, but the trewthe is by reason of somme very earnest businesse of his owne he ~~wi~~ cannott by any meanes comme by the space of thes 14 dayes at the expiration of which time he will nott faile butt comme unto you. I have bespoken you an other butt he is nott yett commen to London neyther he wilbe untill the middle of the ~~next~~ *this* terme. I am desirous to furnish you with honest men and such as shalbe able to serve your turne wherfore you weare better *stay* a littell the longer. As for the horse I thinke if you every morning and evening caused his keeper to walke him abroade to ayre him by the space of an howre and wher hee brought him in to give him a warme mash, that he would doe well yenough. I pray you Sir if you bee already provided send me word by wrighting dyrecting your letters to me into Shooe Lane to the house of one Addam Sewell a womans taylor, he dwelleth right over against the signe of the Hand in Hand, at whose house I lie but if I heere not from you in the meane time then I will send them unto you. A thus [*sic*] with my humble duty remembred to your selfe and my good lady, I rest remayning ever, this present 15th of January 1606

Signed: Your loving cosin Thomas Kyghley.[215] *Holograph.*
Addressed: To the right w'r. Sir Robert Drury Knight at his house at Hausteed or else wheare
2 ff.; remains of seal.

137.   [4185] *Sir Edward Coke to Sir Nicholas and Lady Bacon II, 18 January 1608*

I should be verie unmyndfull of your merite and my great bond of dett, which I owe *unto* you, if I should not give you many thankes for your care like parentes over my poore sonne both in his health and in his late sicknes also. God in his wisdome doth worke by ordinarie meanes, and as alliance is the bond of love and kyndnes, so are the same good motives to confirme ~~the~~ and establish the alliaunce. I have bene aunciently much beholding to you both, and uppon this iust occasion I ame every day to increase my dett unto you. Assuring you both that you might have had a greater allie but none that will be more truly firme to you and yours that [*sic*] I wilbe in all that I cann with all thankfull readines. And so I leave you and all yours to the blissed protection of the almightie and will ever remayne

Signed: Your loving and true frend, Edward Coke. 18 Jan. 1607. *Holograph.*
Addressed: To his honorable and much respected frends Sir Nicholas Bacon and the lady his wife at Culford
2 ff.; seal impression.

---

215   Thomas Keighley was described as of Blackbourne hundred, gentleman, in a loan list of 1590 (TNA (PRO), SP 12/236). He was a JP in Essex from 1600.

138.   [4187] *Joseph Hall to Lady Ann Drury [?January 1609]*[216]

Good Madam, the so good acceptation of that my poore New-Yeares gift I take for a new favour and shall reckon *it* amongst those debts which I would and can not satisfy. I accounted those by-reckonings from my La. Gawdy forgotten upon my last letter, yet since it pleaseth your La. to rub up the mention of them and to desire my valuation of her rent, I *answer that I* referred to two indifferent neighbors before, who need not feare ought on either part in a matter of right; but since they sluff it of as thanklesse, I committ it wholly to your La. [?]alon arbitration. Set downe what you please, I wilbe thankfull. Which yet I would have resolutely set downe a cipher were it not that I am entred here into a purchase which perhaps in my life I shall not wade out of, venturing altogether upon hopes while I have scarc[e] mony to my earnest. Let me be humbly remembered to Sir Edmund Bacon in your next letter; for Sir Robert Drury I heare *he* is at London; and hope to see him [in] the passage. Would God I could yet heare a word from Mr Aldridge of his firme setling at Halsted; whereto I must as I ought beare true affection; and above all to your La., to whom I ever vow my selfe

Signed: A true humble and everlasting well willer Joseph Hall. *Holograph.*
Postscript: I am by promise indebted to Sir Edmund Bacon (to whom I owe more) certayne Lattin verses of Barclais[217] which I am ashamed that for my life I cannot come by. Let him I beseeche your L. know my care of my word.
1 f.; damaged.

139.   [4188] *Henry Keen to Robert Felgate, 12 February 1609*

Mr Felgat youre helthe weshed with the rest of owre good frendes. I hath got Mr Gadies hand too the quetaunse and I praye ~~paye~~ *paye* the £9 too Gabrell Sir Robart Drewry [*word illegible erased*] mane. Thus with mye hartie love I [*word illegible erased*] rest the 12 of Februarye 1608

Signed: Youre frend too my powre Henerye Keen. *Holograph.*
Addressed: Mr Robart Felgat att Colford
Endorsed: I desyre Nun should receave this mony and send itt me by the carriers which is for a horse that Charles Gaudy bought of me. R. Drury. *Holograph. Also two sets of calculations.*
1 f.; damaged.

140.   [4189] *Charles Gaudy to Robert Felgate, 30 March 1609*

Stuward I pray deliver M. Hammot fifty shilling for too payre of sylke stock-kings

Signed: By me Charles Gaudy, the 30 of March. *Holograph.*
Note: Resayve of Mr. Fellgate this 25 of Aprell 1609 By me Richard Hamonde [*word erased*] fefte shellings
1 f.; damaged.

---

216 Suggestions for dating are made in Bald, *Donne and the Drurys*, pp. 63–4, where the text is printed; evidently Hall had already left Hawstead (he took the living of Waltham Holy Cross in 1608). The New Year's gift was probably his *Salomons Divine Arts, drawne out of his Proverbs and Ecclesiastes* (London, 1608).

217 Presumably the poet Alexander Barclay (*c.*1484–1552). See *ODNB*.

141. [4190] *Charles Gaudy to Robert Felgate, 8 May 1609*
Steward these are to desier yow to paye unto this barer my very good frend William Manyng owt of the next quarteres rent which shall be dew unto me the sum of fower powndes. And this note shall be yower discharge for the same. In witnes wherof I have putte my hand the 8 day of Maye in the 7th yere of the Kinges Maiestes Rayne viz.

Signed: Charles Gaudy. *Autograph.*
Addressed: To my loving frend Mr Robart Fellgate Steward of Houshold to Sir Necolas Bakon knight
1 f.

142. [4191] *Charles Gaudy to Robert Felgate, 30 May 1609*
Stuward I have sent my man to you to let you understand my necesitie now to pray you that you would let mee have five pound beefore hand for I have borrowed *it* of a gentleman and I would not for twice the valure but pay it h[im] onely for mi credit, therfore I pray now lef there no intermission but to send it by my man. So I rest *from Ezwell*[218] commiting you to God the the 30 of May 1609

Signed: Your assured frind Charles Gaudy. *Autograph.*
Note by Felgate: The above sayd fyve poundes was delyved [*sic*] to Palfeye the last of Maye by mye Nun *fellowe* Nun at Culfourd Culford.
Addressed: To my very loving frind Mr Felgate. *Readdressed by Felgate:* To my fellowe Nun at Culford
Endorsed by Felgate: [*three words illegible*] to have untill he [*two words illegible*] would be glad to [*word illegible*] of his goodes as [*word illegible*] with all [*two words illegible*]
1 f., damaged; remains of seal.

143. [4192] *Charles Gaudy to Robert Felgate, 8 July 1609*
Stuward I have sent my man to you to pray you that you would send me my quartur for I have great busines and for that which I did set my hand too at Bury to bee payed if you have not payd it already I pray now send mee it for I have very ernest withall which you knowe I stand in great need of clothes and nobody you knowe in Bury will trust mee and therfore I am faine to go to Norwhich to by mee sume ther with the mony you send mee and therfore I pray now dispact my man or else I shall stay for him for I have no mony to by nothing will hee come so hoping this is suffitient ther I rest commiting you to God. From Ezwell the [*word erased*] 8 of Iuly 1609

Signed: Your very loving frind Charles Gaudy. *Holograph.*
Note in Felgate's hand: Receyved by me Abraham Palferye the 10 daye of Julye of Robert Felgate for my master Charles Gawdy Esquire the some of seaven poundes. [*Mark by Palfrey*]
Addressed: To my very loving frind Mr Felgate at Redgrave.
1 f.; traces of seal.

---

218 The addresses at this and no. **143 [4192]** are obscurely written, particularly at the second letter. The place does not correspond to any property of the Gawdy family, but since it is clearly in East Anglia and near Bury St Edmunds, it may be Eriswell or Herringswell.

144. [4193] *Charles Gaudy to Robert Felgate, 25 August 1609*
Mr Stewarde theise are to let yow knowe that my oncle Mr Phillip Gaudy lent me
at London tenn poundes, which I pray paye unto him out of my nexte quarters
allowance, and I will dyschardge yow therof. Wrytten this 25 of August 1609

Signed: Your frende ~~Charl~~ Charles Gaudy. *Autograph.*
Note by Felgate: The 29 of Octobere I pd. William Crosone one part of this £10
£5 which Mr Gawdy allo me in his quote[219]
Addressed: To my frende Mr Robert Felgate Steward of Howsholde to Sir Nicholas
Bacon Knight.
1 f.

145. [4194] *Charles Gaudy to Robert Felgate, 15 September 1609*
Steward these are to let you understand that uppon my uncle Phillipps importu-
natcye hath gote my hand to ane noate directed to you to pay him oute of my next
quarter, £10.[220] These are earnestly to intreate you in respecte as you knowe that
I ame much indebted to poore mene at Bury that you would forbeare payinge of
him untyle you have further order from me. I purpose honestly to paye him and he
shalbe noe looser by me. And soe I ende this 15 day of September 1609

Signed: Your loving frind Charles Gaudy. *Autograph.*
Addressed: To my very lovinge frind Mr Robert Felgate Steward of Houshoulde
to Sir Nicholas Bacon Knight.
1 f.; traces of seal.

146. [4195] *Charles Gaudy to Robert Felgate, before 21 October 1609*
Stuward I have sent my man to you to let you understand that I am without mony
and to pray you that you would send mee ten pound for I am at great need for I am
out of clothes much and you knowe nobody will trust mee. So hoping you will not
faile me I commit you to God. From Harling

Signed: Your loving frind Charles Gaudy. *Holograph.*
Note by Felgate: This letere I receyved by Abraham Perfee the 21 of October
anno 1609 and the same *daye* I pd. hym to the use of his mastire fyve poundes.
Abraham Perfees [*Mark by Palfrey*] marke. The sayd £5 was pd. in the presence
of my fellowe Nun.
1 f.

147. [4196] *Edward Symonds to Sir Nicholas Bacon II, 8 June 1610*
Right Worshipfull; aboute the end of Aprill last, there was founde one drowned
in the river of Thornage[221] of that side, whereupon speakinge with Mr Buers
and some of the aunciente tenauntes, they tolde me that Sir William Buttes and
my Lady Buttes in their tyme upon the like occasion had apointed their bayliffe
there to set as coroner, whereupon I willed Mr Buers to warne a jury of Thornage
tenauntes and to take upon him the place of coroner for your worship for that
manor. Upon the first day of May last I resorted with him to the place, where we
founde Mr Tylney one of the Coroners for the county with a jury of the hundred.

---

219 For 'quota' in an account?
220 See a note of Philip Gawdy's borrowing and his financial embarrassment before his death, *HMC
Gawdy*, p. 110.
221 In Norfolk.

I wished him to stay,[222] acquainted him with your worships libertie there, and to that end before him examined diverse of the said tenauntes who all affirmed the same to him, whereupon he desisted, and I assisted Mr Buers in the said busines and tooke the inquisition, whereof I send your worship one of the counterpaines, which by especiall estatute must be certefied. I thoughte it fitte rather to go some-thinge to farre then to fall any thinge short in meynteyninge your worships liber-ties, wherein if we have gone farther then we should it may yet be holpen. And therefore before any further procedinge, desire to knowe your worships pleasure therein. Thus remembringe my duty and services I humbly take my leave this 8 of June 1610

Signed: Your worships alwaies ready at command Edward Symonds. *Holograph.*
Addressed: To the right worshipfull Sir Nicholas Bacon knight at Culforde
Endorsed: An inquisition upon the death of one Allen
2 ff.; traces of seal.

148. [4197] *Sir Robert Drury to François d'Orleans, Comte de St Paul, 1611.*
Apologises for writing to him on such a small matter and also for any difficulty which will arise from reading his bad French. Since he met d'Orleans, who received him at Amiens with much courtesy than he deserved, he has much desired to visit him once more, but so far has been prevented by business. He now hopes to do so, and knowing that d'Orleans is a lover of hunting, he proposes to bring with him a pack of good hounds, two or three good hawks and seven or eight good horses, and asks him for lodging for his party near d'Orleans's home; this would be a great pleasure to him, being in a foreign country.[223]
Monseigneur, J'ay beaucoup de subiect de vous demander pardon, de la hardiesse que ie prends de vous escrise sur si peu de subiect, et aussi de l'empesement, que ie puis bien penser que vous aurez, pour entendre mon mauvais languadge. Monseigneur, vous scaurez s'il vous plaist, que depuis que i'ay hier l'honeur de vous avoyr ~~eu~~ *baislé les mains* en Amiens, ou ce qu'il vous a pleu de me rescevoyr auecque plus de courtoysie que ie ne merite, j'ay tousiours en un grand desyr, si mes affayres ne m'en eussent doné l'empesement, pour me venir renger aupres de vous, et pour ~~J~~ fayre mon seiour celon ce que ie vous *J* pourois rendre de servise; et ~~si~~ *suis* a ceste heure resolu si ~~pou~~ dieu plaist, d'effectuer bien tost mon desir en icelle, et recognoisant que vous estes bien affectioné a la chasse, j'ay destiné, d'amener avecque moy, une meutte de bons chiens et deus ou trois bons oyseaux et sept ou huict bons chevaux, dont j'auray occasion de supplier vostre signurie, de me permettre *de vous* ~~d~~ estre si importun, de vous prier que par vostre faveur, je puisse avoyr quelque bone maison et esquirie, pour *estre lodge avecque* ~~moy e~~ mon *petit* train *avecque quelque honeste gens et recuilliront volonteer ou* ~~ou~~ de ce que ie pourray estre proche de vostre signeurie, lequell me donnera grand contentement et asseuranse, estant en lieu estrandge; ou ce que ie me'stimeray [*sic*] tousiours for honoré, et bien protecté *en recevant* vos commandements

---

222 That is, to cease his proceedings.
223 Printed in Bald, *Donne and the Drurys*, p. 86. St Paul was second son of the Duc de Longueville; his title came from his mother, Marie de Bourbon, Duchesse d'Estouteville and Comtesse de St Paul. It was no doubt through him that Drury secured his lodgings in Amiens which acted as his base for his time in France.

Signed: Vostre tres- *Holograph; draft.*
Endorsed: To the compte de St. Paul in Fransh
1 f.

149. [4198] *Lady Dorothy Bacon to Lady Drury [October/November 1611]*[224]

Good madam, I have noe neues to salewte you but by this my ell wrytten lettar, that both my penn is naught, my eyncke worse, and my invensyon worst of all. Yt seying it was not my good hape to mett you and Sir Robart at Readgrave, whear so many have wised you both, I must entreat you to eysept[225] of all faltes that you shall fynd and ondly thinke I wish to you as much good as anye antt you have, and God in his marsy gyd you and my fynest nyffy,[226] for hee callethe me his best ~~nese~~ antt therfore I desyre all happynes to folow ~~to fo~~ you both in your jurnye yf you gooe in to France or else wher. My husband and I desyer to be most hartyly commended to Sir Robart Drewri and your ladyship and I must end my lettar for I ame called away to bead, farwell good lady, from Redegrave this presant thursdaye

Signed: Your ever loveng antt Dorothe Bacon *Holograph.*
Addressed: To the Ryght Wor'll and my very good nese the Lady Drewry geve this. *Pen trials:* I A. Drury I A. Drury So blind a fortune *Dum spiro Les.*
1 f.; seal impression.

150. [4199] *Sir Robert Drury to Robert Carr, Viscount Rochester [?December 1611]*[227]

Though I dare be confident that your L'ps noble disposition, wyll affoord a good interpretation to my longe silence, and firbearinge to present my services to your L'p, yet I could not forsake myselfe so much, as not to make a right use of my just excuses, for my occasions havinge stayd mee in England some months after I had the honor to see your L'p last, and beeinge retarded in my way in France, tyll my poor house at Amyens were put into some fittnes, yt ys not now a fortnight, since I began to rest here. And though neyther thys place, nor to shorte tyme, present any thinge, that I could forgive my selfe to trouble your L'p withall, yet I hope yow wyll make thys an argument, that neyther my former abstinence was out of ~~neglect~~ negligence, nor that any distance shall slacken in mee those affections and devotions, which I bear towards your L'p

Signed: Your [abbreviation sign] *Draft in hand of John Donne, and headed* Ld. Rochester
1 f.

151. [4199, dorse] *Sir Robert Drury to Sir David Murray [?December 1611]*[228]

Sir, a ialousy, least my longe abstinence from givinge you an account of myself might be subiect to misinterpretation, and appear like a negligence, makes me

---

[224] Bulk of the text printed (with inaccuracies) in Bald, *Donne and the Drurys*, p. 89. Dorothy Bacon was wife of Sir Nathaniel Bacon, brother to Lady Drury's father.
[225] For 'accept'.
[226] For 'nephew'.
[227] Printed in Bald, *Donne and the Drurys*, p. 91. Carr was then favourite of James I.
[228] Printed in Bald, *Donne and the Drurys*, p. 91. Murray, a talented poet, was gentleman of the bedchamber to Henry, Prince of Wales.

take the first occasion of presenting my true excuses. I was by many businesses held in England some months after my purpose of a present comeing away, and in my way in France, I mett with some necessitye of spendinge more tyme then I suspected: so that in thys, which ys my first restinge place, I have not yet had a fortnight. And from hence, and in so short tyme, no more can be present*ed* by thys poore testimony, that in all places I shall ever retaine the same disposition of doinge yow service, and the same desire of beeinge conserved in your good opinion; as of which I cannot receive a better fruite and effect, that then that yow woulde be pleased, at your best commodity to present my humble services to hys Highnes, and to lett hym continue hym in an assurance, that he hath in these parts a servant, that desires nothinge so much as to have the honor of hys commandements.

Draft in hand of John Donne, and marked My Ld. Rochester and Sir D. Muray *1 f.*

152. [4200] *Sir Robert Drury to Thomas Howard, Earl of Arundel [January 1612]*[229]

Though I had made as serten a promesse to my self as to your Lo. to advertise you bothe to what plases the occasions of your servant shold carry him, *unto*, and what French accydents shold happen whylst he had his frendes dwellinge: the generous activitty of the French nation in my deserving, is so much fallen with the fall of thayr great Kinge, that it hath bine occasion, they fayling of geving me matter, of my fayling in my promesses, sinse I had nothing towards it of matter to present you. But that I had out of want of judgment or the chandge of *the* plase, or *the* chandge of my selfe, or all these taken the plase for my staye, of *in* which I see yett no lyklyhode, of taking so much taske to be gladd of it. Our only little foolish commotion there hath bine in this state by one Vattan[230] a man a man as the *by* reported, as *to have bene often* distracted, I doubt not but your Lo. living at the fountayn of our state hathe had sooner and particular relation of it. There is nothing that I observe remarcable in it, but that the plase being neere to the Duke Sullye who lyves retyred in his government of Poytou. The quene was perswaded by the enimys of Sully, who ar now of the principalls in the counsell of State, that he wold refuse her the artillery and munition, which *she* did requyre of him to furnishe to those companys of her garde, which she sente for the redusinge the poore mad fooles castle to her obediense, *pretending that the disorder beganne with intelligense of those of the religion.*[231] He did not only obaye her but did oute of a castle *plase* of his owne, which he hath [*three words illegible erased*] *extraordinarille* well fortifyed, uppon the river of Loyre, sende *the common company a* quantitty of all royal provisions, offering him selfe, with all his beste meanes, to be imployed in any servise she shold command him. The counsell wold have advysed her to have returned the artillery and munition no more, but she gave her selfe the most prinsely and fastest counsell, returned them, with *and* thanked him. These poore demonstrations of affection to doe you servise, is all that you canne ever expect from the *dis*abillity, and unhappy misfortunes of

---

229 Printed in Bald, *Donne and the Drurys*, pp. 94–5.
230 François de Puy, Sieur de Vatan, executed 2 January 1612.
231 This refers to Huguenots.

Draft: holograph.
Addressed: To my Lo. of Arundel
1 f.

153. [4201] *Sir Walter Cope to Sir Robert Drury, 12 May 1612* [232]

Sir I make noe doubt, but you have often heard ingenerall of my Lord Treasurers sicknes, and I thinke noe man will be more gladd then yourself to heare of his recoverie. But whither yow have hard of the true particulers and progresse of his sicknes, that hath not been in the power of every penn truly to certefie. I will therefore advertise you, as truly and shortly as I canne. His Lordshipp about some foure monethes since beganne to finde a generall dulnes, and distemper in his bodie, and presently upon it a shrode paine in one of his shoulders unto which the surgions applied plasters, and the phisitions administred inward phisick and in the remooving of this maladie, his Lordshipp fell into a little distempered heate, and seemed possessed with a kinde of Lent feaver, whereupon the phisitions by advice of Mr Maierne,[233] tooke from him some six ounces of blood and then his bodie being thought to consist of a distempered heate and coller, they gave him coolers to quallifie and allay those unnaturall heates, which did the woorke themselves desired; after this, so soone as he was freed from his feaver and other distempers, then there beganne a swelling in his legges and lower partes, which was thought first to be the farrwell of the Ague, but after, it grew soe great and rose soe high that the docters were doubtfull it might proove be [*sic*] dropsey. But after some fewe daies, some redd spottes appearing upon his legges, it was presently concluded to be the scorbute,[234] and for a month togeather it was said to be a scorbute, inclyning to a dropsey, many applications and drinckes were given *for* both the disseases, which were now too long to write, some to prevent winde some to prevent water, and his Lordshipp patiently indured all, as a roiall shippe, that had receaved a daungerous leake betwixt winde and water. After he had thus remained full two monethes under the handes of the prime phisitions and surgions of London; the last addresse was unto the Bath[235] where wee have been now eight daies, within which space, wee have been six times in the crosse bath, being hott enough, yet the most temperate of them all; where we finde the swelling of his legges and thighes much abated, and the distention in the bottome of his belly (which bredd in him a little shortnes of breath) to be much quallefied. Wee finde besides his countenaunce and spirittes more chearefull and prettily reumed, and his stomack, and his sleepes somewhat better then at London. But as yet wee finde that the Bath doth rather extenuate and rarifie, then extract this dull and heavie humor (as the moone which hath rather power to raise vapours, then to ripen fruite). But with diott, phisick and the Bath togeather, wee hope to carry him back againe, in a farre better estate then wee brought him hither, which I protest unto yow was very weake and fearfull. How your Duke of Bullyon[236] is used at the Court I cannot particulerly relate, being soe farre from the Court as we are. But wee heare ingenerall, that his troope is very brave and that they are roially intertained. I marvell that my Lo. Treasurer never receaves any letters from

232 Printed in Bald, *Donne and the Drurys*, pp. 99–100.
233 Theodore Turquet de Mayerne, physician, granted denization in October 1611 (*Cal. Hatfield MSS* 21, p. 316).
234 French for the disease of scurvy.
235 That is, Bath (Somerset).
236 Henri de la Tour, Duc de Bouillon.

yow; although Mr Dun and yow have noe place of Ambassador[237] yet I trust you have, that canne and doe observe as much, as the best that have imploiement from the state, and it will be noe ill introduction towardes the setting such idle persons on woorke. But I presume your silence hath growne rather from my Lordes long sicknes, which in me (I must confesse) hath bredd such a dulnes, as I have been carelesse of all, writing or compliment; and this I assure you hath been the cause that my Lo. Treasurer wrote not according to his appointement his letters unto my noble freind Sir Robert Druerie, unto whom with his noble Ladie, I commend my service; not forgetting my best commendations to Mr Donne, who is inriching his treasury, for his countries better service, towardes the which, if I be not able to add a mite, yet I shall be ever ~~able~~ *ready* to cry Amen.

From the Bath 12 *Maii* 1612

Signed: Your loving freinde to commaunde Walter Cope *Autograph.*
Addressed: To my honnorable and especiall good freind Sir Robert Druerie knight
2 ff.; seal impression.

154.   [4202] *Lady Drury to the Duchesse de Bouillon [?June 1612]. Compliments her on her virtues bestowed on her by God and which share in his infinity. Being far from her presence, she still feels her influence and finds traces of her goodness everywhere that she goes. She has found this in the Drurys' welcome at the Elector Palatine's Court at Heidelberg and by the Duchess's other sister Mademoiselle d'Orange; also in the Duchess's letters which she has received at the hand of Mademoiselle d'Orange. Whatever else has been lacking has been supplied by her memories of the Duchess, which have helped her to imitate her virtue, and which oblige her to remain her perpetual servant. In a postscript she thanks the Duchess for passing on news of the arrival of the Duc de Bouillon, and news of the health of the Bouillon children.*[238]

Madame, Come vos vertus sont douéés des autres qualités de nostre bon dieu que vous ~~lus~~ les a donnéés, ainsy participent elles de son infinite. Tellement, qu'estant esloigné de vostre presence je sens encore vos influences, et trove en touts lieus des belles impressions de vostre bonté. Je les ay trouve, Madame, en l'~~au~~ accueil, et autres faveurs, dont sont Alteze, et Madamoiselle d'Aurange, vos tres-dignes soeurs ont este contentés, par vostre mediation, honerer leur pauvre servante et la vostre. Je les ay trouvé dans vos ~~lectures letres~~ lettres lesquelles iay eu l'honneur avoir de la maine de Madamoiselle vostre soeur. Ainsy que par tout je trouve des representations et images de vostre bonte et presence. Mais, quand rien de cela ne m'eust arrivé, ma memoire m'en fourniroit abondamment car ~~encure~~ encore que je [*sic*] suis pas capable d'estre imitative de vos vertus sy suis je neantmoins de les

---

237   John Donne was then travelling in France, Germany and the Low Countries with Sir Robert Drury. Their travels included an informal mission to the Holy Roman Emperor during his coronation at Frankfurt (*ODNB*)

238   Printed with facsimile in Bald, *Donne and the Drurys*, p. 101; Bald notes that this is the only considerable example of Donne writing in French. The Duc de Bouillon was an old friend of Sir Robert Drury and in 1612 was French Ambassador extraordinary to James I. His duchess was a daughter of Prince William of Orange, and another of her sisters was widow of the Elector Palatine (*ibid.*, p. 97). The letter can be approximatedly dated by the reference in the postscript to Bouillon's return from England to France.

admirer, ~d~ et de conserver une perpetuelle memoire de leur fruicts et effects par de vers moy, par lesquels, vous aves obligé a une servitude eternelle

Signed: Vostre treshumble et tresobeissante servante. *Draft in hand of John Donne.*

Postscript: Madame, je vous remercie tres humblement de m'avor faict l'honneur de ~me~ me communiquer les bonnes nouvelles de l'avenement de Monseigneur de Bouillon, et de la santé de vos enfans; car je participeray tousiours de vos affections, et auray ma part en tout ce que vous est a coeur, ou a regret.

Addressed: A Madame Madame [*sic*] la duchesse de Buillion a Sedame[239]

1 f.

155. [4203] *Robert Carr, Viscount Rochester to Henry Howard, Earl of Northampton, 8 October 1612*[240]

My Lord: it hath been objected against me, that I should seeke to get the mastership of the Horse, from my Lord of Pembroke to whom they pretend yt was promised longe ago, when yt fell. Your Lordship heard the Kings protestation that he never made any such promise. And I know no man livinge, whose integrity and memory better ys to be trusted. And for myne own part I protest, I never heard mention of any such promise given, nor did I ever move the King first for that place; but hys Majestie thinkinge yt fitt in generall, that that place should be held by one, who did continuyally attend hys person, made choyce of me, as one upon whome he conceyvd the conferringe of yt could not be unwelcome, as beeinge a peer of thys kingdome, and naturalizd as well by affection and meritt towards yt, as by law.[241] Since, there hath risen another imputation, that my Lord of Worcester should be forced to compound for the possession, for fear of the Kings displeasure, which otherwyse he would not do; which ys no lesse uniust. For at Hampton Court, my Lord of Worcester and I speakinge of that busines, and hys Lordship demandinge, as I thought, somewhat large conditions, I told hym, I was not so fond of the place, as to give unreasonably for yt, but would rather expect tyll yt fell, tyll when I should count my masters trust dignity inough. Thus was I so farr from extortinge hys consent, as that after I had yt, I was negligent in the pursuite of the busines. And all thys can your Lordship the easier beleeve, because your Lordship knoues how carefull I have been, to preserve the nobility here, rather then to invade the right of any: as in that busines of my Lord Montagues escheat, and Cobham Hall; both which your Lordship knoues I refusd; and refused to come by the possession of Sir John Ropers office, by movinge the Kinge to make hym a Baron, because I would not set titles to sale, for my private ends. And as towards the nobility, so towards all men, may I justify my selfe, that I ame the Courtyer, whose handes never tooke bribe; which partly my estate can witnes, which I sought rather to preserve by moderate expence, then to encrease by uniust gettinge, and have been content rather to suffer most by a generall restriction, then to gaine most by a

---

[239] Sedan in Flanders.

[240] Printed in Bald, *Donne and the Drurys*, p. 124. This is one of a number of copies of the letter which have survived; it was circulated by Rochester to vindicate himself amid the intense struggles for office which raged at court after the death of Robert Cecil, Earl of Salisbury, in 1612. James I then gave Rochester the position of royal Secretary on an informal basis, causing much political jealousy. Rochester was already entering on his disastrous adulterous liaison and subsequent marriage with Northampton's great-niece, Frances Howard.

[241] Rochester was by birth a subject of the King of Scots, and hence had required naturalisation in England.

generall confution. And to let me prosper in after tymes, as I have ever in all my wayes, accordinge to my judgement, donne that which was right, reioysed to preserve love between the Kinge, and his people, and ever to ioyne hys, and the publique good, and used my faver, as much as in me lay towards the advaunce-ment of worthy men; out of the conscience of which I ame confident, that when rumor ys left to ytself, yt wyll stand even betwixt me, and any man, but where I am unknouen, or men mis-informed. I would desire your Lordship (because many of these particulars your Lordship knoues best) to rectify them; for which paynes, I shall rest

Royston; the 8th of October.

Signed: Your Lordships to command Ro. Rochester. *Copy in hand of John Donne.*
Endorsed: My Lord of Rochester to my Lord Northampton
1 f.

156. [4204] *Lady Elizabeth Burghley*[242] *to Sir Robert Drury [November 1612]*

Brother, your advantage in one letter which is all I have recayved with out anss-weringe I must acknowleg the ressuns at that tim why I did not was becaus he that brought it could not tell me then which way to convay me a letter to you, sence mallincolly for our great losse[243] has so dulled my sperrits as I know I have bine defecktive with manny of my frends in my prosedinges. I have sturred littell axcept to shuch places as duty or charrity has cumpellde me so as I cane satisfy your axpecktacion *as* littell in gevinge you to understand eyther the humors or pourposses of the tim onlly every boddy makes blacke clothes and have as I hear as morninge harttes. I must nedes tell you beinge at my Lord Cokes[244] and spekinge of the worlde his Lordshipe pleased to tell me darkely that I sholde see when tim was fittinge sum called in question for speches, but when my curriosity wold eyther have urged the words or the *his* gessinge at the partly[245] he went in to outher talke, yet I did and so do more imagin he ment you when you cam uppe. My Lord retunes [*sic*] you all love and has cast whether to finde you out a rider but protestes he cane not finde one he wolde take him self and ther four will not wish anny to you but rather he advisses you to dowe as he dows which is to bringe upppe sum youthe. I will now conclude *with* my rememberance to my sister, though in sum coller that I am not worthy to be partaker of the news of her great belly when it is so gennerally and confidently spoken of but how so ever I hope naturall affeckcione shall never be so wantinge in me as not to take comfort in it as your asured lovinge sister

Signed: Elisabeth Burghley. *Holograph.*
Addressed: To my honnorable and lovinge brother Sir Robert Drury knight
2 ff.; 2 fine seal impressions.

---

242 Sister and coheir of Sir Robert Drury; second wife to William Cecil, styled Lord Burghley, later 2nd Earl of Exeter: *Complete peerage* V, 218.
243 Was this the death of Robert Cecil, Earl of Salisbury, who died on 24 May 1612?
244 Sir Edward Coke, then chief justice of the common pleas.
245 For 'party'.

157.   [4186] *Anne Hungate to Sir Edmund Bacon [late 1612 «» 1615]*[246]
Apon a decre in the chansery with me, I was to make choys of sertin feafes in trust, for the good of my childorn and self, whearapon I made bowld to make choys of you for the chef, senc which tym I have purcheased the fee farm of the Kinge, and am to remofe a teanent that is in it for an improvement of rent, and so to leas it out for ten years until my sonn doe come of age. These things canot be don without you please to joine with me, and the other feaffee. Now if eany doubts may aris whearin you may fear eany incombrances to your self, I will secure you what way you shal thinke fit. This bearer wil inform you how all things doe stand in this besnes. Thus feringe I have bin to trobelsom, with my best wishes I rest eaver

Signed: Your very lovinge cosen Anne Hungate. *Holograph.*
Addressed: To my most hono'bll. cosen Sir Edmond Bakon knight
2 ff.; fine seal impression.

158.   [4205] *William Covell to Sir Robert Drury, 16 February 1613*[247]
Sir, after I had sealed this inclosed lettre I met with some with whome I had some speache concerning the sale of your woods, and for thoes in Hoies fearme I could not be offered above 13 nobles the acre, and for the wood in Mayhewes ground bushwood I was offered but £5 the acre, though I expected to have been bidden a far greater price, and Mayhewe denyeth the way thereto which his father set out for a way. For Cobs wood I cannot get above £4 10s the acre. Stubbings wood will not yeeld above 14 nobles. The thre woods in Pickards fearme will yeeld some £4 some £3 10s the acre and is the most is bidden. I have not made promise of any of theas at theas prices nor seemed to com nere thereto, only this I perceive is the most any man I have yet spoke with is willing to geve, and thought it my duty to certyfy your worship accordingly. I do not purpose to make sale of Hallgrove, but I have sould Newell wood to divers men at £8 13s the acre, which is not so good wood as some of them abovementioned, but that ~~there are~~ it is something better staddled.[248] Thus craving pardone for my ~~re~~ rude and hasty righting I cease, this time. Febr. 16 1612

Signed: Your Worships humble servaunt William Coveill *Holograph.*
Postscript: The buyers do much stand uppon the tythe of theas woods
Addressed: To the right worshipfull my very good Master, Sir Robert Drury knight at Drury House neer the Strand London
2 ff.; traces of seal.

159.   [4205A] *John Green to Nathaniel Bacon, 15 April 1613*[249]
Sir I have inquirete after the daughters of Farie and I am informed that Alice the elder of the two is for certayne in service with Sir Phillip Woodhouse or at lesse wise she was within this thre weeks and for the younger Amy Fary she was

---

[246] These dates are suggested by Anne Woodhouse's second marriage to her Hungate husband, before her third marriage to Sir Julius Caesar on 19 April 1615. For the complications caused by her scheming, of which this letter witnesses one of the earliest phases in the Redgrave collection, see Hill, *Julius Caesar*, pp. 242–5.
[247] Covell was a long-standing tenant of the Drurys at Hawstead.
[248] Meaning that more healthy young trees have been left during cutting to regenerate it.
[249] Although this is undoubtedly a stray from the Nathaniel Bacon archive, it is printed here, since the *Nathaniel Bacon papers* project will probably not reach this point in Nathaniel Bacon's life for some time.

in service with with [*sic*] Edward Yelverton but nowe she is removed to ladye in Suffolk but I cannot learne the ladies name and so much for the recusantes.

Sir concerning Sherringham busines I cannot perseyve but that they are so conceyted of the state of thire right as that nothing will satisfye them which can be shewed in the right of my Lord therfore yf I might but intreat you to signifye unto them, that yf they rest not satisfyed on your oppinion concerning the state of that right which you thinke doth duely belong unto my Lord, and so will refer them selves to take such alloweanc out of the wood, as shalbe thought fitt by Lord [*sic*] to yeld unto them, that then yf some one of them will come upp to London within this ten dayes wher I wilbe God willing, we will agree by consent to frame an action betwixt my Lord and the tennauntes and so will at Lamas assizes have a triall to decide all further controversye for the wood, by which they shall eyther gayne all or losse all, and truely for my part I see that nothing will better stop thire clamorus mouethes both toward my Lord and his officers then the power of the lawe, the men being so strongly possessed of a greater right then I am a frayde wilbe fownde in them. We have forborne to fell any this yeare thinking that they would have sought some allowanc by favour, but I see that Rolffe doth much put them one to try it with my Lord, and it were as good for my Lord so to doe as to offer any other end, but for as much as his [*sic*] he hath intreated your paynes herein so I for my part would be very willing to be advised by you yf you can propownd any corse that may advance the profitt of my Lords and quiet the tenauntes, I shall be willing to followe your directions. Yf you will any thing to London I do purposse yf God will to ride towards London to morrowe, yf you have any service to command me let me understand your pleasure by this bringer and *so* with my duty remembred I take my leave in hast. Wells this 15th Aprill 1613

Signed: Your to his power to comand John Greene *Holograph.*
Addressed: To the right worshipfull Sir Nathaniel Bacon knighte at Stifkey
1 f.; remains of seal.

160.   [4206] *Inhabitants of Wyverston to Sir Nicholas Bacon II, 6 June 1613*
Right Worshipfull, wheras we doe understand that yt hath pleased you to make choise of Mr Andrewes[250] to be our minister, and to that purpose have appoynted that he shall preach at our towne of Wyverston wherby we should have triall of his giftes, may yt please yow therfore to understand that he hath forenoone and after noone this Sabaothe day bestowed such profitable paynes amonge us, as we have great cause to thinke well of him, and for our partes our humble desyre unto your worshipp is that you will continew your good liking towardes this man, not doubting both in in [*sic*] regard of his teachinge as also of his godly liff and honest conversation, that we shall have iust cause to give God harty thankes for sending such a man amonge us, and we shall acknowledge our selfes to be bound to pray still for your worsh. health and preservation, as for many other favors, towardes us so especialy for this in shewing your selfe a most carfull and provident patron for us; in witnesse of our approbation of him we the inhabitants of Wyverston have hereunto subscribed our names this 6 of June 1613

Signed: William Stokes

---

250   Robert Andrewes became incumbent of Wyverston in 1613: Freeman Bullen, 'Beneficed clergy, 1551–1631', p. 295.

Thomas Hovell alias Smyth
John Stokes
Thomas Wilson
William Goodryche
Henry Weste
Thomas [*mark: rough TH*] Hawes his marke
William [*mark: upright arrowhead*] Margerie his marke
The marke of [*mark: rough W*] William Prentys
The marke of [*mark: inverted W*] William Selman
The marke of [*mark: rough P*] John Posford
The marke of [*mark: inverted V*] James Walton
The marke of [*mark: flail?*] Henry Walker
The marke of [*mark: rough F*] Roberte Fulsar
The marke of [*mark: X*] Ivo Bone *Apparently holograph in hand of Stokes.*
Endorsed: A letter from the inhabitants of Wyverston in approbation of Mr Andrews the minister.
2 ff.

161. [4207] *Roger Seman, Robert Shepe, Humphrey Howlett, Abraham Gleed to Sir Nicholas Bacon II, 8 November 1613*[251]

Nether Rickinghall. November 8 1613. Haveing accordinge to comandmente received from your Wor. together with the assistance of a carpinter viewed and considered of the ruens and decayes aswell of the chancell as of the parsonage and all the howses therto belongeinge, we doe certifie that the carpenter will not undertake to finde tymber and workemanshipp to repaier the decaies in the howses aforesaid in sufficient sorte under the some of thirtie poundes and for thackinge daubeinge and other necessary reparations wee thincke it will not be done ~~for~~ under tenne poundes more

Signed: Roger Seman	Robert Chepe
Humphrey Howlett	Abraham Gleed *Holograph in Seman's hand.*

Endorsed: Concerninge Rickingall Parsonage
1 f.

162. [4208] *Sir Robert Drury to Lady Drury, 9 December 1613*[252]

Sweete harte I pray you to cause as much of the clothe to be sente up by the nexte caryer as will serve for fyve liveris, of some 2 yardes and a half or 2 yards three quarters in a livery. I pray aske Susan, what she did with the conserve of roses that Plum did bringe from London. I could wishe ~~if~~ that if you goe to Smalbridge[253] that you went quickly, because I may chance from Roysten to wryte for sommthing I maye misse of. If you shold be gone from home, housoever I pray

---

251   In this and the following letter, the recipient can be deduced since Sir Nicholas was patron of both Wyverston and Rickinghall Inferior in 1603: V.B. Redstone (ed.), 'Condition of the archdeaconries of Suffolk and Sudbury in the year 1603', *PSIA* 11 (1901), 14, 26. The previous incumbent of Wyverston, Robert Ballard, was a graduate and chaplain to Roger 2nd Lord North, a prominent East Anglian Puritan and close associate of Bacon; clearly great care was being taken to appoint a worthy successor in the godly tradition.

252   Printed in Bald, *Donne and the Drurys*, p. 127.

253   Smallbridge Hall, Bures, home of the Waldegrave family. Lady Drury's sister Jemima had married Sir William Waldegrave.

you wryte presently, and send a messadger for the howndes, if it will please my sister to send them, for assuredly, she or I wilbe ansered of them. I pray you cause an entry to be made into Horscroft Ferme, as my coosen Drury shall advise you, and bycause that Albon is runne away, and that Cutrisse is loth to putt Addams oute, he may chouse which ferme he will have, and Adams shall have the other, and I will make a lease for 12 yeres but not a penny under 10s the acre, for as the pryse of thinges ryseth, I will warrant you, you shall see the pryse of lands ryse much or sixe months be passed. If Cutrisse will kepe a goshauk for me I will bring one from Sir H. Drury.[254] I pray take order that Candler suffer no boddy to hauke, and lett my baylys speke to all my tennants about it. I pray that Gabriell[255] take order for tymber for the ryding house to be a stable, and that he have as many carpenters as he care about it, as allso for the leane to, which now they nede not strive to make so broade, but only for necessary houses and some of it for a doggs kenell; and that he doe cause Oalhen Wood, and How Wood to be cutt and mowed with a bushe sythe, and the rayles to be sett up at Thetford, and the water cut to rune thorowe to the ditch on bothe sydes of the causy, and the yong sikamors sett, and osiers pricked in the banks, and bothe ends rayled up presently, and that nothing may cum to byte the sickamors on the cause, till gates and pales be prepared for it. Farwell sweet harte

Signed: Your loving husband R. Drury Stragewell[256] 9 December 1613. *Holograph.*
1 f.

163.   [4209] *Sir Robert Drury to Lady Drury [late January 1614]*[257]

Sweetehart, thoughe as you knowe, I am a very careful jentle man to leave my busines in good order when I comme from home, yett, fewe tymes I misse sending a postscript from my nexte bayte, which is at Sir William Woodhouses, for the Norwidge caryer skared me with his being going to Babrum.[258] I pray you cause ~~my~~ Trippett to be sett by the barbery, and fedd as he is, and the gray colte with the whyte foote sett into the coatch horse stable. Desyer Mons'r Fevre to ryde the whyte barbery and Trippett bothe morning and evening uppon the landes, an ower together *with the bitt* or else you must desyer my coosen William to doe it, with the Scotch sadle and the snafle, that thay may be in good brethe, for on Wednesday, I doe thinke to send for them to Roysten. The barbery must have hunting shoes sett on, and Trippett must have a *rye* ~~wheate~~ sheafe every nyght, and henpseed in his provender, to scoure away his grease; Will Wright to see all the bitts layd up *clene and drye* in brunne,[259] that he tooke the note of, never *a* on lefte abroade when Mons'r Fevre goes awaye, but that which the two mares ar ridden withal. I pray send me a coppy of that note which Gabriell shewed me aboute Emans, and send me your letter of such nues as is at Hargett,[260] sinse I came away. I doubt not but Drue Drury brought you sume. I will send to meet the caryer at Witsford Bridge on Tuesday. I pray *bid* Gabriell not to fayle to

---

254   Sir Henry Drury.
255   Gabriel Catchpole.
256   Possibly Stradishall, on the Haverhill to Bury St Edmunds road.
257   Date suggested by Bald, *Donne and the Drurys*, p. 128.
258   Babraham in Cambridgeshire, probably to stay with Toby Palavicino.
259   For 'bran': see Moor, p. 46.
260   That is, Hardwick Hall.

gett good store of Acorns, to sowe in the plases I shall apointe him about Hargett, and that presently he will sette good store of workmen, to gather yong trees for Snareshill, for I wold not fayle to have them sett there this monthe, or else thay will be mared. He must make the causy presently downe to the ryver where Mr Pointen shewed me the old causy was. It must have great ditches well sett with alders that may growe to make shade, and be 18 or 20 foote wyde a sunder for the walke. It is strandg *seing* what fell oute onse, that Gabriell wold delyver monny agayne, untold or unsealed. I pray commend me to the two honest jentlemen that ar in thayr vertuous exsersyse

Signed: Your loving husband R. Drury. *Holograph.*
Addressed: To my loving wyfe the Lady Drury at Hargett neere Bury
2 ff.; fine seal impression.

164.   [4210] *Sir Robert Drury to Gabriel Catchpole [spring 1614]*[261]

Gabriell, I pray you fayle not to wryte a worde *or to send this letter* to my wyfe to daye to Culforde, that I forgott to tell her that I wold advyse her to use by anny meanes a dyett for her spleane which I have used ever sinse I came up, and have fownd muche good of it, which is to have a presse of a racke of veale, boyled with capers and currans, which is very good lykewyse for the lyver, and tell she be *very* weary of that dyet to take nothing else at her meales, as lykewyse when she will eate ~~capons~~ *capers* for a sallett, to have them boyled a little with currans to take away the rawnes. I would allsoe wishe her to wryte to Doctor Butler, for the rescayte of the brothe which he prescribed to my Lord Denny,[262] which he commendeth for the soveraynst thinge for the spleane, that ever he tooke; allsoe I wold have you to send Burd presently, to looke uppon all my mares, which wer coovered the laste yeere, that you may wryte me nowe word so neere as he canne gesse which ar with foale. Remember that which I writt to you the laste weeke, conserninge Hawkes Wood, and ye to combe bullimong from Mr Brabin. Drury Howse, this Fryday after my oother letter.

Signed: Your loving master R. Drury. *Holograph.*
Postscript: You must thinke of provydinge more monny to sende me up, for my buildings heere will begine nowe to ryse weekly to a greate chardge.
Note by Catchpole: If your La. can send my master any monye I praye do for I have none neyther can I tell wher to gett any this wecke
Addressed: To my servant Gabryell Cashpole, at Hawst.
2 ff.; remains of seal.

165.   [4211] *Gabriel Catchpole to Sir Robert Drury [spring/summer 1614]*

Maye it please your Wor. to understand that I have sould and delyvered fyftye loades of barke at the pryse of fyfty powndes but I have receyved no mony of it; and I have sent to Snares hill[263] fyfty fyve loades of tymber of the houses that are pulled downe. Ther was 28 loades of the barne and 29 loades of the gathouse ~~th~~

---

261   Catchpole was steward at Hawstead.
262   Edward Denny, created Baron Denny of Waltham [i.e. Waltham Abbey, Essex] in 1604 and Earl of Norwich 1626. In 1608 he caused Sir Robert Drury some annoyance by inducing Joseph Hall to resign Hawstead in favour of the living of Waltham Holy Cross: Bald, *Donne and the Drurys*, pp. 62–3, and see no. **138 [4187]** above.
263   Snareshill, near Thetford, Nf. Sir Robert had bought this property in 1611 from Sir Edward Clere (Bald, *Donne and the Drurys*, p. 66).

all which is gon except 2 loades of tymber. The stable is yett to bee carried the most of it shall be carried this week. The fresland mare ~~of~~ with the fole is covered and wee will go one and cover the rest of the mares so sodaynly as the horse will. The hower of covering the mares wee do observe betwen 12 and 2 a clock. The great french mare is not yett recovered ~~yett~~. I am in good hoope she will recover which if she do it is very hardly she is very leane. She is very well fedd with corne continually though she go at grasse. The whelpe that was kept at my howse was putt into the kenell and huntted amongest the beagles and one tewesday last it was lost from the rest of the beagles, Spalding Stuard and Nune being all a hunting and we cann no wheat hear of it. Covell[264] have lost his whelpe and can not hear of it by no meanes. If your Wor. com not home this wecke I pray lett me know your pleasier whether you will have that part of the barne which is left standing at Hausted made up with a pecke end or a leane tto [sic] end lycke the other end next the barne yard or no. If you will make it a leanto end then the wall must be sett so muche the father off, if a pecke end the wall must begone just at the house and so lyckwyse of the newe stable. I have this daye at Newmarket taken bond of Shurt for the 100 com of ottes, and of his suerty Mr Meeade who I thinke is very sufficient for such a debt, and I have also taken order for the delyvery of the ottes at Bury. Thus seassing any further trouble at this tyme, in all remembrance of my duty I most humbly take my leave. Hausted this present Twsday morninge

Signed: Your servant ever to be commaunded Gabriell Catchpoole. *Holograph.*
Postscript: I pray tell my La. Newman is well recovered and ~~also~~ almost well agayne and well able to worke.
Addressed: To the right worshipfull my honorable good Master Sir Robert Drury knight at Drury House neere the Strand or else where.
2 ff.; traces of seal.

166.   [4212] *Edward Kirkham to Sir Robert Drury, 30 August, [?1614]*[265]

Sir Robert, my duty remembred unto you. Weltche has received from you in my absence £5 which is peaid out. Item they have not maide an end of the howse with in and for the conishes they be not done.[266] They shall goe in hand one monday next for I gave them a note to borrow some of the Kinges offiser and they had none to speare. It will be tewesday next before ~~it be done~~ the inside of the howse be done. If that woorkmam [sic] which you sent can be founde hee shall doe it but theise woorkmen will not doe it under £6. Sir my Lord Pagets men have left the twenty pound in towne but I have not received it yet. The howse will be reddy against your coming up for there hath one undertoke to washe and cleane the howse, and thus leaving you I comitt you to God this 30 day of Agust[267]

Signed: Your very assured freind Edward Kirkhame. *Holograph.*
Addressed: To the write worshippfull and my very good freind Sir Robert Drury at Bury.[268]
2 ff.; traces of seal.

---

264   William Covell: see no. **158 [4205]**.
265   Kirkham appears to have been acting as steward for Sir Robert Drury's London property: see Bald, *Donne and the Drurys*, p. 114.
266   Evidently major repairs were being carried out to the house in Drury Lane.
267   Text is entirely without punctuation.
268   First attempt at address on inner fold.

167. **[4213]** *Francis Dodd to Sir Robert Drury, 2 September 1614*

Sir presuminge uppon your worshippfull promyse to pleasure me uppon securytie with the loane of som mony to serve my use, accordinge to your order I gave the name of a brother in lawe of myne one Harrie Weekes, he dwells in Mr Greenes Lane over agaynst the great howses that were Sir George Mores, who I thank him is content to be bound for £20 or £25 for me; the man I assure is suffycyent for a greatter som as your worshipp or any man that enquyers shall heare; and one that will not be bound but he knowes for whome and howe to be sequred. I desyer not to have the mony longer then som 14 dayes after Chrystmas that out of such rentes as I shall receyve that quarter I may repaye it *with* manye thankes for your favors therin. And soe ~~Sir~~ hoapeing therof I take leve and soe rest as at your comaund in any servycce I maye durring lyffe, as a man I protest that willinglie would not deserve yll. Drewrii Lane this second september anno 1614.

Signed: Frauncis Dodd. *Holograph.*
Addressed: To the ryght worshippfull his verie good landlord Sir Robert Drewrii at his howse att Hawsted
2 ff.; fine seal impression.

168. **[4214]** *Sir Robert Drury to Lady Drury [?November, 1614]*

I have sent you this letter, of your wise servante Richard his indyting, to lett yow see yf he bee not mistaken, or if you bee mistaken, which ~~is~~ I hope is trewest, for I had rather, that 3 belimcampoes weare sike, then one bayocaroe.[269] I will by the grase of God see you one Monday att night, att Culford. The stable rome is so misserable heare, that I will not have my coache to com heather, but meaning to goe to Hargett[270] one Monday, before I come to Culford, I would have my coache, with a cople of coache mares only Javorett and Halton, to meete mee att Risby att a brother in lawes howse of Spauldinges, whose name is Hale, and if I bee nott theare by one or twoe of the cloke, lett him retourne bake agayne to you to Culford, for theare is nothinge so unserteayne as the resolutiones of the Corte, uppon which my destynie, which neaver was alotted the beste, doathe now for a while attend. Att Newmarkett this Thrusday att none, 1614.

Signed with holograph postscript: I hope my Lady your sister is by this tyme become maniable (after her beinge coatchfallne)[271] at the least that she will be so by Monday to this lame hande, which never did anny harme to anny of her sexe. Her servant and youre R. Drury. *Main text in Richard's hand.*
Addressed: To the honorable lady the Lady Drury att Culford
2 ff.; remains of seal.

---

[269] 'Belimcampoe' and 'Bayocaroe' are evidently the names of two horses, probably Italian; it was common practice in Italy to give a bay horse such a name as 'Baio caro' [the dear bay]. So Drury is saying that 'Baio caro' is three times the quality of 'Bello in campo'. I am indebted to Dr Arthur Macgregor of the Ashmolean Museum, Oxford, for advice on this matter.

[270] Hardwick Hall.

[271] 'Maniable' i.e. manageable; 'coatchfallne' again seems to be private jocular language relating to horses.

169.   [4215] *Sir Edmund Bacon to Sir Robert Drury [?December, 1614]*[272]
Sir this man that was the overseer at the buyldinge the Tower of Babell[273] hath bene here with me, and as I perceyve by him came hyther upon purpose to have a worde or two of y'r hande for y'r satisfaction about an agreement betwixt Summers the mason and him concerninge the seelinge of the gallerye at Hawsteade. I finde by them both that they are accorded, and that Summers ys alreadye satisfied for the doyinge of yt, which he tells me shalbe perfomed presently after Christmas. I shalbe glad when I come to London to see the fruyts of thy mans labours at Drurye house. Yf his worke be as substantiall in the cytye as in the countrye, for yf yt fall out otherwise, I hope yt wilbe so longe before my occasions shall call me thyther that I shall finde you repayringe that worke that he shall make an ende of. I desyre in this ~~onlye~~ to be *only* remembred to my sister for the past weke she harde from me in the same kinde. And thus I rest.

Signed: Y'r lovinge brother Edm. Bacon. *Holograph.*
Addressed: For his hono. brother Sir Robert Drurye knighte at his house at London
2 ff.; seal impression.

170.   [4216] *Thomas Short to Lady Drury [April 1615]*[274]
Madame, I cannot but send you word of some reportes here at London to counterpoyse those which you perhappes here at Bury. The Kinges Maiesty told my Lord of Arrundel going to Marybon Park[275] on Tuesdaye after Sir Robertes departure from this lyfe, that he heard of his deathe and swore by his soule, he was a gentleman that he could not tell how had bene frustrated of some suites but he was willing he should have bene cofferer, for he was a good husband for him self and would have bene frugall for his sonn, he was of sufficient estate as it was convenient and otherwise he was so well qualified as her [*sic*] Maiesty verely thought he would have bene a great honour to that service, with much more, and some thing of a neighbour nere you who is thought to be gracious, but I beleve farr from it. My Lord of Arrundell spake of him very often and protested he was sorry for him and he knew none about the Court of his rancke, but had more faultes; none that had so many good partes. My Lady Burleighe[276] Madam I hope will well accord with you; she gives you the best wordes that any frend can doe, more sparingly of hir brother rather then of you as I heard by my Lady Kitson[277] and by another. So in hast Madam preying God Almighty to send you comfort I take my leave.

Signed: Your worshippes to commaund Thomas Short. *Holograph.*
Postscript: Good madame let one of your servantes tell my wyfe I wilbe at home on Thursdaye at night.
Addressed: For the right worshipfull the Lady Drury at Halstead.
2 ff.; fine seal impression.

---

272   Printed in Bald, *Donne and the Drurys*, p. 134.
273   Presumably a jocular reference to the builder's long experience, or claims to it.
274   Printed in Bald, *Donne and the Drurys*, p. 135. Dateable by reference to the death of Sir Robert Drury. Short was a physician of Bury St Edmunds: see *ibid.*, p. 146.
275   That is, Marylebone.
276   See above, no. **156 [4204]**.
277   Or possibly 'Bilson': Sir Thomas Bilson was knighted in 1613.

171.   [4217] *Richard Brabon to Lady Drury, 25 April 1615*[278]

Madam, this is my purpose and this is graunted unto, that you shall have letters of administration *pendente lite*, and commishion to prove the will *per testes*. They wishe it might be heare proved but I tell *them* that ther is apotticary that is soe well imployed that it would be to his great hindrance, with many other things, that I hould it best for many circumstances to have it proved in the cuntry. It wilbe more sure thoughe it be more charge. The question is what suertye shalbe got for your iust administration of the goodes. It is a thinge of course in this prerogative court to enter bond with suertye unto his Grace of Canterbury, the circumstances would be longe to writ. If you *have* the goodes in your handes I hope it is the best saffety for you. I tell Sir Henry Drury that it is fitting for him and my self to give way for your credit untill the will be proved; what his answer was and what else dependeth upon it hereafter I shall lett you knowe. It is your good and your credit with honor that I desire; lett others stand upon ther owne good. If you may doe well I hope your freinds shall not doe ill.

   Mr. Thomas Drury is very inward with Sir Henry and is of his counsell and giveth him what information he can, but he doeth cum over Sir Henry Drury with an anuity for £5 for paynes taken and doeth warrant Sir Henry that he will doe well enoughe for Drury House and those partes. And Mr Parker[279] is benifited by Sir Roberts death by some writinge made longe since. The Lord Burly and his Lady with the rest doe purposse to be at the funerall, and what is fitting for him to doe ther about that busines he protesteth he will doe it most willingly, and to that purposse he desireth me to goe to Clarentius[280] and that he would give me direction for him; upon that I shewed him your care ~~your~~ and respect you had of his honnor and howe you had given me in writinge to that purpose to goe goe [*sic*] unto Clarentius. They doe protest peace and great good affection towardes you, but yet I [*?*]praise[281] ther is sumthinge in the wind about the inheritance in the land, and Drury House is in ther eye if it be not in ther hart. If I may fittly dispatch as aforesaid, it shall be well *de bene esse*. April 25

Signed: Your La'ps servant R. Brabon. *Holograph.*
Addressed: To his honorable and most worthy Lady the Lady Drury at Hausted House
2 ff.; seal impression.

172.   [4218] *Lady Drury to Sir Francis Bacon [May 1615]*[282]

Sir, I have receved both by my brother and Mr Brabon so much assurance of your care and favour to me in my business, as I blush to retorne you those poore thankes this paper can carry for itt deserves a great deale more, but ~~when I consider your love of goodnes for ther owne beauty~~ I hope you wilbe pleased to accept this poore widdowes ~~might~~ mite untill ~~opertunyty~~ *better opertunyty* be presented ~~for better. I shall~~ give me leave still to besech *you* to continue your love and

---

[278]   Note that this is misdated in *Bacon handlist*. Mostly printed in Bald, *Donne and the Drurys*, p. 139. Richard Brabon was former tutor to Robert Drury and his brothers and sisters at Hawstead Place, and had also been presented to the parish of Whepstead by Sir William Drury: Bald, *Donne and the Drurys*, p. 19. He was one of the executors of Sir Robert Drury.
[279]   George Parker: see above, no. **122 [4169]**.
[280]   William Camden, the celebrated antiquary, Clarenceux King of Arms 1597–1623.
[281]   Apparently for 'appraise', but the reading is not clear.
[282]   Mostly printed in Bald, *Donne and the Drurys*, p. 140.

care for your poore neece whom you see like to fynd many opposers and none hable to succor *hir* but your selfe of whose and [*sic*] love *and power* I am so confident as I confess itt armes me agaynst all feares; I know I have all justice and equyty on my side; but that is not of such strength in these dayes as to pass without frendes ~~and doo therfor esteeme itt a great favour from God too have one so near in blood~~
~~and must were loth~~ [*sic*] *to have you* provided for my refuge
To

No signature. Holograph draft.
1 f.

173.   [4219] *Gabriel Catchpole to Lady Drury, 20 June 1615*

Maye it please your Ladyship to understand in what sort I purpossed to have delt with your shephard. When I sawe that he fell short in his accoumpt I had inquired wher he had sould 10 shepe and asking him wher he had bought them he would not tell me. I went ~~th~~ to the ~~iustyce~~ iustices and gott a warrant purpossing to have him examyned wher he bought those shep he had sould, or else to procure him to enter a bond to awnsware you your shepe that ware wanting but in the meane tyme ~~he~~ he toke him to his leges demaunding no wages nor cloake. I would intreat your La. to bestowe his cloak uppon an honest old workeman of your who much morneth for the dethe of my master, old Creme, who befor was forgotten. Wee cannot yett gett all the bills of the poore people of Bury; wee yett want two. I am promyssed them one Wendesdaye next, which if I cann gett I purposse to cause Foxgill one Wednesday in the after none to proclame in every stret in Bury that your La. geft to the poore shalbe geven one Thursdaye by eyght of the clock. I ~~pur~~ will buy your wyne this wek god willing; if your La. do look for any company this sommer I would intreat your La. to send word what tyme you think to com downe that we may provyd some young gesse duckling and some puett[283] and to have them fedd agaynst your coming. John Overend is to paye unto your La. rent wheat and rent ottes. His desyre is to buye it. I think if your Wor. do herafter take his rent corne you maye very well spare it, for I am suer that you had the last yeare 40 or 50 combes wheat growing besydes your rent corne. God send a good accoumpt of it. ~~but~~ And if you do not herafter receive these rent cornes then I thinke fitt your La. do not sell Overend corne. I intreat your La. if you cann call to mynd the covenaunt of Overend leases for the payment of his rent corne, which as I remember though it be due for the half yeare ending at our La. yett by the covenaunt of his lease he is to paye it at mydsomer. I praye consyder of it and send word whether we shall receive it or no, or sell it him. I have ~~seene~~ had a syght of my La. Walgrave woode. It is made far unfitt for sale, it was deere bought and it now must of nessessytie be had out of the woode. I cannot sell it to any other body butt one di. acre to Mr Short yett your La. shall do the La. Walgrave a pleasuer to take it and red the wood of it which must be don within a fortnight at fardest. There will be no great losse to your La. because I purpose call your tenaunt to helpe her with it. This yeare your La. shall have no ned of the rent haye of ~~of~~ Bury Medowes and they will geve butt 20s a loade for it. If your La. will be pleased to lett me have it I will geve you as muche as any other and I will promysse better payment then you shall fynd at your tenaunt Harrold handes. Ther shalbe 12 acres

---

283   Meaning 'peewits'.

of the best medow spared for Mr Felton and if your La. do not sell or leat your shepe at Snarshell at Mych. next then ~~you~~ ther must be some haye made for the shepe in winter. Thus seasing any further trouble at this tyme in all remembraunce of my duty I humbly take my leave. Hausted this 20 of June 1615

Signed: Your La. servant ever to commaund Gabriell Catchpoole. *Holograph.*
Addressed: To the right worshipfull my honorable good La. the La. Drury at Drury House neere the Strand
2 ff.; remains of seal.

174.   [4221] *Gabriel Catchpole to Lady Drury [October 1615]*[284]

May it please your La. to understand that I have sould 20 of your cowes ~~at~~ for good profitt. I have sould them for the mony they cost, and for so much as will bere the charge of the tenn that dyed and for a eleven powndes eyght shillinge more. If your La. had not lost no cattell wee should have made a great proffitt by greassing this year. I hard that Mr Robert Bacon hath a great losse of catell of late. Covell told me he have lost senc he was here 3 ~~of~~ *in* a day. I would fech all your thinges from Hausted if I myght knowe your pleasuer what writtinges you would have brought out the closset. I had some thing to have spoken to you a bout halving with your tenaunt Stallom. I here he hath a great losse by fyre. Beleve me if he remayne your tenaunt he will bothe hurt him self and hender you taking the corsses he dothe as shall appere by dyvers reasons I can truly sett you downe. I could not yett fech the stuffe from Snarshell; we made an end of harvest but one Satterday last. And if your pleasuer be I shalbe your tenaunt to Making Hall;[285] my wyfe dislycke shall not make me refusse it, but truly I thinke it a good sharpe peneworth of £4 score a yeare. I desyere to have it so as I may make my rent to lyve lycke a poore fermer, and that I may so use it, that it maye be rather the better for me and not the worse. Therfore I desyere to have it for 21 yeares; I shalbe the boulder to bestowe good cost of it. And as I have allwayes found you my very good La. so I hoope you will remayne ever. Good Madame if you purposse to make me a lease I pray sett downe those princepal covenauntes that you will have observed and I will gett the lease drawne and then bringe it to your La. agayne to take your lycking of it. Thus seassing any further trouble in all remem. of my duty I take my leave

Signed: Your servant ever to be comaunded Gabriell Catchpoole. *Holograph.*
Addressed: To my honorable good La. the La. Drury
2 ff.; remains of seal.

175.   [4222] *Bartholomew Cook to Lady Drury, 13 October 1615*

Madame, theis may be to let you understand that Sir Drew Drewry hath taken order that your ladiship should have the best stuffe in his howse, together with hanginges for your greate chamber. John Brewer[286] hath paid unto my Lady Cooke one hundred poundes and hath taken her acquittance under her hand and seale for the receipt thereof. Mr Holmes hathe not yet paid Sir Edmond Bacon his rent, but saith he will this morning paie it, and take an acquittance; he saith he would have

---

[284]   The date is the suggestion of the *Bacon handlist.*
[285]   Malkins Hall, Snareshill: he was granted the lease, which is mentioned in two leases from Lady Bacon, Bacon Collection MS nos. 2771–2, cited in Bald, *Donne and the Drurys*, p. 147.
[286]   See no. **182 [4228]**.

paid before now, but Mr Manley was not in towne. Howsoever, this day at some tyme I will be there my self to see yf he paies it, and yf not then I will tender it and pay it my self. I delivered my Lady Walgraves letter and delivered it to Mr Ramsey, at which tyme, being the same day I came to towne, he sayd that yf it required an answeare he would send it as this day for the carrier. I doubt not but I shall have the howse ready this week against your Ladyship come. I have nothing els to write at this tyme and thus for present I remaine, comitting you to the protection of thalmighty, ~~your loving serva~~ your most humble servaunt. London this 13 October 1615

Signed: Bartholomew Cook. *Holograph.*
Addressed: To the right worshipfull the Lady Drewry at Hargatt neere to St Edmonds Berry
2 ff.; seal impression.

176. [4224] *Richard Brabon to Lady Drury [November 1615]*[287]

Honorable Madam, I spake with your most worthy father upon Munday at the Angell in Bury. When he first sawe me, he said I was welcome from London and next asked howe his daughter Drury did and whether she had got her an husband. My answer was, that you loved Sir Robert Drury soe well that your eye could behould as yett not aney answerable unto hime and therfor all men or any man to you was as nothinge in repect of him. He must have me to dyne; with him at the Angell ther was Sir John Heygham, Sir William Poly, Mr Claxton,[288] all of them very glad to hear of your health and good end you have made.[289] Your father asked me how much money you did give to make your end; I answered not a penny. He said it was strange that it should be soe reported as it is, if you gave not much money to make an end. I answered him that you had that strength in your owne handes and they them selves soe honorablie affected unto you that they wer as willinge to come to an end as yourself, and that appered, for what you required you had, and that you wer choser for your thirdes; also you took your lott wher you would and althinges done in as great luve as might be. He said I fear *aliquid latet quod non patet.*[290] I tould what so ever it was it could not hurt you. My paper willeth me to saye to you from him that he hathe his health very well and that this Chrismas he hath a lodgine for you. I perceive by him that you shall bringe much joye unto him by your presence. He willed me to tell you that your brother Mr Nicholas matter is ended very well. Covell thinketh him self disgraced much that I have got his fearme from him; in that and what else I rest your true servant

Signed: R. Brabon. *Holograph.*
Postscript: Your father said he received his wine but this weeke. If you bringe a cummission to prove your will by wittnesses, take tyme sufficient thoughe in truith you will and doe purpose to prove it afore that tyme. Good Madam remember my

---

287   Printed in Bald, *Donne and the Drurys*, pp. 149–50.
288   John Claxton was a Suffolk JP.
289   I have suggested punctuation for this sentence, but some alternative punctuations would be equally valid.
290   'Something is concealed which does not appear'.

service to that good Lady Gaudy and my honeste Mr ~~Colby~~ Coldby.[291] I praye doe not forgett me to Doctor Dune[292] and my most necessary thanks for ther kindnes.
Addressed: To his honorable Lady the Lady Drury at Drury House by the Strand
2 ff.; seal impression.

177.   [4223] *Gabriel Catchpole to Lady Drury, 7 November 1615*
Maye it please your La. to understand that I send by this carrier 260 powndes sealled up in two pursses which I praye lett it be carfully feched home to Drury House and attend the carriers cominge least it should be ill delt with by long lyeing their. I could not by any meanes paye it by exchange, for I understand that uppon exchange they will dryve longe tyme after the payment of our mony in the cuntrye before we shall have our mony of them at London and the carradge will not cost muche the bringing to London; besyd it is sent up with 7 or £800 more of ther mens. I purposse by Gods grace to be at London one Frydaye next, I riding to the woddes to bringe you a perfitt note what yeares grose[293] they all be of, and what quantitie of acres. What I cannot well perfitt here I will by your direction better parfitt at London after I com thether. The *pott of* butter ~~cannot be~~ *is* sent this weck. I wonder muche the bende boxe[294] should be left. Ther was directions sett uppon every parsell and an note sent howe many parssells weare sent. Thus seassing any further truble in all remem. of my duty I humbly take my leave. Bury this 7 of November 1615

Signed: Your La. servant ever to be comanded Gabriell Catchpoole. *Holograph.*
Addressed: To the right worshipfull my honorable good La. the La. Drury at Drury House neare the Strand
2 ff.; remains of seal.

178.   [4225] *Sir Nicholas Bacon II to Thomas Lord Ellesmere, 21 November 1615*
Ryghte honorable and my verie good Lord accordinge unto the tenor of your Lordships lettuer [*sic*] directed unto me being dated at Yorke House the third of Julie last past for the endinge of a controversie betwene Ogle and Chrysall dependinge in Chauncherie [*sic*] for the right of certen customarie landes houlden of my mannor of Foxerthe, presently I willed my steward of that and other my mannors, beinge a counceler at lawe, to cale a courte and so to procead from courte to court until a triall was had for my better understanding of the righte therin, which shortlie after was performed, wherin a playnt of trespase was entered by Chrysall against Ogle for trespas supposed to be don in yt of the coppihold landes in question. Theruppon processe was awarded against Ogle but he would not then appeare and thre weekes after that an nother court was kept; then Ogle appeared by his attornye and craved a copie of the playntif his declaration and also a daye to answere untill the next court, which was graunted unto him; at which court Ogle by his said atturney pleaded unto him not giltie to the said trespas and therupon did put him self upon the lordes homage wherupon processe was awarded to my

---

291 Dorothy Bacon, sister of Lady Drury, married first Sir Bassingbourne Gawdy and second Philip Colby; Brabon addresses her by her more honorific title.
292 John Donne.
293 That is, total value.
294 Ambiguous: this could either be a band-box, a light cardboard box for millinery or hats, or a stout box bound with iron bands (bends).

balye of that mannor for the customarie tenauntes to be at the next court and the balie beinge called returned his presept served, and twelve of the said customarie tenauntes did then appeare and were sworne and charged to enquier upon the issue, wherupon the playnt. did beginige [*sic*] to set forthe his title but the defend. Ogle althoughe he was thre tymes solemlye demanded in court to appeare and to make answere to the said Crysall in his said attient of trespas refused soe to doo but did make default. Theirfor the jurie did give the verdit that the said Ogle was guiltie of the trespas in such sort as Crisall did set forth and he had complayned of him in his declaration, and therfor they found for the playnt and did give him twoe pence for damages and 2 pence for costes wherupon judgement was craved on the behalf of the playntif which was also granted accordinglye. Nowe my good lord my meaning was after I understode howe the jurie had passed in the controversye to have don something therin in equitie as I thinke your honors entent was that I should, but Ogle never did come at me sithince ther [*sic*] said triall nor yet mad any means to me therin. Thus having signified unto your honor as breflie as I maye my proceadinge therin and in what sort I have employed my endevor in the care of your Lorships [*sic*] comande, being lothe to troble you with more wordes I humblye take my leave and rest alwayse your Lorshipes in all dutie to comande

Signed: N. Bacon. Culford this 21 of November 1615 *Copy in secretary's hand.*
2 ff.

179.   [4220] *Sir Edmund Bacon to Lady Bacon [?27] December 1615*
Madame, I most humbly thanke your L'p that yt pleases you to call us so soone unto you; but to tell you the truth howe we stande at this tyme, the last night I had a fitt of my olde malady for 2 howers, but I thanke God yt was not so violent as to make me rise. My wife hath bene subiect to a payne in the joynts of hir handes since we sawe you last, and the last night sett in one of hir shoulders. So that we entreate your La'p to dispence with us till Munday, to which purpose yf yt please you to send your coach upon Saterday, Olyver for himself and his ~~horses~~ mares shalbe as well accommodated as this place can afforde. And in the meane tyme yf we growe [*word illegible erased*] worse you shall have knowledge of yt to spare the journy; but God willing there shalbe nothing to kepe us from you, but the providence of him to whome we must all subscribe. Redgrave this St. Jhons day[295] 1615

Signed: Your Ladi'ps most loving sonne Edmund Bacon. *Holograph.*
Postscript in another hand: ~~Mada~~ Madam I remember my love to your La. with a lame showlder. Phillip Bacon
Addressed: For his dearely beloved mother the L. Bacon at Culforde
2 ff., torn; seal impression.

---

[295] This is almost certainly St John Evangelist's Day, 27 December, since in 1615 it fell on a Wednesday. This makes more sense than the Nativity of St John Baptist, 24 June, which in 1615 fell on a Saturday. The letter envisages the coming Monday preceded by a coming Saturday, which would not be possible if one were writing on a Saturday, but is natural if one is writing on a Wednesday. Moreover, Lady Bacon has very recently seen Edmund and his wife, which would be plausible with Christmas Day having fallen two days before St John's Day.

180. **[4226]** *Elizabeth Lady Burghley to Lady Drury [?1616]*

My good sister,

~~Sister~~ I have recayved your linnes safe by the carrier and in them your respecktive satisfacktion to uss conserninge thous speches. It semed Mr Neve mistouke outherwise I asuer you we hade bine muche mistaken but I dout not we shall take no longe tim if we live to geve ~~in that poynt~~[296] good testimonny you ar not all together desaved in belevinge so well of our prosedinge in that poynt. Conserninge your desier English showld survay the ground you hould of uss, we will no ways be agaynst your likinge, thow we did ever intend no outher *manner of* survay if the outher did it but with in the hegges as is the common usse to tennants. Sister let me I pray intreat you if your self or sarvantes know anny thinge may at this tim be advantagus eyther in generall or particular to further to the survayer the knowleg of what is our rittes, dow uss the favor and kindnes to let him be instruckted, for we desier much to make a just and a cleare worke of what is in hande to which pourpos we are in great hope we have met with a sufficient and honnest mane our survayer. When I have discharged my self of my trust to salut you with much love from my sisters I will geve your passience fredum from the trubel of *my* scribles which shall onlly holde your iees[297] ~~to~~ *at this tim to rede* that which I desier to posses all your senses with all, which is that out of your one worthe you cummande my Lord and me

Signed: as your affecktionnat lovinge sarvante for ever Elisabeth Burghley. *Holograph.*

Addressed: To my honorable and much respeckted sister the Lady Drury at her hous at Hargill.[298]

2 ff.; 2 fine seal impressions.

181. **[4227]** *Robert Bacon to Lady Drury, 24 June 1616*

Honorable Sister, It hath pleased God sithence our parting to visit me with such a daungerous sicknes as *I* have bin altogether unable to effect aswell that which I formerly promised for your self as also that which I purposed of myne owne. Notwithstanding I sent my man to buy the horses, but one Sir John Jowles who is landlord to him who did owe[299] them had bought them for £22 before his coming. Whereof I thought yt fit to certifye you. Thus remembering my love I take my leave, resting

Signed: your verie loveing brother Roberte Bacon. Ribrowgh this 24 of June 1616. *Holograph.*

Address torn off, except: in Suffolk.

Several calculations on two sides.

2 ff., torn; traces of seal.

---

[296] Apparently altered from 'of the poynt'.
[297] For 'eyes'!
[298] Hardwick House.
[299] Meaning 'own'.

182.   [4228] *John Brewer to Lady Drury, 5 July 1616*[300]

Madame, I have sent your Ladishippe by Simpson the carrier, a boxe which Mr Cotgrave[301] intreated me to send downe for your Ladishippe wherein as I conceive are writings which appertaine unto you. He hath the key of the boxe himself and purposeth to be with your Ladishippe ~~to~~ one Monday or Tuesday the next weeke; in the meane time he desiereth the boxe may not be opened. I have paide Sir John Hollis rent yeasterday[302] thoughe this seavennight might serve the turne, the rather because I would putt that care from your Ladishippe. I woulde I could also aswell lett Drury Howse to your Ladishippes content; there have been divers chapmen of late, but none that ~~staye~~ sticke to the busines. My Lord Harbart would have had it, but not untill Mich'as, and then but for a yeare, and yet concluded it was to little for him. I would not wishe your Ladishippe to make anie effect of abateing anie thing of £100 pound [*sic*], for those that will take it now are but pidling customers, and doe not bite home, and it maie hinder the letting of it at your owne price about Mich'as, at which time if I cannott drawe it to £100 I could wishe ~~then~~ that the best offer might be accepted. So I humbly rest your Ladishippes to my power

Signed: John Brewer. London the 5th July 1616 *Holograph.*
Address: To the right wor'll the Lady Anne Drury at Hargate. With a boxe [*in a different hand*], *per* William Simson at the Eagle in Bury.
2 ff.; fine seal impression.

183.   [4229] *?Lucy Harington*[303] *to Lady Drury [date uncertain]*

Madame, I was offred the service of a gentlewoman that did serve yow but not minded to receive her tyll I had notice upon what termes she lefte yow, for thoughe I had little acquaintance with your La. yet knowinge that yow had marryed a coosen of myne I would have it thought I so much respected yow as not to take any servant that had belonged to yow without your approbation: but now that I finde the gentlewoman leaveth your service with yowr good lykinge and your La. delivereth so good comendation of her fytnes to serve, and her wel deservinge, I shalbe the more willinge to receve her; and thoughe my present want requireth the havinge of one, yet I can be content to expect her cominge tyll the tyme by yow lymieted, and yf in the meane tyme yow well suffer her to come hyther, it maie geve us both the better satysfaction and by sight, reason to judge how we shall lyke the one of the other, and for this I shall expect her, as your La. may most fytly send her, but the sooner the better. Thus wishinge the meanes that maie geve assurance of my redyness to be approved,

Signed: Your La. lovinge coosen and true freind [?]L. Haryngton. *Holograph.*

---

300   John Brewer, a London mercer, acted as a London agent for the Drury family: Bald, *Donne and the Drurys*, p. 93.
301   Randle Cotgrave was in the service of Lord Burghley: his work as a lexicographer has gained him admittance to the *ODNB*.
302   Sir John Holles owned extensive property in the area north of the Strand.
303   I am puzzled as to how to attribute, let alone date, this letter. The signature is not clear. The Chicago listing gives it to Anne, Lady Harington of Exton, but I cannot see how the signature can be turned into 'A'. The tone of the letter is clearly as from a female. John, 1st Baron Harington of Exton married Anne Keilway, and had daughters Lucy and Frances. Lucy, a noted patron of the arts, was a friend of the Bacon family, and erected a monument by Nicholas Stone over her parents' grave; she married in December 1594 Edward Russell, 5th Earl of Bedford, and d. 1627 (*ODNB*). The only other possibility would be the wife of Sir John Harington of Kelston, Mary Rogers; again the signature does not suggest this.

Address: To my honorable good coosen the Ladie Drury.
2 ff.; traces of seal.

184.   [4230] *Sir John Crofts*[304] *to Lady Drury, 6 May 1621*
Maddam, Your Ladyshipes desyre must ever carry a power of commandmente
with me, though yow shall fynd in this nothynge worthye the relatynge, the
effectes beinge so poore; if your noble disposytion will not advance it self, yow
shall fynde nothyng to rayse it by presedente, which in that respecte, I had mutch
rather have observed, then discovered, had not my promyse tyde me otherwise,
but that so overrules me, as yow muste reaceyve hereinclosd a brefe of that which
two breflye paste amongsste us at our sessyones. If I heare of no change from yow,
I will prosede accordynge to your former reasolytion, and that is all the servise
I can performe for your La'pe at this tyme. I praye doe me so mutch favor, as to
delyver my beste love to my wife, with a kysse from me to boote, and if yow please
acquaynte hir with this pertyculer I sende yow that she maye see hir husbandes
wise follye; and if your La'p can brynge hir home with yow in tryumphe, yow
shall purchase a moste faythfull and affectionate servante of

Signed: John Croffts. Saxham 6 of Maye 162~~2~~ 1. *Holograph.*
Postscript: I praye presente my servise to the Master of the Master of [*sic*] the
Roules[305] and his worthy Ladye
Address: To the noble, and my mutch estemed worthye Ladye the Ladye Drury at
the Roulles.[306]
2 ff.; fine seal impression.

185.   [4231] *Sir Edmund Bacon to Nicholas and Nathaniel Fowle, 20 July*
1623
Wheras, since my comminge from London, I have understoode that at the last
courte holden at Redgrave, ye did agree that I should appointe a guardian for ye
during your minorityes,[307] I have thought yt fittinge to appointe Jhon Parker my
servant, of the same towne, thinkinge him to be every way very fittinge to undertake yt. To which choyse yf ye shall give your consents, I desyre ye to signifye the
same by subscribing your names to this which I have written

Signed: Your loving frende Edmund Bacon. Redgrave this ~~19~~ 20 of Julye 1623.
Holograph. Signatures: Nicholas Fowle Nathaniell Fowle Thomas Fowle
Addressed on same sheet: To Nicholas and Nathanaell Fowle
Endorsed: An appointment of a garden to Mr Fowles sonnes.
2 ff.

---

[304]   The *Bacon handlist* describes the writer as Sir John Hollis [*sic*], and indeed the signature might
be read thus. However, Sir John Holles had been made Baron Houghton in 1616, and his son
John was not knighted until 1625. Moreover, the writer is also a Suffolk JP (NB the reference to
the 'sessyones'). The identification of Sir John Crofts is clinched not only by the address from
Saxham, home of the Crofts family, but by the seal, which has in first and fourth quarters of the
shield the arms of Crofts of Saxham, three bulls' heads cabossed. No Hollis coat of arms has a
similar blazon.

[305]   Sir Julius Caesar. He married Anne Woodhouse, Sir Nicholas Bacon's granddaughter, on 19 April
1615: Hill, *Julius Caesar*, pp. 242–3, and no. **157 [4186]** above.

[306]   In Chancery Lane, London.

[307]   Thomas Fowle was appointed incumbent of Hinderclay and Redgrave by Lord Keeper Bacon in
1561 and held the living until his death in 1597. Were these his grandsons?

186. [4232] *Sir William Withipoll to Sir Edmund Bacon, 14 March 1626*

I have receyved from the gentlemen of the Fraunchise of Bury a coppye of the commyssion for this second subsidye, and another copye of letters from the Lo. of his Majesties Privy Counsell, both which I send you herinclosed. The commyssioners being fewe, the tyme short (and myselfe by reason of Sir Henry Glemhams sicknes being to attend this servyce for the libertye of St Etheldred, besides the hundreths of Stowe, Bosmere and Cleydon and Sampford), I cannot be spared to joyne with you for Hartismere and Hoxon. But if you shall please to appoint your daies of sitting and give notice therof to Mr Bedingfield who borders uppon Hoxon hundreth, h[e I] doubt not will give his best assistance in that servyce, [his] division being sufficiently furnished with commyssioners for tha[t] purpose. Thus wishing your happines I rest

Signed: Your frend and servant William Withypoll. Christchurch[308] Marche the 14 1625. *?Holograph.*
Addressed: To my noble frend Sir Edmond Bacon knight and Baronett
2 ff., slightly damaged; fine seal impression.

187. [4233] *Thomas Bedingfield to Sir Edmund Bacon, 18 March 1626*

Right Worshipfull, I am and wilbee readie at all tymes to doe my e[? ndeavour] to give yow content in what I may. I have peruse[d Mr] Withipolls letters sent to yow, wherein I perce[ive he is] misinfourmed: for there are not any nomin[? ated more] for Beccles division,[309] but Sir Thomas Playt[ers, Sir John] Wentworth, Sir John Rous and my self [? of whom Mr] Rous is att London at the Parliament; so i[? t is that] Blithinge hundred must bee done onely [? *two words* Mr] Playters and my selfes. And wee ha[ve [? *two words*] warrantes which are delivered already [? *three words*] to appeare before us at Wrentham the 28 of this [? month *two words*] for I sawe at Bury the comission and had the coppi[e of the] Counselles letters, where I stayde untill the knights and justices the[re did] joyne to in a letter to the Lo. in aunswere of their letter, the copp[ie] whereof I send yow heereinclosed. May yt please yo[w to] understande, I was desired by Sir George Waldgrave [to] joyne with him at Ipswich about this service, but I a[nswered] him I could not attend yt. Sir I am nowe 74 yeeres [of] age and therefore I am not able to take theise journe[ys] and therfore am desireous to bee freed thereof. Yo[w can], Sir, I doubt not, procure other commissioners of be[tter] ablenes of bodye to travayle; I thinke Sir William Sp[ring] for your sake would joyne with yow in this business, but if neither hee nor any other (with more conveniencie then my selfe) can meet for this service, then to give yow content, I will doe my best to meet with yow at Eye, soe as yow wilbee pleased to appoint another daye of meeting which may bee after the abovesaid 28 of this instant March next, for till after that daye yt is not possible for mee to perfourme this yow require, and that yow will send mee a warrant for Hoxton Hundred with the Assessors, and chiefe constables names thereto, for I am altogether unacquainted with what proceedinges they have had in that hundred. Sir whereas yow mention in your letter that yow sent 2 warrantes by mee to bee subscribed, there was in your packet enclosed but onely this warant for Hoxton hundred, which I have alsoe sent yow heerewith (without my name

---

308 Christchurch House, Ipswich.
309 That is, in the subsidy commission referred to in the previous letter.

subscribed) for the reasons above mentioned. And thus I leave yow to the protection of the Almightye. And rest

Signed: Yours to bee used in what he maye Thomas Bedingfeld.[310] Darsham the 18 of Marche 1625. *Autograph.*
Addressed: To the right worshipfull Sir Edmond Bacon knight and Barronett at Redgrave
2 ff.; slightly damaged; remains of seal.

188. [4234] *Sir John Higham to Sir William Spring, 20 March 1626*

I send you herewith Sir Edmund Bacon his letter togither with warrantes and other letters, as I receyved them from him, which does more properlye concerne yow, being a comissioner of the subsidye, then the deputye lieuetenantes. I praye you sett your hande to his warrantes, and joyne with him upon Satterdaye next at Eye. And if you can send the letter to Sir Lionell Talmatche, whoe maye joyne with you yf it please him.

This morning I receyved from Sir George Waldegrave a list of names of the recusantes dwelling in the Franchisse of Burye whoe being convicted, as you knowe, are to be asseassed in the subsidye, at a double payment. Those therfore that concerne Blackburne and Thedwestrye, Hoxon and Hartsmare I send to you herewith, to be alsoe delivered to Sir Edmund Bacon respectyvelye. I have appointed Sir Edmunde Bacones man to wayte upon you with their letters; by whom I praye yow returne there warrantes with your name subscribed unto them. And soe with my hartye commendations, to yow and all your companye, I betake you to God. And doe reste

Signed: Your lovyng cosen and assuered frynd John Heigham. Burie 20 Martii 1625. *Autograph.*
Addressed: To the right worshippful my loveing cosen Sir William Spring knight
2 ff., slightly damaged; remains of seal.

189. [4235] *Sir Edmund Bacon to Sir Lionel Tollemache, Sir John Higham and Sir George Le Hunt, 20 March 1626*

After I had written my *last* letter to you, I receyved the inclosed from Sir William Withipoll, which within a day after I sent to Mr Beddingfeyld, from whome I have yesternight his awnsweare brought me. The jentleman dwelleth far of, and other excuse he hath sett downe wherby he might be freed from this service, which I desyre you to consider of, and yf in regarde of what I wrote unto you for myne owne exemption at this tyme I cannot be spared, yet I would entreate you that some body may be joyned with me that the busynes may be speadily gone in hande with all, which otherwise will hardly be concluded in the tyme lymited. I had sett downe to Mr Beddingfeyld Satterday next being the 26 25 of this present moneth to have mett at Eye, but you may perceyve by his lettere, that his ingagement in an other place about the like busynes cannot suffer him to doe yt. And thus I leave you being

Signed: Your assured frende Edmund Bacon. Redgrave this 20 of March 1625. *Holograph.*
Postscript: I have sent you two warrants to which I desyre yf you joyne any body

---

310 The signature is tremulous.

with me he may sett his hande that I may with the more speade goe forwarde with the busynes.

Addressed: To his honorable frendes Sir Lyonell Talemach knight barronett, Sir Jhon Higham, and Sir George Lehunte knights

2 ff.; traces of seal.

190.   [4236] *Nicholas Bedingfield to Sir Edmund Bacon, 23 March 1627*

Sir, Wher I have had notice of your worshipps sittinge in comission at Bodesdale on Wedensdaye in Easter weeke next where (yf it please God I shall attende you) aswell for the examininge of witnesses betwene one Gerard Wright pl. and my self defendant as for the produceinge of my accompte to satisfie the courte concerninge the profittes of his wyefes portion in her mynoritie in his Bill multiplied by suppositione I hope improbable; and Sir, for the clereinge of this pointe have made meane to my nephewe Yaxlee to shewe the lease of Bickerton and some other accomptes and convayances therof made with the counterparte of the indenture of the mannor of Falcons Hall by him sould to Sir Nicholas Bacone your late father, these writinges and some accomptes pertinent, he hath had a subpena to produce before your worshippes, but excuseth for sicknes, and *for* that he hath lost some of them which he had of my delivery. Now Sir the tyme of sale of Falcons and the full age of Mary by computation of both, by the Register and a note taken of the date of the counterpaine of the indenture of Falcons Hall (not like to be produced) fall out to be in one yere of anno 42 Eliz. but ame like to fayle of profe thereof, unlesse it would please yow to doe me the favor for justice to permitte the bearer purposely sent to attend you, to take only a note of the date of the[311] said indenture of Falcons Hall, and of the names of the parties to the same and the somme of money receyved for the same, which £1500 wherof I am charged with by acquittances produced may appeare with £500 more to be paid to the legatees nere 30 yeres past; wherfor I humbly peticion unto you ~~upon my commission~~ to doe me this necessarye favour at this tyme that the date and somme receyved may be taken to be attested before yow ~~upon~~ upon my comission which was first granted, where the Pl'es cautelusly[312] have since obteyned an other commission retur*nable* before the next terme, the first returne therof purposeinge to frustrate my comission as I ame informed by a cursiter of the court yf his be first certified. So leaveing the consideration of the prejudice to your wisdomes for equitie crave pardon for *my* last old age not *meete* attend~~inge~~ humbly take my leave

Signed: At your service and comande Nicholas Bedingfelde. Gislingham 23 Mar. 1626. *Holograph.*

Addressed: To the right worshipfull Sir Edmond Bacon knight banoret at Redgrave Halle

2 ff.; fine seal impression.

191.   [4237] *Thomas Athow to Sir Edmund Bacon, 12 and 14 December 1627*

Sir, I have received yowr letters by yowr nephew Mr Robert Bacon, and have thought good to signifye unto yow that since my last letters written to yow by Mr

---

311   'The' erased and replaced by 'ye'.
312   Deceitfully.

Chittocke,[313] Mr Noye[314] saith that he is injoyned by some great one to forbeare to be of yowr counsell, but he swore he will not be against yow. Thus much he said to Mr Weston[315] and after to my selfe. Nowe Vernon[316] followe him hard, and as Mr Weston tould me, and I thinke will soe write to yow, that Vernon is contented to referre the matter of account to Mr Noye, if yow will doe the like, and to free yow from all former pattentes and leases of post fynes issues and such like, and yow to make one composition for all. It will not be amysse if yow were at London upon Satterday before the begynning of the next terme, to se if Mr Noye and Mr Weston cann mediate an end to yowr likeinge, for if the charge be once entered *in schedula pipe* yow must stand it out to the end without any composition which will be verye tedious. I desire much to have a note of the breife of the last charge which come to £29000, where we may see what the post fynes come to in the first nyneteene yeares of King James, and what the issues of jurors came to in those yeares, for Vernon give out that the post fynes in those nyneteene yeares come to 29 hundred powndes which I conceyve is not soe. He doe mostly relye upon them to be good money; for the rest he must be dryven to proove the receipt which is difficult. If yow have a coppy of that charge I pray yow lett my servant write out all for the 19 yeares of King James.

The wordes of the provisoe in the pardon of 21 *Jacobi* wherupon Mr Attorny[317] relye ar these: 'alsoe excepted all and singuler accountes all and every collector etc. and all accountes of every other person whatsoever that ought to be accountant to the Kinges Highnes for or in respect of any receipt or other charge which have growne sine [*sic*] the 25 day of March *Anno 1 Jacobi*, and the heires, executors and administers of every such person that ought to account for all thinges touching onely the said accountes, and all and singuler arrerages of accountes and untrue accountes made or rendered since the said 25 day of March *Anno 1 Jacobi*, and all impetitions etc.'

Mr Attorny saye yowr father was an accountant; we aunswere that his account was every yeare allowed, and a *quietus est*, and those accountes were not untrue, for the thinges in question were turned over to him by judgement of the Court, first by the clayme made by yowr father and allowed by judgement of the Court *anno 23 Elizabethe* wherin post fynes and issues were allowed although they were not in the *quo warranto*, and yowr fathers *quietus est* for every yeare of the said 19 yeares, soe that we say ther were neither arrerages of accountes nor untreue accountes at the tyme of the makeinge of the statute of 21 *Jacobi*, and it were hard to make the judgement in the *quo warrento* [*sic*] to relate soe farre as to make yowr fathers accountes untrue. But I dare not trust the Barons of the Exchequer with it, for in my opinion in two pointes they gave judgement against yow contrary to the law *videlicet* that the judgement in the *quo warranto anno primo Elizabethe*

---

[313] No doubt Henry Chittock of Thrandeston, who was involved in transactions with Sir Nicholas Bacon in 1620: *Bacon handlist*, nos. **2768–2770**.

[314] William Noye, distinguished lawyer (1577–1634).

[315] Sir James Weston, Baron of the Exchequer.

[316] Christopher Vernon (see below, no. **197 [4242]**), who in 1624/5 initiated the investigation of the Bacons' Liberty of St Edmund as concealed lands. See *Suffolk in the XVIIth century*, p. 287, quoting *HMC 12th report*, I, 182–4. For extensive papers in connection with all these actions see [Anon., ed.], *Memorials of the past relating to Bury S. Edmunds and West Suffolk reprinted from the Bury and Norwich Post* (Bury St Edmunds, 1889–90), pp. 89–107. Judgement was entered for the Crown against the Bacons in the Exchequer Court on 14 November 1627 (*ibid.*, p. 107).

[317] Sir Robert Heath, the Attorney-General.

did not bynd till it were reversed by error, and alsoe upon the point of the *salvo iure*, for that save noe title to the Kinge but such as were not in question when the judgement was given.[318]

When yow come to London if Mr Noy cannot prevaile, I thinke it were good to intreat my Lord Cheife Baron[319] and the other two which argued yowr case to mediat an end betweene yow. They promise yow great kindnes, but I had rather trust them in that course then to stand to their judgement in the Court for some reasons that I perceive.

I have some of yowr evidence at London, but I thinke I have not the clayme made by yowr father 23 *Elizabethe* and the judgement therupon. I take it Mr Gosnold[320] had it from me and brought not that agayne as he did the rest; I pray yow if he or yowr selfe have it, to bring that with yow, and as many of the yearly *quietus est* as yow have; the clayme will be very necessarye. And soe with my best service remembered I rest

Signed: Yowr very assured loveing friend Thomas Athow. 12 *Decembris* 1627. *Autograph.*
Postscript: I had sent these letters to yow this Frydaye by Jaques, had not this bearer come with yowr letters the last night, and I thinke they conteyne a full aunswere to yowr letters, saveing that I desire to be spared in the nomination of any of yowr counsell untill yow come to London and have Mr Westons advise therein as well as myne.
I am very desirous to see the breife of the charge heretofore ~~entered~~ *intended* for £29,000 whereby I may see what the post fines were in the first 19 yeares of Kinge James; I pray yow to send me a coppy of soe much thereof as soon as yow cann. Mr Mosse the attorny did supp with Mr Weston and me at Starford, and heard us speake of yowr cause, but wee did send noe message by him, for I intended to write to yow as yow may perceive; and I thinke Mr Weston will eyther write to yow or come to yow this Christmas. 14 *Decembris* 1627.
Addressed: To my much honored friend Sir Edmond Bacon knight and barronett
Endorsed by Bacon: divers letters from Serjeant Athow, Mr Vernon and other with other papers of sondry contents. Divers letters.[321]
2 ff., slightly damaged; traces of seal.

192.   [4238] *Thomas Athow to Sir Edmund Bacon [?mid December 1627]*[322]
Sir, you shall perceyve by two orders in [the] exchequer which Mr Ashley Brampton will s[end] you, the first uppon Mr Attorney motion to h[ave] two charges sett, the one from the death of your grandfather to the first yere of Kinge James, the other from the first yere of Kinge James [to] this tyme, and the court gave daye till Tuesd[aye] last for ~~ux~~ us to shew cause whye the charges should not be sett. Uppon the same Tuesdaye I came and shewd cause for the first that the Kinges general pardon *anno 21 Jacobi* discharged them without question (as I sayd); for the other, nothynge was receyved after December 21 *Jacobi*, and for all before 21 *Jacobi* and scithence *primo Jacobi*, I ~~was~~ was of opinion that they were all

---

[318]   For the *quo warranto* of 1559, see TNA (PRO), KB 9/1006, m. 31.
[319]   Sir John Walter, Chief Baron of the Exchequer.
[320]   Anthony Gosnold: see below, no. **193 [4239]**.
[321]   Evidently this letter was used as a wrapper for a bundle of papers, probably including nos. **192–198 [4238–4243]**.
[322]   Dated by reference to nos. **191 [4237]** and **193 [4239]**.

discharged by the pardon, and therefore desired that no charge should be sett but that you might have a coppye of the charge entended to be sett and to give aunsere the next terme ~~whye it~~ whye it should not be sett; and withall I shewed that what officer or clarke soever should make out any proces upon any thinge pardoned, they were to paye treble damages to the partie grevid. The next daye being the last daye of the *terme*, Mr Attorny and I mett in the exchequer and after ~~deb~~ debate of the matters ensuyd, he sayd he would leave the first charge and desired to have the last charge scithence *anno 1 Jacobi* entred but the order was as you shall shee [*sic*] *to staye* ~~staye~~ *staye* that ~~also~~ till the first weeke of the next terme in which youe will have liberty to shewe that it is pardoned. Mr ~~Noye is~~ Noye was present and seconded me that it was pardoned, and I am very glad that he is of your counsell and in deed he so promised me to be with ~~you~~ you in this point. My Lord Thresaror was there at the motion and ordre ~~giving~~ givinge this last daye of the terme. When Mr Brampton send you the orders you shall see it more playnly. I ~~pray~~ praye God that you maye be there your self the first weeke of the next terme for it will be most needfull and so I rest your very assured to be commanded

Signed: Thomas Athow. *Holograph.*
Addressed: To my much honored frend Sir Edmond Bacon knight and baronett
2 ff., damaged; traces of seal.

193. [4239] *Anthony Gosnold to Sir Edmund Bacon, 17 December 1627*
Good Sir, I have herein enclosed sent a copy of Ter[?mino *two words missing*] mentioned in your letters. The clayme ma[de *?two words missing*] in *anno 23 Elizabethe* was, amongst the rest of [*?three words missing*] which Mr Serjeant Athowe, who, noe [*?three words missing*] same by him; for that and the rest w[ere *?two words missing*] the ~~quo w~~ plea to the *quo warran*[to *?three words missing*] agreed uppon, and after that tyme, here [*?three words missing*], that I know of, to use the same. But [?Sir sure] I am that I for my parte never had the sa[me *?one word missing*] after. Sir I doe conceive, upon such inf[ormation as] I could ~~receive~~ *learne*, that upon the judgement nowe against you in the *quo warranto* although [*?one word missing*] Greenewax be ~~adjugd~~ adjudged to the King, yet [*one word missing*] of the things therein mentioned are ~~saied to be~~ left, [*one word missing*]. I caused my man to stay after the terme to hav[e] a copy of the judgement, but they had not then entre[d it and] it was affirmed to him by Mr Wilson, clerke to [Mr] West your attorney, that they were so secret therein [that] he could not get any knowledge how the ~~judgement~~ *same* shou[ld] be entred. It may please you the next tyme you write t[o] London, to write to Mr Brampton to send you a cop[ie of] the judgement *verbatim*, which without question, they have by this ty[me] entred. It were not good, you should be deprived of any thing which the meaning of the courte was to leave still unto yow. Sir the rent for the hund[red] due at Mich. last I affirmed to Mr Quarles I would pay as before, ~~but mony~~ and the same is ready. If Mr Quarles or any other of your servantes hath any other occation to come to Bury, a good part of it is out of my purse, and I must when I shall growe more able to travaile in this tyme of the yeare attend you for some course to be taken therein, and in some other things. My not yet perfect recovery may crave pardon for not performyng my dutie in giving attendance uppon yow since your retorne home, and my hast of busynes this day, for this hasty writing. I humbly take my leave and remayne

Signed: Your good worships at commaund Anthony Gosnold. 17 December 1627.
Holograph.
Addressed: To the right worshipfull Sir Edmond Bacon, knight and baronett
2 ff., damaged; seal impression.

194.   [4240] *Sir John Walter and Sir John Denham to ?Lord Treasurer Marl-*
borough [end of 1627«»1628][323]
May it please your Lordship, According to your Lordships reference to us
touching the claymes made to parte of the arrerages turned over to the Libertyes of Bury St. Edmunds by the farmers of the post-fynes, issue of jurors and
clerke of the markett, wee have heard the reasons and allegations of the farmers
for the post-fines delivered by their learned counsell at severall tymes, in which
wee finde that they clayme not onely the post-fines included with in the Judgement given in the Exchequer for his Majestie, but alsoe diverse other post-fynes
taken by Sir Nicholas Bacon and Sir Edmund Bacon uponn fynes levied both of
landes holden *in capite* within the Liberty, and likewise of lands lying parte in the
Liberty and parte without; to which last duty wee conceive they have title by their
patents, without question. But because it is uncertayne how much the same were,
and that it is a difficult thing for them to prove, wee have principally uponn that
reason mooved that they should have the summe of two hundred pounds which
Sir Thomas Culpeper, under farmer of the sayd postfynes, was content to accept
in full discharge of all claimes for the premisses, which is soe agreed unto of all
parts. But as touching the farmers of the issue of jurors and clerke of the merkett,
they have not attended us, and therefore wee can certifie nothing which concernes
their title.

Signed: John Walter John Denham. *Copy.*
No Address.
2 ff., damaged.

195.   [4241] *Richard Elton to Sir Edmund Bacon, 21 December 1627*
Sir Edmund Bacon, My umble duty remembred to your worshipe. The weke
paste I receaved your letter whearein you direckted me to see fild the same white
malligo[324] or as good as you tasted of at Meades which I have done and sent by
this bearrer your carriare of Berry as this note in clossed makes mention of the
quantety, but for the price it rest unpayde untill it be spent, for he will take noe
mony but upon the liking therof, for I will not pay this price for it. You knowe he
asked lesse when you ware last with him. Thus praying for your worshipes good
health long to continew in hast I umbly take my leave

Signed: Your worshipes in all duty and servis to commaund Richard Elton. London
the 21 of December 1627. *Autograph.*
Postscript: I hope you have ~~have~~ receaved your goodes sent by Walter long sence;

---

323   This represents a late stage in the Exchequer proceedings in the accompanying correspondence
nos. **191–193 [4237–4239]**, and hence is placed at this point. Walter was Chief Baron of the
Exchequer 1625–31 and Denham a puisne Baron 1617–39. The Lord Treasurer is the likely recipient: Sir James Ley, 1st Lord Ley 1624, 1st Earl of Marlborough 1626, was Lord Treasurer from
11 December 1624 until succeeded by Richard Weston on 15 July 1628.
324   A white wine associated with the port of Malaga.

they ware sent by the first that came, for the tempast was so sore that none could passe soner.

Endorsed: Mr Elton for a roondlett[325] of mallego

1 f., damaged.

196. [4244] *Sir Edmund Bacon to Sir William Spring and Sir William Spring to Sir Edmund Bacon [c. 1628]*[326]

Sir, Yesterday a pilfrey[327] was discovered to me to be done at the signe of the Crowne the weeke before Christmas, and hereupon I sent for dyvers to come before me; and yt is layde upon one Jhon Croxon, by Henry Croxon his brother, who was fownde to have given a ~~forehead-clo~~ coyfe, and a payre of gloves which weare stolne to a wench, and he sayth he had them of John Croxon to be delyvered to a suter of theyres. Nowe Sir I have stayd proceeding in this busynes bycause I am tolde that John Croxon who was formerly committed to the jayle of Bury ys gone for a souldyer. I would entreate you to knowe whether he remaynes in Friton still or not. Yf he be there, I shall bynde over the witnesses against him to give in theyr evidences, at the next quarter sessions,

Signed: Your assured frende Edmund Bacon. *Holograph.*

Addressed: To his honorable frende Sir William Spring knight

Sir, beeing here in the sheerehouse[328] when I receyved your letter and having neyther other paper or place convenient to write you an answer, I am inforced thus to doe itt. For Croxon supposed to have beene in the gayle, hee is not there nor knowne where, by the gayler. I should thinke itt safest to send him to the gayle if hee have no suerties for bayle until the next sessions, and to binde over the evidence, for though itt may bee probable that the partie with whome the goodes are found is butt accessory (and cannot bee tried without his principall), yett itt is best to have yt to the bench rather then to determine itt privately. If hee finde bayle (after examination of the partie and ~~wit~~ evidence) your man may take the recognusance in your name and mine (for two justices there must bee) and before you certifie itt to the sessions, lett him not forgett to have both our hands to it.

For your busines of Cotton I have mooved the judge who from any information of the minister and townsman could give noe resolution in itt, and finding itt a difficult case was loth to meddle in itt, yett the minister tells mee that Mr Sherman urges them to lett him moove itt agen, whether expecting a fee or a check I yett knowe not, but I beleave yett that uppon some farther examination of the wench wee shall yett find a justefiable way to settle hir; to which end I will (if I can) attend you soone.[329] Your weavors have thought fitt to commend their business and petition to the judg by the sherif but if hee doth propound itt I will second itt.

Signed: Your sarvant William Spring. *Holograph; on same sheet as previous.*

Addressed: To the honorable and my most honored frend Sir Edmund Bacon knight and barronet att Redgrave

---

325 A 'runlet' or cask.
326 This date is suggested by mention of the settlement dispute between Cotton and Thwaite, also dealt with in nos. **198–199**.
327 Meaning a robbery.
328 The shirehouse in Bury St Edmunds.
329 This refers to a dispute about which parish would have to admit 'settlement' and therefore to support a pauper girl, no doubt with an illegitimate child: see nos. **198, 199**.

2 ff.; fine seal impression of Bacon's arms, and remains of second seal impression.

197. [4242] *Christopher Vernon to Sir Edmund Bacon, 28 March 1628*

Noble Sir, I received your letter dated the 16 of this present March according to promise, for which I give you thankes. And now to give you an accompt what hath byn done in your busines since your departure. It may please you to understand that wee have obteyned his Majesties full direction for granting all the arreares according to the certificate of the Lord Th'r[330] and Mr Chancelor,[331] whereuppon theyr hon'rs have allso given warrant to Mr Attorny Generall for drawing uppe the grante accordingly in the name of Mr Shaw[332] and my self, with full power to release and discharge all sommes of money dew in the tyme of your grandfather or sithence. And the grante is now in drawing uppe by Mr Attorny. I shall see that your directions be observed touching Mr Noy, who shall peruse the paper booke before it be ingrossed, to see that it be every way sufficient for your discharge, which Mr Attorneys warrant (as it is drawne) will every way beare. Soe as I doubt not to have all thinges in a redines for you against your coming uppe, and Mr Attorny himself hath promised to take care that all thinges shalbe to give you satisfaction.

For Parliament newes, all thinges are yet in agitation, nothing concluded of.[333] The Higher house being now compleat of it [*sic*] members, the Erles of Arrundell, Hartf.[334] *and* Bristoll being called thether, and the Bishops of Canterbury and Lincoln. The E. of Bristoll sate in the house Fryday last,[335] and frendly salutations past betwixt the Duke[336] and him etc. They begane somewhat roughly in the lower house by Sir Robert Phillippes, but they proceed temperately in somuch as there is greate hope that this wilbe a consort-able [*sic*] and a comfortable Parliament. The necessytyes and pressing occasions of the tyme being propounded on his Majesties parte for quickening there resolutions, they are falne to certen queryes, viz. whether they have any thing to give or noe, before they grante subsydyes, in regard of the course lately held, for sending for imprisoning etc. refusers to paye etc. So as the first quere is whether by the lawes a mans liberty shalbe restrayned for refusing. 2. Whether he may be sent uppon forraine imployment as Sir Peter Hayman, Glandvile etc.[337] 3. Whether his Majestie hath any dominion over a mans goodes without a law which is touchinge the propriety of a mans goodes, and lastly

---

330 Sir James Ley, Earl of Marlborough, Lord Treasurer.
331 Sir Humphrey May, Chancellor of the Duchy of Lancaster; his second wife was Judith daughter of Sir William Poley of Boxted, Suffolk, and they had married at Bury St Edmunds (*ODNB, s.v.* May, Humphrey).
332 William Shaw, who worked with Vernon on the concealed lands suit. See *Suffolk in the XVIIth century*, pp. 287–8, quoting *HMC 12th report, Cowper MSS* I, 184.
333 For a useful account of the background to the events described here, see R. Cust, 'Charles I, the Privy Council and the Parliament of 1628', *Transactions of the Royal Historical Society*, 6th series 2 (1992), 25–50.
334 Hertford: William Seymour (1587–1660).
335 Friday 21 March.
336 George Villiers, Duke of Buckingham (1592–1623).
337 Sir Peter Hayman had been summoned before the Privy Council in 1622 for refusing to contribute to the benevolence raised for the defence of the Palatinate. As a punishment – and since he also refused to serve as a soldier at his own expense – he was made to accompany Sir Arthur Chichester's diplomatic mission to the Palatinate. Sir John Glanville was punished for protesting against the dissolution of the 1625 Parliament by being pressed into service later that year as secretary to the military expedition to Cadiz (*ODNB, s.v.* Hayman, Peter; Glanville, John).

concerning the billetting of soldyers. These thinges *or the most of them* they past through yesterday, and as is well hoped, shall have good satisfaction given therein from his Majestie touching the priveledges of the House and libertyes of the subjec[t] in this kinde, which will make them the more chearefull givers. There is a ~~fast~~ fast for the House and for London and Westminster appointed Saterday ~~nexte~~ *come sevenight*,[338] the generall fast for the Kingdome must have more distance. I beseeche God blesse all theyr proceedinges with good successe. And thus praying you to take in good parte this short digression I take your leave to remayne

Signed: Your poore freind and servant to the best of his power Christopher Vernon. London 28 *Martii* 1628. *Autograph.*[339]
Postscript: Sir Drew[340] is not of the House as you were pleased to signify, for which some of his frendes are sory. I pray doe me the favour as recommend my service to him when you see him.
Addressed: To his hon'ble good freind Sir Edmond Bacon knight and baronett at Redgrave
2 ff., slightly damaged; fine seal impression.

198. [4243] *Robert Reve to Sir Edmund Bacon, 20 July 1628*
Sir, Oure towne of Thwayte being an exedinge poor towne have had a twoe or three unjust chard[ges] put upon it within this twelve moonthes; and no[w] we are petitioners unto you that you will be [?ready] to assist us in this just cumplaynte. Owre n[ear] neyghbour justices we dare not mutch rely upon [for] some particuler respects. We know you will pity owre poverty and way the justnes of the cause as my Lorde hathe declared the lawe. The woman to us is a mere stranger, neyther had she or her husband ever lawfull setling or ever payd one peny rent in owre towne. She was last lawfully setled in Cotton and borne in Mendelsham, but neyther borne nor setled with us, and if she showld have bin putt upon us, we haveing noe towne howse nor any place to lodge *her*, must have bin forsed to build up a howse, which is fare beyond the habilety of owre towne. Sir I doubte not but you will be owre noble freind herein and the rather at my importunate and unmanerly instance. You knoue *you* may cummaund me to rest

Signed: Your faythfull servant Robert Reve. Thwayte 20 July 1628. *Holograph.*
Postscript: Sir for your better ease I have drawne the order which you may if you please subscribe, or else your clarke may wryte it over againe more fayer.
Addressed: To the righte nobe [*sic*] and my most honored freind Sir Edmund Bacon knight and baronet Redgrave
2 ff., slightly damaged; seal impression.

199. [4245] *Thomas Goodwin to Sir Edmund Bacon, 22 July 1628*
Noble Sir, I am sory this poore creature made your appoyntment to heere her cause no sooner knowen unto me. I wold moste willin[gly] have weighted uppon you, to have informed you of [the] whole passage, but my present occasions are such that [I] cannot attend you *at this present* haveing no knowledg of it but th[is] morneing at 8 of the clocke. Yett you may accordi[ng as] is desiered receive

---
[338] Saturday 5 April.
[339] The friendly tone of this letter is notable after the recent major litigation between the two men.
[340] Sir Dru Drury.

some touch of it, by these papers [here] inclosed wher the truth of the cause in her petiti[on is] sett downe which moved the court of Sessions at Eas[ter] last to make an order for the setling of this poore woman in Thayte according unto which order she repayering to the towne to be provided for, as was required, the townesmen have not only contemned the sessions authority but taken *away from that benefitt which inableth her to complayne for further redresse, yett by providence a coppy of the session order I doe likewise send hereinclosed. Thus recomending my best service and respect unto you I will ever rest

Signed: Your humbele servant to be commaunded Thomas Goodwyne. Lytle Stonham this 22 of July 1628. *Holograph.*
Addressed: To his *noble and* much honored coronell[341] Sir Edmund Bacon knyght and barronett
2 ff.; seal impression.

200. [4246] *Abraham Viell to Sir Edmund Bacon, 14 August 1628*
Noble Sir, According to your worshipfull deriction, I have bought a drume and have sent it by the Berry carriear this weeke; it is in a barrill case, and locked with a pad locke. I bought it of one of the drumers of our artilery gardon;[342] it hath ben all oon his drume this nine years to my knowleg, and is estemed to be so good a drume as any is in all England. Ther is a small cracke in the rime, next to the nales, but hee dothe warrantt that it shall never goe any ferther, for it hath bine so ever since it was made. I cased him to tacke out one of the heads, that I might looke in to the rime, and I found it to be very sound. If I had not had some great trust in him, I could not have bought it of him for any mony. I have sent the key of the locke hear inclosed. If your worshipfull have any other service to comand me att any other time, or nowe, I shall be ready att your worshipfull comand. Soe with my service to your worshipfull remb. I *leave* you to the protitition [*sic*] of the most heigh, and rest

Signed: Your worshipfull to comand to his power Abraham Viell. London this 14th August 1628. *Holograph.*
Postscript: it is sertinly thought (and also reported) that we shall have pece with Spaine, wich I thinke will be good for us in thes times.

	£	s	d
For a drume and stickes	2–10–0		
For a case and padlock	0–08–0		
For a porter	0–00–6		
	2–18–6		

1 f., slightly damaged; traces of seal.

201. [4247] *Henry Montagu, Earl of Manchester, Lord Privy Seal, to Sir Edmund Bacon and Thomas Goodwin, 5 May 1629*
After my hartie commendations; I am informed by Mr Faweltier that one Coppin an attorney att lawe hath raised upp an unjust suite against him in the name of one Eminges a turner, who receving into his howse one Raven thatt did runne awaie

---

341 Meaning 'colonel'.
342 The Artillery Garden in London. This was one of the places appointed in 1614 by the Privy Council for the newly formed London Artillery Company to drill (see *Acts of the Privy Council 1613–14*, pp. 667–8), and Viell and the drummer may have been members of the Company.

with another mans wife, and with one Grove his apprentice, and left his owne wife and five smalle children to the charge of the parishe, were all harboured by the said Eminges then not knowing any one of them, they rooveing out of another countrey full fortie miles from their owne habitation, who beeing pursued by diverse inhabitants of the towne from whence they fledd, and they repairing to Mr Faweltier with a petition subscribed by a Justice of Peace, and by the minister and other of the said towne for the apprehending and punishing the said fugitives, and for the resending them backe for the releeffe of the said Ravens wife and his poore children, did obteine a warrant from Mr Faweltier for the finding out of the said parties. By vertue whereof the said apprentice was brought beefore him, who upon his examination did confesse that his master Raven and his harlott did lye in one and the same bedd as man and wife in the howse of the said Eminges for diverse weekes together, and that they were then fledd awaie. And did then also acknowledge thatt he had constantly reported the said harlott to bee his masters lawfull wife, impudently alleadging that hee was bound to keepe all his masters secreates, and beeing charged to make knowne where Raven and his harlott then were, hee did scornefully reply thatt hee would nott reveale itt though he knewe itt. For which foule misdemeanor Grove beeing *particeps criminis*, Mr Faweltier did committ him as by lawe hee might, which committment itt pleased the Judge to approve in open court, the which tryall would not bee brought to hearing butt by Mr Faweltier his humble suite unto the Judge himselfe, nor could hee prevaile therein untille the very end of the Assizes, so as itt was the last cause thatt was called upon. And after full opening of the cause on the pl't's side, and the Judge his declaring the imprisonment to bee just, hee did referre the ending thereof to *him and* Sir Edmond Bacon and to Mr Goodwyn and did curteously write to you both in Mr Faweltiers justification and favour. Now for thatt I have upon examination beene made privie heretofore ~~of~~ unto many lewde partes doune and comitted against many men by the said Coppin *and* ~~unto his~~ his desert of punishment for his wicked practizes against Mr Fawlther, and against publique justice, as also to Mr Faweltiers integritye and painefull endeavors in his Majesties service, I have thought fitt to informe you of thone and thother, assuring you that itt seemeth strange unto mee thatt Eminges keeping an howse of baudery and pretending Grove to be his apprentice sett over by Raven should dare so injuriously to sue a justice of peace for doeing the duety of his place, in whose power itt was to have punished him sevearly for the same. Whereof I hartely praie yow and doe presume you wilbee pleased to take good consideration and duely to respect a discreete and painefull magestrate whome I have a longe tyme knowne to have right well deserved, so as I wilbee ready to incourage and countenance him in the due execution of his Majesties service. Thus assuring myselfe of your most speciall care herein for the better furthering of publique justice, and the speedy restreyning of the said Eminges his insolencye, I bidd you very hartely farewell. And rest

Signed: Your very loving frend H. Manchester. White Hall, 5 *Maii* 1629. *Autograph.*
Addressed: To the right worshipfull my very loving friends Sir Edmond Bacon knight and barronett and Thomas Goodwyn esquier.
2 ff.; fine seal impression.

202. [4248] *John Dinley to Sir Edmund Bacon, 26 June/6 July 1629*[343]

Sir, All this time that I have bin silent, was not that I laid aside your commaunds, but rather that I was searching within myselfe the nearest waie to effect them. At last they are done, I hope according to your owne desire. Sooner they might have bin but that the Queen and Prince of Orenge[344] were farr from this place, and both asunder, insomuch that it required some time, for me to passe betwixt them. The conclusion is, the Prince of Orenge bad me write unto you to send him when you pleased; he should *be* welcome, as all thinges were from the recommendation of the Queen. He liked my description of him in all thinges, but his age, which he thought some what too old for a page, but I told him he might the sooner serve him as a souldier when he saw capacitie in him, for that was his owne desire, and the designe of his freinds. I have acquainted Sir Henry Wotton with other particulers, which may concerne his comming over, and his admission.[345] I shall be very to glad to see and assist him the best I can, hoping to receive many thanckes for introducing him; for whome I assured the Queen, she should not need to feare any dishonour, having bin bred up in your noble familie, wherin are and alwaies have bin, so many examples of vertue. As you thincke I have served you in this, so I beseech you spare mee not in any thing els within my compasse. I am borne to do honest services, and it is my comfort, when I may do them for gentlemen of honour, such as you are knowne to bee, and shalbee ever so esteemed by

Signed: Your humble and faithfull servant John Dinley. Leyden 6 July *stylo novo* 1629. *Holograph.*
Addressed: To my honourable and worthy freind, Sir Edmund Bacon knight esq.
2 ff.; fine seal impression.

203. [4249] *Richard Elton to Sir Edmund Bacon, 23 October 1629*

May it please your worshipe, I have receaved your letter and £69 19s 6d and by your direcktiones have under neath made an account with the acquittances hear hear in clossed. Mr Reades was 20s more then your bill fol *for* the lining and fassing of your toney satten dublet. Sence your bill was delivered, the price of stirgine is 30s a kadg. It is very good but noe firkines to be had, because the price is so deare. I have sent a pound of burrace[346] by this bearrer as cheap as mony could bey and it cost 11s 6d. Thus praying for your worshipes long life and happey dayes I umbley take my leave and rest

Signed: Your worshipes umble servaunt in all duty to commaund Richard Elton. London the 23 of October 1629. *Holograph.*
Postscript:

---

[343] Dinley was a long-term servant to Elizabeth, exiled queen of Bohemia, sister of Charles I, who was resident in the Netherlands, and who is the queen referred to in the letter: see *Calendar of State Papers Domestic 1629–1631*, p. 528. Dinley specifies that he is dating his letter New Style, i.e. by the Gregorian Calendar in use in the United Provinces of the Netherlands; this was ten days ahead of the Julian Calendar still in use in England. Hence 6 July translates in England as 26 June.

[344] Henry Frederick, Prince of Orange, married to another sister of Charles I.

[345] Wotton was an old acquaintance and a supporter of the king of Bohemia, and had been English ambassador to the United Provinces in 1614–15.

[346] Meaning 'borax'.

	£	s	d
Payd unto Mr Bynnion[347] silkeman in full payment	18–	0–0	
Payd unto Mr Read mearsler[348] in full payment	15–	6–0	
R. on my owne account for all formor billes deliverd	36–	15–0	
Payd for a grosse of tobacco pipes sence delivered and a box to send them in	0–	5–0	
For a pound of burrace now sent	0–	11–6	
R. £69–19–6d	70–	17–6	
So ther remaynes due unto me unpayd	0–	18–0	

Addressed: To the right worshipfull Sir Edmund Bacon knight and Barronet at Readgrave.

2 ff.; fine seal impression.

204. **[4250]** *Richard Elton to Sir Edmund Bacon, 25 November 1629*

May it please your worshipe, by your formore letter having now receaved an other, gave me order to bey wines, and other provision from Mr Nicholas are now all sent. The wine was delivered unto Edward Rivatt master of the Hey.[349] The parseles are under written, I hope all to your worshipes good liking, but as it[350] ther is noe new wine to be had. I have bine three times with Mr Pey at Court and likewise with Mr Letchland, who lookes every ower for some for the King's use, but proclamation was that none should come untill the first of Febrewary; it[351] I doubt not but to send you some be fore Cristmas. The fish mungers bill is heare in closed who did under take to furnish the hollen chese as well as the rest you then write for in your last letter, but I have sent but one, fearring it will prove like Viales chease, but the soming up of his bill makes a menes of his price, which I did refuse to pay unlesse you like it, but if you will have me trey further you may have what you please, and I will doe my best servis ther in that or aney thing else you will please to commaund me in. So praying for your worshipes good health I umbly take my leave ever rest

Signed: Your worshipes in all duty to commaund Richard Elton. London the 25 of November 1629. *Holograph.*[352]

Postscript:

	£	s	d
Rest unpayd of your formore account	8–	18–0	
For a hodgeshed of ould shearro sack	11–	5–0	
For 10 gallenes and a pottell of cannary 4s 8d	2–	9–0	
For 11 gallenes 3 quartes of muscadine 4s	2–	7–0	
For 2 Rondletes	0–	4–0	
For porters, copers and sponing	0–	3–0	
For cassing and pack thred	0–	1–6	

---

347 George Bynnion.
348 Possibly a 'mercer'.
349 For 'hoy', i.e. a ship?
350 For 'yet'.
351 For 'yet'.
352 Cf. a further transaction in which Richard Elton acted as agent for Sir Edmund in securing liveries for servants in Paul's Churchyard, 18 February 1630: *Bacon handlist*, no. **4005**; cf. also bills from Elton of 3 December 1628 and 18 January 1630, *Bacon handlist*, nos. **3133, 3153**.

For a car man	0– 1–0
For canvas to pack them in	0– 7–0
	17–15–6

Addressed: To the right worshipfull Sir Edmund Bacon knight and Barronet at Readgrave.
Endorsed: Londoners bills and acquitt. dd. to me by my master
2 ff.; fine seal impression.
Enclosed slip **205.** **[4251]:**

Mr Nicholas bill

One ould Holland cheese waighing	
11 lb 4 oz at 8d per lb is	00 07 05
A potle of small Ollives	00 03 04
4 1b of Genoa capers	00 04 08
3 lb of Genoa Anchoves	00 06 00
The 3 barells	00 01 02
	00 19 07[353]

1 f.

206. **[4252]** *Sir Thomas Woodhouse to Sir Edmund Bacon, 5 December 1638*
Noble Patrone, *Post varios casus post tot discrimina rerum*; our businesse is now brought to a parenthesis, I dare not say to a period, but we have defended the foorte of our trust and [*word illegible erased*] *testament* against the assaults of our troublesome adversarie so longe as we could with loyaltie befittinge English subjects. For to oppose regall orders and legal decrees, shall ever be as far from our dispositions as London from Edenburghe.

I have had no leisure all this tearme untill now to send you any newes, but now I beginn; yt is reported by the last packett which came late from Maunchester, that the Prince of Hungarie[354] will laye downe his armes for a season, and suffer your two servants to goe downe to their garrison in poore Thetfoorde, from whence they intend after some convenient tyme of rest to make their approache at Redgrave, and there to salute the noble Governor with hoate Hart-illerie of fervent affection; here companie cutts me off, I must owe you the rest *è cosi Dio voglia chè Vestra Signoria sta sana et alegra semprè*

Signed: Your inseperable servant Thomas Wodehowse. *10bris* 5 1638.[355] *Holograph.*
Addressed: To my most honored Sir Edmond Bacon knight and Baronett.
Endorsed by George Gardiner: a letter from Sir Thomas Woodhouse: June 1638
2 ff.; fine seal impression.

---

353 The addition is wrong; it should be 22s 7d.
354 Probably a jocular reference to Sir Henry Hungate, if the content of this letter can be related to the business described in the following letter (no. **207 [4253]**).
355 It is difficult to be certain about this date: 5 December 1638 would relate well to the date of 6 December in the following letter, no. **207 [4253]**. The facetious tone of the whole letter makes it difficult to interpret, but it almost certainly refers to the great Hungate legal dispute which was preoccupying the two men. The metaphors to do with Scotland may simply refer to the tension during summer/autumn 1638, which did not break out into open plans for an English invasion of Scotland until January 1639. The endorsed date June 1638 is not reliable; there are various mistakes in George Gardiner's endorsements of this batch of letters (nos. **206 [4252]** onwards), which must have been examined and arranged in 1648.

207. [4253] *John Godbold to Sir Edmund Bacon, 6 December 1638*

Sir, I have nowe at the last finished your great worke touching Sir Henry Hungate. The decree is passed ~~and~~ the assurances made and the overplus mony payd; accordingly I have sent you the assurance to your selfe and the other 2 executors of £120 *per annum* which in the first place is to save you harmeles, and then to the use of Sir Henry Hungates sonnes successively in tayle as is limitted by the will of the Lady Caesar. That assurance doth consist of an indenture of bargayne and sale for a moiety and a grante of the revertion to the said uses. And then Sir William Russell assigneth his morgage for 99 yeres to the 3 executors for £400 parte of the mony in your handes payd, Sir Henry Hungates consent. And for your security ag't St. Katherins, Sir William Russell is bound as suerty with Sir Henry Hungate to save you harmeles ag't St. Katherins[356] to the value of £300, and Sir Henry Hungat decreed to satisfy the rest and to make it good out of the terme of 40 yeres limitted to the executors in the grand conveyance if there be cause, but not till the executors be saved harmeless if any other charge should happen. Soo as every way you are sufficiently provided for and well freed of a troublesome and tedious imployment and the decree doth warrant all which is done, which being in a coercive way as you may see by the decree in Sir Thomas Woodhouses handes, you are freed allso ag't the children from further account, they being allso parties to the decree and a gardian appoynted by the Court ~~to~~ defend them therein. I have sent you Barbars leas for £200 rent which though it be not expired, yet a newe leas is to be made *to Tristram Staply a newe tenant* by the 3 executors when it is required ~~to a newe tenant~~ who hath contracted to have it at £120 rent *per annum* and as may appeare by the grand conveyance. As for the incumbrances in Sir Henry Hungates answer in Chancery, they are all discharged and soe manifested to Sir Thomas Woodhouse and my selfe, and soe declared by the decree and the writs cancelled and delivered up. As for the particulers, I wrote them in the margent of Sir Henry Hungates answer, the copy wherof Sir Thomas Woodhouse hath. To relate unto you the particuler passages and difficultyes would exceed the boundes of a letter, but uppon your viewe of the decree (which I had the happines to be trusted to drawe for want of a register) you may fynd I lefte out nothing which might be for your safety, and soe I provided in your grand assuraunce to bind Sir Henry Hungat in strong covenauntes to performe all thinges with you and his children. He nowe desireth a letter of attourny to collect some small detes due to his mother which I wish would defray one halfe of his dilapidations, and that you may please to let him have into the bargayne, for he hath payd well for it. And as touching a leas of ~~St K~~ parte of the possessions of St. Katherin he promiseth to doe his best endeavor to get it for his children at his owne charge, but the event of that wilbe doubtfull to what good passe he can bring it. But it will not concerne you unles it proveth of value and than you may therin doe a further helpe to the children as executor if neede requireth. Sir Thomas Woodhouse hath all the writinges but these I send you by your servant whoe hath carefully performed his trust and weighty imployment. My task is nowe done and all is well as can be desired. I knowe not what we could have added which we have not but am assured if we had gone any other methode much troble and vexation would have ensued. It yet remaynes that I shold testify my hearty desires of your heath [*sic*] wherof if any man can exceed myne I shall nevertheles remayne in all due respectes and faythfull service

---

[356] The Hospital of St Katherine by the Tower, London, in which Sir Julius Caesar had taken a particular interest: see Hill, *Julius Caesar*, p. 256.

Signed: Yours John Godbold *sexto Decembris* 1638. Serjeantes Inne, Chaunc. Lane[357] *Holograph.*

Addressed: To his much honored Sir Edmund Bacon knight and Baronet at Redgrave Hall.

Endorsed by George Gardiner: Serjeant Godboldes letter concerning Sir Henry Hungates busines, as the Decree etc. 6 December 1638

2 ff.; fine seal impression.

208.   [4254] *Sir Thomas Woodhouse to Sir Edmund Bacon, 27 April 1639*

Sir, I am sure by this tyme, you are saluted with a citation out of the Arches, which I hope will hasten your intended jorney to London, where I beseech you soone to choose an honest Procter (if any be) to appeare for us both. I being joyned with you in theis unhappie troubles (God willinge) I will not fayle to share with you in the chardge and travells of them; howsoever this tearme I̶-[*two words erased illegible*] I must entreat your excuse; for by reason of my over early goinge abroade after my sharpe feaver I feele my self brought backe into an aguishe disposition, which deterrs me from a London voyage untill my health may be better confirmed. Sir Henry Hungate hath left us naked, without any wrightings to defend this sute; and we must labour to bringe the same to a sentence with all safe expedition, for the avoydinge of chardges, which now must be layd out of our owne purses. The bond of Sir William Russell for £300 towards yt, was left with you, the rest whatsoever yt be, must come out of the smale portion of lande assured upon the children. Sir, you now see that daynger of St. Katherins debt, doth n̶o̶w̶ fall upon us, which I did feare from the beginninge; wee must endeavour to redeeme our selves, at as smale a̶n̶ ̶e̶x̶p̶e̶n̶s̶e̶ *a rate* as we may, for I doubt most of the chardge will be oure owne. If you please to reviewe the decree out of the Court of Request, you may *there* see how violently we were over ruled upon this poynt (*O tempora! O mores!*)[358] Sir I pray let the indenture be carried up with you, wherein we are chardged to employ certein moneys raysed out of Fremnells for one of Sir John Caesars daughters; it is an office I wish we were free from, and deserves a quere of some good leardned [*sic*] advise. I beseech you take yt into your secound thoughts and so I remayne

Signed: Your entirely lovinge servant Thomas Wodehowse. Aprill 27th 1639 *Holograph.*

Addressed: To my ever honored Sir Edmund Bacon knight and Baronet at Redgrave.

Endorsed by George Gardiner: a letter from Sir Thomas April 1639

2 ff.; remains of seal impression.

209.   [4255] *John Godbold to Sir Edmund Bacon, 3 May 1639*

Sir, I rec. your letters and caused an apparance to be entred for your selfe and Sir Thomas Woodhouse according to your direction, and the next weeke or else soe soone as need requireth will take forth a commission for your answers. Meane while let it suffice that I have given you notice that I have that farre proceeded, and being heartily sorry for your inhability to travayle, however this occasion would not have enforced a journey, but all may be done your absence [*sic*]. Sir Henry

---

357   That is, Chancery Lane in London.
358   Cicero, *In Catilinam* I, i, 1: 'O what times! What conduct!'

Hungate is out of towne but I will write to him and put the [?]care uppon him which though he neglect you have 2 good securityes for your indemnity and soe with my best service and hearty wishes of your wellfares I rest

Signed: Your ready servant John Godbold, Serjeantes Inne, Chaunc. Lane *tertio Maii* 1639. *Holograph.*
Postscript: Mr George Gaell is the proctor.
Addressed: To his much honored Sir Edmund Bacon knight and Baronet at Redgrave.
Endorsed by George Gardiner: Serjeant Godboldes letter May 1639
2 ff.; remains of seal.

210. [4256] *Sir Thomas Woodhouse to Sir Edmund Bacon, 24 March 1642*

Much honored Sir, I received your late expresse about the rents of Fremnalls,[359] to which I must truly answere that my depencie [*sic*] was upon your care in that particulare; for since the last receipt thereof by your servant my fellowe Gardiner, the rest (for ought I know) remeineth in Mr Humphries handes the farmore; which sum may be easely computed, from the tyme of his last payment, and I desire you wilbe pleased to call for the same togethere in Easter-tearme, when as I hope in God to see you here in London.

My want of health and leisure in this tyme of publicke trouble and distraction[360] hath rendred me unactive in my private businesse; wherefore I must entreat your pardon herein, untill we may be hapely permitted to adjorne and then God willinge I shall not fayle to wayt uppon you in any matter you will vouchsafe to commande,

Signed: Your faythfull lovinge servant Thomas Wodehowse. Westminster Marche 24 1641 *Holograph*
Addressed: For his right noble friend Sir Edmound Bacon knight and Baronet.
Endorsed by George Gardiner: Sir Thomas Wodehouse [?]letter 24 March 1647 [*sic*]
2 ff.; fine seal impression

211. [4257] *Richard Humphrey to Sir Edmund Bacon, 17 February 1643*

Noble Sir, These are to certifie yow that I have not my rent as yett; the tymes are soe troublesome that I cannot receave my owne rents neither have I sold any corne as yett to make itt. By the grace of God yow shall have itt all, shortly after Lady Day; in the meane tyme I make account to speake to Sir Thomas Woodhouse about itt. I am dayley in danger of haveing my goods taken away by the plunderers that I dare not ride to London to take any course for moneys till the tymes be more settled which I hope will be shortly. Sir my wife and I present yow with our best love and service soe God keepe yow and ever commaund

---

359 Tremnals, Hemnals or Fremnalls Park in the parish of Downham, Essex: ''Tis vulgarly called Frimnells' (Morant, *Essex* I, 206). This was a property of the Caesar family which would cause Sir Edmund Bacon much trouble over the next few years. See Dame Anne Caesar's attempt to raise a dowry from the property, 4 November 1645 (though note the wrong location in Kent): *Bacon handlist*, no. **2811**.

360 By now all Ireland was in revolt against English rule, and the king was embarked on a tour of northern England trying to rally support.

Signed: Your cosen and servant Richard Humfrey. Fremnolls 17 of February 1642
Holograph.
Addressed: To his much honored cosen Sir Edmund Bacon knight and Barronett.
Endorsed by George Gardiner: Mr Humfrey 16 February 1642
2 ff.; traces of seal.

212.   [4258] *Lady Anne Caesar to Sir Edmund Bacon, 26 March 1643*

Sir, With aknowlledgment of your many noble favors and the presentment of my
humble thancks and servise, I beeseech you bee pleasd to helpe mee with thoes
monies due nowe at our Lady day (Sir it is 700 pounds) for wich I shall remaine

Signed: Your oblidged kinswoman and humble sarvant Anne Caesar. March the
26 1643. *Holograph.*
Addressed: To her noble kinsman Sir Edmond Bacon knit and Barronet.
Endorsed by George Gardiner: The La. Caesars letter 25 [*sic*] Mar. 1643
2 ff.; remains of seal.

213.   [4259] *Philip Woodhouse to Lady Anne Caesar [?May/June 1643]*[361]

Honor'd Madam, I receiv'd your Ladyships letter by my cozen your sonn, to which
I am sorry I can returne no fitter answer at this tyme, being hastily importun'd to
accompany a freind at this instant *a journey* into another country, but especially
that I can not satisfy your Ladyships desires, being heer in a country farr from
home so as I have not wherwithall by me *to serve you* nor indeed were I in a
place wher I could, am I fully ~~satisfyed~~ resolv'd whither I might do it out of that
already receiv'd for the benefitt of some of yours, being responsible to them for it.
If I may do it *safely* I shall be very gladd to serve your Ladyship which I will
be advis'd in, as soon as I can conveniently, being suddainely going into Norfolk.
In the mean whyle I desir~~ing~~*e* your pardon and best acceptation of thes hasty
scribles from

Signed: Your truly honoring kinsman and servant Philip Woodehous. Bedford-
shire. *Holograph.*
Addressed: For his honor'd kinswoman the Lady Caesar in Hertfordshire.
Endorsed by George Gardiner: a letter from Mr Phillip Woodhouse with a letter
from the La. Caesar in it[362]
2 ff.; seal impression.

214.   [4260] *Lady Anne Caesar to Sir Edmund Bacon [?May/June 1643]*

Sir, My humble servis presented with the aknowlledgment of your favors. I have
as I was dirrickted by you, intreated those money (nowe due) of my cosin Wood-
hous: at our Lady Day I sent: but had noe a*n*swer. A bout a month sence I sent
againe and received this letter, which hath putt mee out of hope to have them of
him. Sir I beesech you *be* pleasde according to your wonted goodnes to helpe
mee and I shall remaine your most obliged kinswoman and humble servant

Signed: Anne Caesar. *Holograph.*
Addressed: To her noble kinsman Sir Edmond Bacon kni*gh*t and Barronet.
2 ff.; traces of seal.

---

361   The content of the next two letters suggests a date rather more than a month after letter no. **213**.
362   The letter to which the endorsement refers is clearly no. **214 [4260]**.

215. [4261] *Richard Humphrey to Sir Edmund Bacon, 30 November 1643*

Sir, I have received yowr letter wherein yow write for yowr rent due for Fremnells, but I well hoped I should have received withall some expressions from yow and Sir Thomas Woodhowse in answer to my severall requests made formerly unto yow for to give me some ease in my to extreame hard bargaine which was to deare by £50 a yeare when times were at the best (Judg then what it is now the farme consistinge most of tillage, and I have had all my horses taken away, whoe can bowldlie and trulie say am noe delinquent either in word or acction, and have paid all payments whatsoever as it is well knowne).[363] But it seemes the present necessitie was the cause and I hop I shall obtaine some order from the Comittie for sattisfaction for them.[364] But my request unto yow and Sir Thomas Wood-howse once more is, that yow will take into consideration the damage I sustain in howlding the farme. ~~with~~ And if possible yow can in some convenient time dispose of it to some other; if yow neither will nor can, pray advise together of abateinge me £50 *per annum* (for I protest I cannot see that I can lett it within £60 of what I pay yow) and then the remainder due I shall pay speedily, otherwise I can but answer yowr sute uppon yowr covenant, which I hope yow will not put me toe, in regard I was a young man little knoweing the world when I ventured uppon it, then haveing married the graundchild of her whose guift it was whome certainely would never have willed that we should howld it at to deere a rate (allmost to owr undoeing) in regard of the much money I owe allready and in theise times am forct to abate rent in everie farme of my owne not withstanding a lease under seale. Let me and my wife intreat yow to speake unto Sir Thomas Woodhowse of this, and then be pleased to write me both your intentions, and we shall both pray for your health and happines both heere and heereafter; soe rests

Signed: Your poore kinsman and servant Richard Humfrey. Fremnolls the 30 of November 1643 *Holograph.*
Addressed: To his much honored freind and kinsman Sir Edmund Bacon knight at Redgrave.
Endorsed by George Gardiner: Mr Humfreys letter 30 November 1643
2 ff.; traces of seal.

216. [4262] *Ann Humphrey to Sir Edmund Bacon [?April 1644]*[365]

Sir, My humbell sarvist remenbred unto you. I had thought befor this tim to hav bine a ~~siu~~ sutor unto you in my husbands behalf and myne about the leacse of Fremnalls which wee hold that you and Sir Thommas Woodhowses would be pleased to release Mrs [*sic*] Humfrey of itt and to take it into your owne hands and desposed of it to som other for I find it puts ous much ove[366] behind hand, Mr Humfrey being left by his fathar some monys to paye and having rune into som ingeagments since himself which ~~himself~~ will speeddely fall oppon him and his

---

[363] On the acute problems of finance and military supply in Essex in 1643, particularly on seizure of horses, see C. Holmes, *The Eastern Association in the English Civil War* (Cambridge, 1974), pp. 79–81, 97–9.

[364] This letter was written in the aftermath of the crisis of October 1643, when Newport Pagnell was briefly captured by the Royalists: Holmes, *Eastern Association*, p. 103. 'The Committie' is the Parliamentary County Committee for Essex.

[365] The reference to Michaelmas shows that this was written after the other due day of the year, Lady Day, 25 March, but the content suggests that it is prior to the resolution of the difficulty over the Fremnolls lease indicated in no. **217 [4263]**, written on 2 May.

[366] For 'over'?

132

stock. My humble request unto you and Sir T*h*omas Woodhowse is that you will be pleased to send over as speedly as you can and seas on the stoke on the ground for rentt allreddy due and att michalmas to take it into your hands. Sir for my granmother sake and mine deny not tha request of hear that is

Signed: Your sarvant and kinswoman and servant Ann[e] Humfrey. *Holograph.*
Addressed: To her much honored freind Sir Edmund Bacon knight and Barronet att Redgrave in Norfolke.
Endorsed by George Gardiner: Mrs Humfreys letter
2 ff., slightly damaged.

217.   [4263] *Richard Humphrey to Sir Edmund Bacon, 2 May 1644*

Sir, I have bin with Sir Thomas Woodhowse and delivered him yowr letter and he seemeth verry willing to joyne with yow in doeing me all lawfull favour in the request I make unto yow, but desiers time to advise with councell which way it may be best donn with safetie to yowr selves, which at present he hath not time to doe with by reason of his being at the Committee,[367] but he promiseth me to doe something in it assoone as possible he can wayte upppon yow: and when yow both shalbe advised and resolved what to doe in it, there shalbe a messenger sent to me. Now my humble suite unto yow is that yow wilbe pleased to expedite it and be as favourable to me as lawfully yow may. I have left the particulars of my request with Sir Thomas according to his desier, whoe will bring them with him I presume when he comes to waite uppon yow. Sir by reason I was like to have noething donn in it now, and in regard of some buseness I have in the Ile of Ely, I could not retourne to Redgrave to give yow thankes for owr kinde entertainement and yowr favours which I hope yow wilbe pleased to excuse. My brother Bernard and the other gentleman present their service humble service unto yow, and I rest

Signed: Your humble servant and kinsman Richard Humfrey. Norwich 2 May 1644 *Holograph.*
Addressed: To his much honord freind and kinsman Sir Edmund Bacon knight and baronet. Redgrave.
Endorsed by George Gardiner: Mr Humfreys letter 2 March [*sic*] 1644
2 ff.; seal torn off.

218.   [4264] *Richard Humphrey to Sir Edmund Bacon, 2 June 1644*

Noble Sir, I have receaved yowrs of the 29 of May last and doe give yow manie thancks for yowr favours and returninge me an answer, but I had hoped that Sir Thomas Woodhowse would have advised a little with a conscionable counceller as with a learned, in my soe reasonable requests; and I must hope yett that by yowr good perswasion and my speakeing with him againe att London I shall find some ease in abatement, consideringe these hard tymes for tennants, and my extreame losses by being soe. My brother Bernard presents his service to yow and hath sent by this bearer the nutts and 2 recipes for the goute with a roule of salve with his prayers for a good effect. My wife presents her service to yow. Soe ceaseth to trouble yow any farther

Signed: Your humble servant and kinsman Richard Humfrey. Fremnolls 2 of June 1644 *Holograph.*

---

367   That is, the Parliamentary County Committee for Norfolk.

Addressed: To his much honored freind Sir Edmund Bacon knight and barronett att Redgrave.
Endorsed by George Gardiner: Mr Humfrey 2 *Junii* 1644
2 ff.; traces of seal.

219. **[4265]** ***Mary Warren to Joseph Hall, Bishop of Norwich, 6 March 1645: as patron of the living of Brandon Ferry for one turn, she petitions Hall for the institution of George Warren MA to the rectory on the resignation of Edmund Cartwright DD.***

Reverendo in Christo patri ac domino, Domino Josepho providentia divina Norvicensis Episcopo obedientiam et reverentias tanto patri debitas cum honore. Cum ecclesia parochialis de Brandonferry in comitatu Suff. et diocesi vestra vacari nuper contigerit per voluntariam resignationem Magistri Edmundi Cartwright Sacrae Theologiae Professoris[368] et advocatio ac libera dispositio eiusdem dictae ecclesiae pro hac vice ad me spectat:

ego Maria Warren vidua, vera et indubitata patrona dictae ecclesiae pro hac unica vice, dilectum mihi in Christo Georgium Warren in artibus magistrum reverentiae vestrae praesento, rogans, et humiliter petens ut dictum Georgium Warren in dictum rectoriam de Brandonferry cum suis juribus universis instituas et induci facias caeteraque omnia quae paternitati vestrae in hac parte incumbant facienda, proficias cum favore. In cujus rei testimonium manum et sigillum meum praesentibus apposui.

Datum hoc sexto die mensis Martii anno regis Caroli etc. vicesimo annoque Domini 1644.

Signed: Mary Warren *Autograph: text probably in hand of George Warren.*
Postscript, holograph of Hall: Exhibita mihi fuit haec praesentatio per Magistrum Georgium Warren: Martii 12 1644. Joseph Norvic.[369]
2 ff.; seal impression of Mary Warren.

220. **[4266]** ***Sir John Caesar[370] to Sir Edmund Bacon, 6 April 1646***
Honorable Sir, The accumulation of your cardinall favours makes mee blush at my owne incapacitie of giving requitall, butt thus much I dare saye without vanitie, you could not have conferd them upon any that more highly aesteems you. My wife often in her sicknesse desird me to bring my daughter to kisse your handes, hoping you would bee pleased for their sakes, who living lovd and honored you, to afford your effectuall furtherance for her preferment to some deserving husband. I promised to fullfill her will, butt will not attempt it, without your invitation, therefore desire to knowe your pleasure. My selfe and children present our humble respectes, beseeching the Allmightie to poure downe the choicest of his blessinges

---

[368] Cartwright is recorded as having been sequestered from his living of Norton by the earl of Manchester in 1645: A.G. Matthews (ed.), *Walker revised ...* (Oxford, 1948), p. 330.

[369] See a further transaction of 1651 involving the Brandon advowson by Mrs Warren, involving Martin Warren of Fordham (Cambs.), clerk: *Bacon handlist*, nos. **2815, 2816**. Martin Warren had been sequestered from his livings of Drinkstone and Worlington by Parliament during the 1640s. He mentioned his brother George (clerk) in his will of 1655: Matthews (ed.), *Walker revised*, p. 347. All these connections with clergy who were Royalist or unacceptable to Parliament show what a defiant gesture to the Parliamentarian establishment of East Anglia Mrs Warren's presentation represented. It is unlikely that the presentation of George Warren took effect.

[370] Son of Sir Julius Caesar.

upon your selfe and noble familie; to his most gracious protection I betake you, resting ever your humble servant most readie to receive your commands

Signed: John Caesar. Hydehall[371] this 6 of Aprill 1646 *Holograph.*
Addressed: To the honorable and worthily honored Sir Edmund Bacon knight and baronett with my humble service at Redgrave.
Endorsed by George Gardiner: Sir John Caesars letter about his daughter: 6 April 1646
2 ff.; fine seal impression.

221.   [4267] *William Beaumont to Sir Edmund Bacon and Philip Woodhouse, 7 July 1647*

Honorable Gentlemen, upon the decease of the Lady Cesar whose executors you are, there was due to me £18 2s 3d for prosecutinge of the cause of *Quare Impedit* against the Bishopp of Norwich, Thomas Springe and William Strode Clarke for the Church of Braddenham, which suite concerned the tithe of all the land late Hoogans, questioned by Downes and Springe.[372] I did once in Chauncerie Lane in the presence of Mr Earle informe Sir Edmond Bacon of this debt, and he comanded me by Mr Earles advise to sue Mr Strode to exigent for the execution money. I did so, and Mr Strode stand outlawed at your suites, but cold not be arested beinge then universitie orator of Oxford. I after made my addresses to Sir Thomas Woodhowse; he told me that Sir Henry Hungate had undertaken to pay all the Ladies debts. I wayted often upon Sir Henry Hungate but cold get no money. Sithence his decease I wayted on his lady for this money; she denyeth me saieinge she had nothinge left wherewith to pay Sir Henry Hungates debtes. Nowe agayne I humbly retorne to your selfes, desiringe you wold please to pay this £18 2s 3d out of the Lady Cesars estate. I knowe Mr Earle, yf he be inquired of, well [*sic*] remember that I faithfully followed this greate suite for the Lady Cesar, and that I was a suitor for payment thereof ymediately after the Ladies decease, who lived but a small tyme after the suite was ended. My humble suite is you will be pleased to take such consideration hereof, as I may receive speedy satisfaction; I havinge much suffered for want hereof. And you shall not want the prayers of your humble servant

Signed: William Beaumont. London 7 July 1647 *Holograph.*
Postscript: I pray be pleased to vouchsafe me your answeres.
Addressed: To the right worshippfull Sir Edmond Bacon knight and baronett and Phillip Woodehowse esq.
Endorsed by George Gardiner: Mr. Beamontes letter 7 July 1647: for a debt. Md. this letter was brought by Mr Woodhouse to my master 24 July 1647.
2 ff.

222.   [4268] *Richard Humphrey to Sir Edmund Bacon, 29 July 1647*

Sir, I had an intencion to have been with yow before this tyme, but the hardness of the bargayne and the great payments of the tymes hath hindered my resolucion of wayting on yow, but if it please God within this month I shall not fayle too bee

---

371   Near Sawbridgeworth, Hertfordshire.
372   East Bradenham, in Norfolk: this property had come to the Caesars through the marriage of Sir Julius Caesar to his third wife, Anne Woodhouse, widow of Henry Hogan of East Bradenham. See further correspondence below, no. **231 [4277]**.

at Redgrave. So presenting mine and my wives humble respects to yowr selfe and Sir Thomas Woodhowse I rest

Signed: Your affectionate servant and kinsman Richard Humfrey. Malden[373] this 29 of July 1647 *Holograph.*
Addressed: To the much honored Sir Edmund Bacon at Redgrave.
Endorsed by George Gardiner: Mr Humfreys letter 29 July 1647
2 ff.; remains of seal.

223. [4269] *Sir John Caesar to Sir Edmund Bacon, 1 September 1647*

Much honored Sir, It has pleased God to take my daughter, and my humble suite is that my sonne Robert according to his mothers will may receive the moitie of her portion, if it bee raisd, as I expect it should bee long since.[374] For the other part, and what else my deare wife did assigne to my sonne Henry (if yourselfe and those other gentlemen in trusted shall soe please) I will take into my hands for my childs use, and by the advice of councell secure you from future trouble. Upon your answere I shall waite on you, for I desire with passion to see you. With a most cordiall expression of thanckes for your cardinall favoures and presentment of my humblest service shall ever rest

Signed: Yours most deservedly to bee commanded John Caesar. Hydehall this first of September 1647. *Holograph.*
Addressed: To the honorable and truly noble knight and baronett Sir Edmund Bacon at Redgrave.
Endorsed by George Gardiner: Sir John Caesars letter 1 *Septembris* 1647 with a note of Mr Robert and Mr Henry Caesars age. To ~~be~~ direct the letter to be left with Mr Thomas Smyth at the Signe of the George in Barkeway,[375] to be sent to Mr Caesar ~~in~~ at Hidehall in London.
2 ff.; seal torn off.

224. [4270] *Memorandum [1 September 1647]*

Robert Caesar of Sir John Caesar and Dame Ann his wife bapt. November 14 1625.

Henry Caesar of Sir John Caesar and Dame Anne his wife bapt. Aprill 10 1635.

Ita testor Nicholas French Vicarius de Sandon.

Holograph.
2 ff., torn.

225. [4271] *Philip Woodhouse to Sir Edmund Bacon, 4 September 1647*

Noble Sir, My cozen Robert Caesar commen over to me this Saterday hath demanded of me, such part of the monyes as I have in my hands towards the £1000 which should be rays'd by the Feoffe's for his (late dead) sisters portion, it being dispos'd by my Lady his mother to him and his brother upon her death. My answer to him is that till I be satisfyed by councell whither it may safely by law be deliver'd to him by parcells as t'is gatherd before the whole summe be raysed I desire to

---

[373] In Essex.
[374] Cf. *Bacon handlist*, no. **2811**.
[375] In Hertfordshire.

be excused, and that I am resolved to doe nothing in it but as your second, and therfore Sir I shall desire to know (when you thinck fitt) ~~your~~ what your pleasure and resolution is in it, being ready to follow and attend your proceedings heerin. Sir I desire your pardon for not wayting upon you as it becomes me, and I desire, my abode heer being for a very short tyme and that fully taken up with my petty affayres, but shall be always ready to serve you and your commands

Signed: As your faithfull honored servant Philip Woodehowse. Downham Lodge September 4 1647. *Holograph.*
Addressed: For his ever honor'd friend Sir Edmond Bacon knight and baronett at Redgrave.
Endorsed by George Gardiner: Mr Woodhouse his letter 4 *Septembris* 1647
2 ff.; traces of seal.

226. [4272] *Richard Humphrey to Sir Edmund Bacon, 5 November 1647*
Sir, I present my humble servis to yow with my wives. It hath pleased God to visitt me with a long sickness or else I had been at Redgrave with yow and have payd yow the money, but so soon as it shall please God to give me any strength of body I shall wayte on yow. In the meane tyme if yow please to appoynt any to receave £200 and deducting the charges (which I have been for contribucions) and receaving yowr acquittance thereof I shall willingly pay it to him at London *this terme* where I am now going in a horse litter to morrow being otherwise unable. I hope yow will excuse my not comming according to my last letter, sickness hindering of me, and wishing all health and happiness to yowr selfe I rest

Signed: Your affectionate kinsman and humble servant Richard Humfrey. Fremnolls this 5 of November 1647. *Holograph.*
Postscript: My brother Barnard presents his humble servis to yow
Addressed: To the much honored Sir Edmond Bacon at Redgrave.
Endorsed by George Gardiner: Mr Humfreys letter 5 November 1647
2 ff.; fine seal impression.

227. [4273] *Sir John Caesar to Sir Edmund Bacon, 24 December 1647*
Honorable Sir, I intended to have waited on you, butt the multitude of soldiers which quarter at my howse will hinder mee. I desire to knowe your pleasure concerning my sonne Henry his portion; if you shall thincke fitting and the other noble knight to putt it into my handes for the childes good, I will give such securitie, as your councell shall like of. If I maye bee assured of performance, I will then bee in London the next tearme, that all thinges maye bee there fairely concluded, else I will save that labour and charge. I beseech the Allmightie to poure downe the choicest of his blessinges upon your selfe and family, and with presentment of my humblest service unto you, to his most gracious protection I betake you, resting ever

Signed: Yours most deservedly to bee commanded John Caesar. Hydehall this 24th of December 1647. *Holograph.*
Note in hand of Bacon's secretary: Answere returned the same daye receyved.
Addressed: To the honorable and truly noble Sir Edmund Bacon knight and baronett.
Endorsed by George Gardiner: Sir John Caesars letter 24 December 1647
2 ff.; traces of seal.

228. [4274] *George Waters to George Gardiner, 7 January 1648*

Honest Mr Gardner, My mastar Sir John Ceasar would intreat you to doe him the favor to speake to Sir Edmond to send him an answer of his latar. It semes thar was on sente all redey and the poste hath loste it which doth inforce him to trobell you once more to send about it. He would intreat you to ~~send a~~ retorne the answer backe by this barore that the poste may bringe it this retorne. And in so doinge you shall for ever command your ~~respectes~~ most faithfull and loving frind

Signed: George Waters. January the 7 1647. *Holograph.*
Note in hand of Bacon's secretary: Answere wrott by my master 8 Jan. 1647.
Addressed: To his very loving frind Mr Gardnar at Redgrave Hall nere Bodesdell or to Mr White
Endorsed by George Gardiner: George Waters Sir John Caesars mans letter 7 Jan. 1647
2 ff.; traces of seal.

229. [4275] *Philip Woodhouse to Sir Edmund Bacon, 15 January 1648*

Sir, My fathers affliction of the gout continuing still upon him, so as he is unable to wryte unto you himselfe, I must entreat you to accept of my scribling answer to you about Mr *Robert* Caesar's busines, which is thus that, if you be persuaded that the deed wheroff he shews a copy be authenticall, we ~~should~~ *shall* be very willing the mony shall be payd in according to your opinion, so as a sufficient legall discharge may be given us for the same. As for the mony therof which is in our handes, you shall be *made* acquainted therwith, in the begining of the next week, when as I intend God willing to attend you my selfe, or to send a messinger with a lettre to declare it unto you. Sir I must tell you, that what mony there is, is totally in my hands (my father ever refusing to intermeddle therwithall). Sir Mr Caesar seems to be very importunate to receive a hundred pond therof for his present occasions which he sayth you are contented withall, so as I may disburse £50 of the same, which motion of his being unmentioned in your lettre I am some-what diffident to agree unto untill I have understood it from your selfe. And ther-fore till my wayting upon you or sending unto you, I thought fitt to deferr which I hope I shall not fayle in accordingly, wheras I will take order to concurr *with* ~~with your~~ and observe your safe directions therin. Thus with my fathers and my affectionate desires for your health and happines I remayne

Signed: Your humble servant Philip Wodehowse. Kimberly Lodge[376] Jan. 15 1647. *Holograph.*
Postscript: Sir I desire you in the mean tyme to understand that I never receivd any monyes from Mr Humphryes since my last reckonings of accompt with you about Fremnalls.
Addressed: To his ever honored friend Sir Edmond Bacon knight and baronett at Redgrave.
Endorsed by George Gardiner: A letter from Mr Phillip Woodhouse Jan. 15 1647
2 ff.; fine seal impression.

---

[376] In Norfolk.

230. [4276] *Sir Edmund Bacon and Philip Woodhouse to Richard Humphreys,*
21 January 1648

Cosen Humfreys wee marvele, that after our soe long patience, yow neither come
nor send to pay the arrerages of yowr rent, which is now amounted to a great
summe, and yow know that wee are but trusted for others, who doe now call
earnestly upon us for the monyes which wee would willingly paye ~~yow~~ according
as it is due, if wee had receyved it from yow. If yow give us not present satisfaction, yow must not take it ill if wee comence a suite against yow by course of lawe
to recover the same. Wee desire yow therefore ~~to pa~~ suddainely to ~~come~~ come
~~and~~ paye s in ~~yowr all~~ *all* the monyes due unto us, that wee may satisfie them
that now call upon us, and performe the trust reposed in us. And soe wee shall
remayne

Signed: Your truly loving freindes and kinsmen Edmund Bacon Philip Woode-
hose. 21 Jan. 1647. *Copy in hand of endorser.*
Postscript: This letter was sent by Mr Roberte Caesar then, who promised to
procure an answere.
Endorsed by George Gardiner: The copy of a letter sent to Mr Humfrey Jan.
1647
1 f.

231. [4277] *Philip Woodhouse and Sir Edmund Bacon to Henry Hungate, 21*
January 1648

Sir, There is a gent. one Mr ~~Bennet~~ Beamont *an* attorny, whoe hath often impor-
tuned us, as thexecutors of your late grandmother the Lady Ceaser, to paye him
a debt of £18 2–3d due to him for prosecuting of a suit against the Bishopp of
Norwich Thomas Spring and William Strode clarke for the church of Braddenham
which suite shee imployed him in (being a busynes of that consequence, that it
concerned the whole title of the land late Huggens questioned by Downes and
Spring).[377] Wee are very well assured that it is a due debt, he haveing the repute
of a very honest man. And besydes Mr Earle whoe was your grandmothers coun-
sellor in all these affayres does testefye the same. This is therfore to desyre yow
in a fayer way, to send to one of us this monny, otherwyse wee must be forced in
a more troblesome, to come upon your landes of Braddenham which wee have a
right in for the discharg of your grandmothers debtes, wee being threatned to be
sued for the same. Thus with our respectes to you wee rest

Signed: Your lovinge kinsman Edm. Bacon Philip Woodehouse. 21 Jan. 1647.
Copy.
Postscript note: The letter was sent then by Mr Phillip Woodhouse.
Endorsed by George Gardiner: The coppy of letters sent to Mr Henry Hungate at
Bradnam concerning Mr Beamont. Jan. 1647
1 f.

232. [4278] *Richard Humphrey to Sir Edmund Bacon, 21 March 1648*

Noble Sir, Presenting mine and my wives humble servis unto yow, having had a
full intencion to have wayted on you at Red Grave this weeke and to that intent
did certifye my cosen Robert Caesar as much, but it pleased God to visitt with
sickness a sonn of myne who wee doe expect every day when it shall leave this

---

[377] See no. **221 [4267]** above.

life [*sic*], and not willing to leave my wife in soe sad a condicion, also my owne strength being not perfected since my last sicknes causeth my not attending on yow, but (if it please *God*) the weeke after Easter weeke I shall not fayle to wayte on yow for the evening of the accounts and the money most part if not shall bee ready to bee payde according to yowr appoyntment, although I must confess my long sickness hath been a great loss and chardge unto me with the hardness of the bargayne. Sir in the meane tyme I shall wish all health and happiness to your selfe as from him that desires to bee esteemed

Signed: Your affectionate kinsman and humble servant Richard Humfrey. Frem-nolls this 21 of March 1647. *Holograph.*
Addressed: To the much honored Sir Edmond Bacon at Redgrave.
Endorsed by George Gardiner: Mr Humfrey his letter 21 March 1647
2 ff.; seal impression.

233.   [4279] *Philip Woodhouse to George Gardiner, 21 April 1648*
Sir, I desire you to present my humble service and respects to Sir Edmund being very sorry that I cannot according to his commands attend him at this tyme by reason of my present illnes of health, which makes me unfitt and fearfull to travayle so farr as to my fathers Lodge (which is but a mile of) *and* being indeed in physiq, this day. I desire you therfore to obtayn my pardon of Sir Edmund for the busines. Whatsoever Sir Edmund shall think fitt to do in it, I shall submitt therunto. I can not think of any thing else than what we advised together the last tyme I was at Redgrave. We can take no more than he gives us, and what must be allowed him the law will order, and Parliament ordinance, if they stand till the busines be out of our hands. I have sent you heer Mr Hungats answer to the letter we sent *him* from Redgrave. Mr Payn Chab'nr [*sic*] brought it, and by word of mouth told me from him that he will take submit to what we shall think fitt, so I sent desir'd that he would meet with Mr Beaumont and Mr Earle and give himselfe the best satisfaction he could. Thus with best service and thankfullnes tender'd to my cozen Gaudy, and her *my* fayre [*word erased and illegible*] yong cozen and to Mr Butts, I rest

Signed: Your faithfull friend Philip Woodeh. April 21. *Holograph.*
Addressed: For his very much respected friend Mr George Gardiner at Redgrave.
Endorsed by Gardiner: Mr Woodhowse his letters to mee, April 1648
2 ff.; traces of seal.

234.   [4280] *Henry Hungate to Philip Woodhouse, May 1648*
Noble Sir, I received a letter bearing date the 21 of Februar Januarii from Sir Edmund Bacon and you [*sic*] selfe, the contents wherof seeme somewhat strange, concerning a debt which should be dewe from my grandmother to one Mr. Beau-mont. I knowe she was a woman soe often carefull of her affaires as she never imployed anie man in them but she largely payd them, but since her death the estate hath binne in my father, since in my brother, and nowe after a long time of sequestration, in my selfe, and for Mr Beamont in all this time to make noe meanes for his monies, if anie due, is very strange. I will not be refractory to any debt that may justly be layd uppon me as a dewe from her, but if uppon one mans bare affirmation I shall have a debt layd uppone me, my whole estate may be in the like kind questioned. If dewe as he pretends why did not Mr Beamont seeke

it while the estate was under sequestration. But I knowe you to be soe nobe [*sic*] as you will rather take of burthens from me, then impose anie that are noe way visible, under whose banner I desier ever to be protected, who will ever remaine your faithfull servant and kinsman,

Signed: Henry Hungate. *Holograph.*
Addressed: To my much honore [*sic*] kinsman Phillipp Woodhouse esquier.
Endorsed by George Gardiner: Mr Hungates letter sent by Mr Woodehowse with his letter May 1648
2 ff.; seal impression.

235.　[4281] *Philip Woodhouse to Sir Edmund Bacon, 6 May 1648*

Sir, I am extreame sorry, and even asham'd that I must now agayne be fayling to your commands of coming over. The last tyme my indisposition of health detayned me; now my plea of excuse must be my present going out of the contrey, with my wife to her grandmother who hath importunately sent for her, but Sir were I with you, I could say no more than now I wryte, which is that in this busines I shall referr my part therin to you, and concurr with you in whatsoever is fitt for me to do. You were pleas'd when I was last with you to think fitt to employ Mr Moss *who I think is a very fitt man* to have care of the busines upon occasion; nor can I tender any thing more to be remembred than that we be very tender what disbursements of Mr Humphrey's we give allowance to, and that some court of justice may order us therin, for our indemnity. In the mean tyme I think we may safely take what monyes he will pay us in. Thus Sir with the tenderaunce of my humble and thankfull acknowledgement of your noble favours to me, I am

Signed: Your truly honoring servant Philip Woodehowse. Downham Lodge May 6. *Holograph.*
Addressed: For his most honor'd friend Sir Edmond Bacon knight and baronett at Redgrave.
Endorsed by Gardiner: Mr Woodhowse his letter, *Maii* 1648
2 ff.; seal impression.

236.　[4282] *William Bernard to George Gardiner, 19 June 1648*

Sir, Presenting my humble servis to Sir Edmond and my respects to your selfe, I am not knowing how the actions of Essex men may bee interpreted or punnished[378] and *there* being much arrears of rent dew for Fremnolls and being a great stock on the grownd if it should bee taken *away* and the estate sequestred, the tenant will bee utterly unable to pay the arreares of rent. It is conceyved the safest way for Sir Edmond is to send tymely and seaze on the stock and goods for his security, which if it please you to communicate thus much to Sir Edmond from him that wishes all fayre dealings on all parties. This day is payd to Mr Caesar two hundred powndes part of the same. Soe wishing all happiness to yow, hoping to meet at Berry *once* agayne, remayne

Signed: Your affectionate frend and servant W.B. London this 19 of June 1648. *Holograph.*

---

[378]　A reference to the Royalist rising in Essex: a Royalist army had gathered at Chelmsford on 9 June and had occupied Colchester on 12 June; Parliamentarian forces began to besiege the town on 18 June. See the account in Morant, *Essex* I [Colchester], pp. 59–61.

Addressed: For his very much respected friend Mr Gardiner at Sir Edmond Bacons at Redgrave.
Endorsed by Gardiner: Mr Barnardes letter rec'd 4 July 1648 at 10 at night
2 ff.; traces of seal.

237. [4283] *Robert Caesar to George Gardiner, 22 June 1648*

Mr Gardiner, Your masters letter I sent to my cosin, but could not suddenly get *an* answere, because of the troubles in Essecks but at last Mr Bernad came to London, and offerd to pay 2 hundred pounds, which I excepted of, and gave him one *of* the dicharges. The remainder hee would have paide, but because the discharges had not witnesses hands to them, hee was cautious of paying any more before hee had fuller satisfaction from Sir Edmunde (which now hee hath write a letter about *it* inclosed in this) to whom present my humble service, and his longe live and health shall incessantly by prayid for. Soe hee hath oblieged mee by his multitude of courtesies. Futher more my service to all my cosins I pray, and be confidend your loves shall bee laid up in a grate full breast, promting mee to bee most faithfully

Signed: Yours Robert Caesar. London June the 22. *Holograph.*[379]
Postscript: The fishes I tooke order should bee sent with all expedition pray let mee heare from you.
Addressed: To his much esteemed freind Mr Gardiner at Redgrave. *In another hand:* leave this letter att Sir Edmond Baccon his howse neer St. Edmonds-Berry
Endorsed by Gardiner: Mr Caesars letter rec'd 4 *Julii* 1648
2 ff.; fine seal impression.

238. [4284] *William Bernard to Sir Edmund Bacon, 13 July 1648*

Noble Sir, I did write to Mr Gardiner desiring him to intimate unto *yow* that Captayne Humfreys your kinsman had payd according to yowr order to Mr Caesar £200, and now being as is imagined in an estate not too dischardge the remaynder of that debt behind soe soon as he desires, that yow *will* be pleased (if yow expect any farther sume soudaynly to bee payd unto yow) to take possession of the stock and corne on the grownd at the farme, whereby yow will performe that trust reposed in yow and he to his power of his disingagement. Conserning which I shall humbly request a speedy answer from yow so with my humble servis to yow I remayne

Signed: Yowr humble servant William Bernard. London this 13 of July 1648.
Holograph.
Postscript: If yow please to direct yowr answer *to me* to the Queens head in Bishops gate street.
Addressed: To the much honored Sir Edmond Bacon Baronett at Redgrave neere Budsdale.
Endorsed by Gardiner: Mr Barnardes letter rec. 16 *Julii* 1648
2 ff.; seal impression.

239. [4285] *William Bernard to Sir Edmund Bacon, 3 August 1648*

Sir, I have writt two severall letters to intimate unto yow the desires of ~~of~~ *me and* Mr Humfreys to complye and pay that debt, dew for the rent of Fremnolls to which

---

[379] A naive hand.

end desires that yow will send over some body to entre on the corne and stock on the grownd otherwise he shall *bee* utterly unable to pay it, soe desiring yowr answer herein this next weeke if yow please to direct yowr letter to the Queens Head in Bishops gate street. Soe remayneth from farther troubling of yow

Signed: Yowr most humble servant William Bernard. London this 3 of August 1648. *Holograph.*

Addressed: To the much honored Sir Edmond Bacon Baronett at Redgrave neere Budsdale.

Endorsed by Gardiner: Mr Barnardes letter rec. 6 August 1648. And sent an answere the same daye to London by the carrier.

2 ff.; seal impression.

240. [4286] *Philip Woodhouse to Sir Edmund Bacon, 24 August 1648*

Sir, Be pleased to understand that upon the 21 of this August Mr Barnard, my cosen Humfryes kinsman, mett mee in Westminster Hall, and after telling mee that by reason of his kinsmans being in Colchester, all his goodes and estate was taken awaye by the Parliamentes sequestrators, and after a great complaint, that he was now utterly disinabled to paye the arreres, especially since your agent had refused to seise upon the stock and corne upon the ground, according to his advise, and also adding that they tooke £200 in money awaye which yow might have had upon allowance of his taxes, he finally desired mee to take notice that he was resolved to cast up the lease of Fremnalls into yowr handes this Mich'as. I only tould him it was too short a warneing; he replyed, there is noe helpe in it.

Sir I have since asket [*sic*] yowr kinsman Mr Nathaniel Bacons opinion in it; he is of the mynd yow had best accept of it (since there is no remedy) and make the best of it; which if yow shall thinke fitt to doe I make noe question, but upon the giveing of it upp yow will cause him to paye the due arreres, or give yowr sufficyent security for them (which as I remember he intymated to mee to doe he would doe, upon the acceptance of the lease into yowr handes).

Sir for this and what other safe waye yowr councell shall advise yow to take in this busines, I doe subscribe my consent thereto; for my owne occasions are soe doubtfull as I feare I cannott give any personall attendance upon yow or this busines in due tyme (my staye here being but short and uncertaine, and when I doe remove heare, I goe not directly home, but about by the countrey where my wives kindred live). Therefore I humbly desire my not being present may be no hindrance to the setlement of the busines, for I fully submitt what concerneth my concurrence therein unto yow. Thus Sir with my humble thankefullnes, for all yowr noble favoures to mee. I am Sir

Signed: Your truly honoring and faythfull servant Philip Woodehowse. Westminster August 24 1648. *Copy by Gardiner.*

Postscript: A true coppy of Mr Woodhouse his letter sent to Sir Thomas Woodhouse, who kept it. Rec'd this letter 5 *Septembris* 1648 by Knott.

2 ff.

241. [4287] *Thomas Woodhouse to Sir Edmund Bacon, 7 September 1648*

Noble Sir, I perceive by your letter with that inclosed from my sonn, that Mr Humphries would throwe up his lease of Fremnolls. Truly Sir on the sodein I can say no more, but that I thinke it an unequall thing that he should receive any advantage or we should endure any damage by his inconsiderate errores. I expect my sonn very shortly, who will attend to consult farther with you, of what course wilbe best for our owne safeties. My disease doth disinable me to wright, or stire in any businesse of perplexitie, wherefore I pray your pardon and remain

Signed: Your affectionate servant Thomas Wodehouse. Kimberley 7 of September 1648. *Whole text in secretary's hand.*
Postscript by Gardiner: Md. Mr Thomas Woodhouse kept Mr. ~~Bernard~~ Woodhouse his letter by him and returned it not; this inclosed being a true coppy thereof.[380]
Addressed: To his much honored friend Sir Edmond Baccon knight and barronett at Redgrave.
Endorsed by Gardiner: Sir Thomas Woodhouse his letter dd. 7 *Septembris* 1648
2 ff.; seal impression.

242. [4288] *Robert Caesar to Sir Edmund Bacon, 4 January 1649*
Sir, Since my beeing last made your servant, by many favours, which with a gratefull person, are ever tyes and by much experience, knowing your aptnesse to right every one in the verge of your power, makes mee presume to relate Captaine Humfreis not paying in of all my mony (according to my dicharge given at Redgrave) nor any satisfactory answere as yet, this my condition, to your noble consideration, I leave, but shall never from beeing your truly honorer, and humblest sevant,

Signed: Robert Caesar. Hidehall January the 4. *Holograph.*
Note by Gardiner: Brought from Newmarket by William Padnall 23 Jan. 1648. 4 *Martii* 1648 Sent an answere of this letter to be left at Barkwaye to be sent to Hide Hall
Addressed: To the right honorable Sir Edmunde Bacon knight and baronet at Redgrave.
2 ff.; remains of seal.

243. [4289] *Robert Caesar to George Gardiner, 4 January 1649*
Mr Gardiner, I could not satisfie my selfe, till I had dicharged my remenbrance, and charged my letter with comendation to you, intreating a presenting of my letter to Sir Edmunde Bacon, with my service to all my cosins and a answere of my letter, pray direct *to* Sir John Caesars, who present his service to your master, soe by this meanes, what is sent, will come to him, who is very faithfully

Signed: Yours, Robert Caesar. Hidehall January the 4. *Holograph.*
Addressed: To his much esteemed freind Mr George Gardiner living with the right honourable Sir Edmunde Bacon at Redgrave.
Endorsed by Gardiner: Letters from Mr Roberte Caesar, *dat.* 4 *Januarii* 1648. R. 23 *eiusdem Januarii* from Newmarkett by William Padnall
2 ff.; fine seal impression.

244. [4290] *Philip Woodhouse to Sir Edmund Bacon, 3 February 1649*
Noble Sir, Whatsover you shall be pleas'd to think of for the stirring up and quickening Mr Humphreys my father and I shall be willing to consent with you therin and this my father will'd me to advertisd [*sic*] you, he lying at this tyme so

---

[380] See no. **240 [4286]** above.

extreamly afflicted with his old disease the gout, as he is unable to wryte, or to think of ani busines. Sir we are both very confident of your wisedome and care to *that you will* employ so able a lawyer in the busines, as shall preserve us all from detriment, and further expences, than by the Lady is allowed.

Sir my intent had bin to have wayted upon you and tender'd my thankfullnes for your last noble favour when I was with you, but indeed my tendernes, and indisposition of body make's me very unfitt for winter journeys, and therfore crave your pardon if I do putt it of till the dayes be longer and warmer in the mean whyle assuring you that I shall always remayne

Signed: Your faythfull honorer and obliged humble servant Philip Woodehowse. Kimberly the 3 of Feb. 1648. *Holograph.*

Addressed: For his most honored friend Sir Edmond Bacon knight and baronett at Redgrave.

Endorsed by Gardiner: Mr Phillip Woodhowse his letter, 3 [February 1648]

2 ff.; seal impression.

245. [4291] *Serjeant Francis Bacon to Francis Bacon, 23 August 1651*[381]

Cosin, Synce receit of yours the Doctor hathe not beene with mee but not longe before hee was. Hee had then some discourse of such a proposition to lend such a some for 3 yeares uppon security and as that my cosin his brother Paynell wished him to take my councell in it and his desyer was to knowe yf I shoulde continue here, all this vacation which I toulde him I purposed to doe. For vallues he seemed hee would rest uppon yowe to informe him. I shall bee reddy to doe that which is equall betweene them but I shall desyer yf the busines and my employement proceede, I maye have the ~~form~~ evidences aswell of the former entayles by Sir Edmond, his father and grandfather, as of the last setlement sent up, the better to satisfye the Doctor of a carefull endeavor to doe him right. Indeede I thinck yowe advise our good kinsman verry well to drawe his detts and engagements all in to one. I perceived the Doctor had somme inclination to a purchase proposed, which is not yet free from anothers treatye, but shortly maye bee, therefore delaye not longe concluding yf theare bee a desyer to perfect the worke treated of betweene yow and the Doctor. The tempest of thunder lightninge wynde and rayne that hath and houlden most parte of the last nighte ~~and~~ houldes nowe at highe noone so with such darkness that I canne hardly see to wryte more yf more were requisite. God deliver us from all daunger of this and any further tempest and other evils,

Signed: Your verrye lovinge kinsman Francis Bacon. 23 ~~Sept~~ August 1651. *Holograph.*

Addressed: To his lovinge friend Francis Bacon esq. at his howse in Ipswich.

Endorsed by Gardiner: Serjant Bacons letter and Doctor Wrightes

2 ff., torn; fine seal impression.

---

[381] Of these namesakes, the writer Sir Francis (*c.*1587–1657) was a distinguished Norfolk lawyer (see *ODNB, s.v.*); the recipient was Francis Bacon of Ipswich (1600–63; see also *ODNB, s.v.*), who was fifth son of Edward Bacon of Shrubland, third son to Lord Keeper Bacon. Sir Francis was apparently no relation to the Bacons of Redgrave, so the kinship which he claims to the Ipswich Francis Bacon may be by marriage, unless he is simply referring to their common surname.

246. **[4292]** *Thomas Kemp to George Gardiner, 15 July 1652*
Sir, Mr Athwoode hath had conference with Mr Bacon to whom I delivered your letter; he is still much unsatisfied (as appeares) by his queries under his owne hand, which I have sent you, by this bearer, and desires to see all the old evidences, Sir Nicholas will and both Mr Bacons joyntures and wishes he might together with those writings speake your selfe at Chelmesford or at his house in Bromefeild betwixt Brayntree and Chelmesford upon Thursday next the 22 of this instant when he wilbe purposely at home. Sir yf you please to send the writings and come yourselfe to Brayntree upon Wednesday night I wilbe ready to ride along with you to Bromefeild the next day, if I may have your answer by this bearer to determine me. In the interim be pleased to present my humble service to Mr Bacon and accept the respects of Sir

Signed: Your freind and servant Thomas Kemp. From Brayntree July 15 1652. *Holograph.*[382]
Postscript: I should have desired you sooner at Brayntree, but that Mr Coun'll' will not be at home sooner.
Note by Gardiner: Thomas Rupp at the Cock at Braytree Mr Keene
Addressed: For my worthy freind Mr Gardner at his chamber in Redgrave Hall.
2 ff.; seal impression.

247. **[4293]** *Elizabeth Chester to Sir Robert Bacon, 11 August 1652*
Noble Cosen, I have an humble sut to you if I may obtayne it truely it will be allmost as great as the former favour which I shall ever acknowledg and doe really desier to mett with sum happy occation to serve you or yours in. Sir my sut is for the contenewance of tenn pound of the twenty which yet remayns due to you but till our Lady next if you can posible and then God willing you shall not fayle of it and the cuse allso if ye please truely Sir it goes yet sum what to hard with me by reson my joynter was since these tims set at so under a vallew which I could not reays agayne last our Lady, Sir Anthonys death being so neare to it, but I shall doo it then, if you will doo me this great faver, it will infinatly ade to my ingagments and to me last bereath I shall be, Sir

Signed: Your oblidged honourer and fathfull knoted cosen Elisabeth Chester. Barham in Lenton Parish[383] August 11 1652. *Holograph.*
Postscript: My humble service to my honoured cosen your wife and all my cosens I beg to heare of yo if you sent yo letter to Mr Sharfe he may convay it by the Cambridg carriers to my cosen Le Hunt who lives at Mr Lukins in Cambridg
Addressed: To my ever deare and honored kinsman Robart Bacon Esq. at his house Reedgrave
Endorsed by Gardiner: Mrs Chesters letter to Mr. Bacon
2 ff.; seal impression.

248. **[4294]** *Sir William Doyly*[384] *to George Gardiner, early 1654*
Mr Gardiner, There is soe great a necessity of making present sale of Foxheath[385] that I would not by any meanes have it now neglected, therefore I desire you to

---

[382] The sale under discussion was probably of Foxearth Hall: see nos. **248–51 [4294–7]** below.
[383] Barham Hall, Linton, Cambridgeshire.
[384] Of Shotesham, Norfolk; first baronet.
[385] Foxearth, in Essex, a Bacon property. Doyly was son-in-law to and among the feoffees for Sir Robert Bacon: see *Bacon handlist*, nos. **4023–4, 4026–31, 4035–7**. Bacon on 1 August 1650

presently order and conclude it if it bee possible. I pray take John Spendlow, and carry with you such evidence as may cleare the title in particular those deedes from Mr Robert Bacon and Mr Edmund to the feoffees together with the fine thereupon levied. For that deede of partition betwixt Sir Nicholas Bacon and Mr Barrow I understand not; I hope it will bee sufficient that Sir Edmund Bacon[386] had quiett and peaceable possession during the whole course of his lyfe. Mr John Wilkin had order from Mr Bacon and Mr Reeve[387] himselfe to procure a chapman for the mannor and landes at £3000, the mony all to bee p'd at, or before Our Lady; and the purchaser to rec. that halfe yeeres rent, referring to the feoffees the gift of the livinge, and alsoe all arrearage of quitt rents, farme rents and the profitts of any's death or alienation before or since the last Court; but if he comes roundly up to the summe and tyme of payment, lett not the advowsion of the living or profits of the courts, hinder the sale, or if hee will give any reasonable consideration for eyther or both those; 'tis left to you, as you shall see cause; for I am confident Mr Bacon receives greater prejudice by paying interest for mony than the profitts of the courts and the living amounts to, were they tenefold greater than they bee. I pray shew Mr Reeve this letter, and take his authority and approbation to this letter, and I shall rest;[388] however if Mr Reeve bee not at home, I pray proceede and I am confident 'twill bee acceptable to Mr Bacon

Signed: Your lo. freinde William Doyly. *Holograph.*
On dorse: Mrs Gardiners; that married to one in Cambridge died in childbedd and was buried on Wednesday last.
Addressed: These for Mr George Gardiner att Redgrave Hall
Endorsed by Gardiner: Sir William Doylyes letter
2 ff.; fine seal impression.

249.   [4295] *George Reve to George Gardiner, 13 February 1654*
Sir, I have perused the severall letters concerning Foxhearth and likewise Sir William Doyley his comment or raither his approbation. There upon I cannot but conclude with him and you in all the particulars he mentions, for tis noe other to the best of my remembrance, then what we concluded on at our last meeteeing at Redgrave and if you can save the advousion and sell the residew att £3000 it will be as much service as can be expected. My occasions will not possible admitt my attendance but I hope you may as well, if not better performe this servis, which I beseeche you by noe meanes neglegct for you verie well knowe how much it concernes yourselfe and freinds and him that is

Signed: Your trew freinde and servant George Reve. Feb. 13 1653. *Holograph.*
Addressed: To my much respected freinde Mr George Gardener att Redgrave Hall
Endorsed by Gardiner: Mr Reves letter
1 f.; fine seal impression.

---

vested the manor of Foxearth with several other estates in these feoffees for the payment of his debts and legacies, as specified in his will, 1 September 1650: Morant, *Essex* II, 327.
386   From the context, this has to refer to Sir Edmund Bacon the second baronet, i.e. son of Sir Nicholas Bacon II, not Sir Edmund Bacon the fourth baronet.
387   George Reve, Esq. was also a feoffee for Sir Robert Bacon: see below, no. **249 [4295]**.
388   From here, after a note 'verte fol.', the text is written down the margin.

250.   [4296] *James Cobbes to George Gardiner, 6 May 1654*

Sir, I have seene Foxherth, which I fynd rented according to the particular, but in lease for 9 yeares next Mich's (as Mr Wilkyn informes me). But if the leases were now expired, how any considerable improvement could be made, as the tymes are I see not. All that is able to beare corne is broken upp. The houses (for tymber) are to be sustayned by the landlorde; and none there to doe it with. Wood there is not for the use of the farmour; nor possibility of ever having any; so is it beguirt with poore townes besides the out rent is extreme great. These things considered (and diverse others which I could expresse) the most indifferent valuation I can make of it is, the scite of the mamor [*sic*], lands, wood, mill, all £137[389] per annum and 18 yeares purchase (deducting £167 for the rents to Clare) cometh to £2299–0–0. The rents of assise att £18 per annum and 30 yeares purchase £540. That is *in toto* £2839. As far the profitts of Court (they being not certayne) I know not how to bring them under a certayne valuation; and therefore thinck it the more equall *way* (as it is allso most usuall) to value the rents of assise att 30 yeares purchase which considering the charge and trouble of collecting, and keeping courtes is a full value of them. Sir if to this summe I shall add £61 and for the groweth of the wood, and reputation of the advouson *etc.* and so make upp £2900 I am confident your judgment will tell you there is nothing wanting to the full value of it, and so (in one worde) I will give; if the assurance be good (as I nothing doubt it is) your tymes of payment not too sharpe; and the condicions of the tenants be ases[390] reasonable. I add this laste, because I see ~~that~~ the landes have not beene well used, and doubt the tenant may have too much libertye. Sir I desire to knowe what will be your finall resolution touching this matter; that I may dispose my selfe accordingly and I shall ever rest

Signed: Youres in all readines to serve you James Cobbes. Bury 6 *Maii* 1654.
Holograph.[391]
Addressed: To his honoured freind Mr George Gardener att Redgrave Hall
Endorsed by Gardiner: Mr Cobbes letter
2 ff.; fine seal impression.

251.   [4297] *John Woodcock to George Gardiner, 29 May 1654*

Sir, Both my master and Mrs Bacon comanded me to lett yow know, that shee hath commenced sute against Parkins for incloseing without licence, and that hir attorney saies he is advised by councell, that he can neither bring ~~it~~ *the tryall* downe against next assizes, nor can doe any thinge securely unles he hath both the ground conveyance from Sir Robert Bacon to my masters father and also *the fine with* the conveyance that leads the use of the fine with the originall will of my masters fathers, and saith that to have coppies without perusinge and examineing them with the origenall is to no purpose because he cannot make affydavit that they be true unlesse he examine them with the origenalls himselfe. Therefore my master and shee desires that yow wold send them forthwith to Thornage because if they be not suddenly sent they will not be coppied out *and examined* before hir attorney goes to London intendinge to goe next Munday at furthest. And this is all which was commanded, from

---

[389]   Also noted in the margin.
[390]   For 'assessed'?
[391]   Cobbes did not buy the manor. By 1 April 1656 Major-General Hezekiah Haynes was holding his court, and thereafter the Haynes family held the manor for a century: Morant, *Essex* II, 326.

Signed: Your humble servant John Woodcocke. 29 May 1654. *Holograph.*
Postscript: After they be coppied out and Mr Discipline hir attorney hath examined them they shall saffely be returned againe.
Holograph note: Mr Gardiner, You see the necessitie of having these writings; pray send John Spenlo over to Thorneage presently with the writings and allso with the coppy though it be not fully finished and I shall rest

Signed: Your loving friend William Doyly. Munday 4 of the clock.
Addressed: For Mr Gardener att Redgrave Hall
Endorsed by Gardiner: John Woodcockes letter for wrightings, which were sent by John Spendlove
2 ff.; traces of seal.

252. [4298] *L. Wright to Francis Bacon of Ipswich, 28 August 1656*[392]
Thursday 28 August 1655
Sir, Thorough Gods providence I am safely returned to my owne home: I do find no present obstackle to hinder my writting unto you; nor likelihood of any so suddayn impediment, as may make the least retarding of perfecting our busines next weeke, if you or your freind to not make it which if you do, I pray lett me heare of it as soon as is possible; and so put one end or other to our proceedings, for I am not willing to be entreated to stay longer, haveinge as you know other offers els where, but as I kept my word in my journy unto you (though with much prejudice) so will I rest disengaged untill by the next post I may heare from you. Sir I am

Signed: Your loveing freind L. Wright. *Holograph.*
Postscript: Sir you remember what I have sayd concerning the sending upp all ~~wright~~ writings, that ther be no hindrance to councell etc.
Addressed: For my worthy freind Francis Bacon Esq. at his house in Ipswich
2 ff.; seal impression.

253. [4299] *Christopher Smeare to Mr. Blowers, 19 April 1681*[393]
Tenent Blowers, I desire that yow should pay unto my Brother Mr Thomas Smyth of Backton in the County of Suffolk gent. or to Mr. ~~Thomas~~ Abraham Wright of Norton in the said County of Suffolk gent. the summe of Twelve pounds sterling in manner following viz. the summe of six pounds thereof upon the fourteenth day of October next ensuing and the summe of six pounds residie thereof upon the fourteenth day of Aprill which shall bee in the yeere of our Lord one thousand six hundred eighty and two and soe upon the same dayes in every yeere untill the expiration of yowr terme soe long as the mortgage shall continue and Mr Smyths or Mr Wrights accquittance for soe much money rec'd shall bee your discharge and shall bee abated out of your rent. Witnesse my hand and seale this nineteenth day of Aprill *Anno domini* 1681

---

392 The year written is 1655, but 28 August in 1655 was a Tuesday. It was a Thursday in 1656. To get the day of the week wrong is a much less likely mistake than to write the wrong year by a slip of the pen.
393 Christopher Smeare was described as of South Lopham (Nf.), gent., after 1678: *Bacon handlist,* no. **2843**. This letter seems to be associated with the bargain and sale (part of a lease and release) of 12 April 1681 by Smeare to Wright and Smith of lands in Burgate and Gislingham: *Bacon handlist,* no. **2857**. See also *ibid.,* no. **4044**.

Signed: Christopher Smeare. *Autograph. Seal.*
Note: Sealed and deliverd in the presence of William Burrough.
1 f.

254. [4300] *William Beeke to Daniel Cooke, 10 February 1684*
London the 10 of Feb. 1683.
Lo. frend Mr Cooke, I received your letter ~~from Mr~~ by Mr Skiner and have sent
you an answeare by him but feareinge that should miscary I thought good to wright
by the carryer to sertifie you that God willinge without fayle I shall send downe
my sone Turgis on Munday next who will be with you on next Tuseday aboute
the busynes of the land, and therefore desier your frend that the knight[394] and the
fafees may not fayle to be at Sudbury on Wensday next and bringe the evidences
with them that ther may be a full end or else to breake of, for beinge far of, it is a
greate charge to me and my frend to come downe, but if the title be good, and the
knight will be but reasonable I make noe question but there will be a conclusion.
I am in your debt and if we goe through in this busynes I shall be thankfull. If my
sonne Turges or his frend want money I pray you procure it, and I shall se you paid
with thankes, vs

Signed: Your frend William Beeke. *Holograph. Seal.*
Addressed: To his frend Mr Danell Cooke in Sudbury
Endorsed: Mr Beekes letter
1 f.; traces of seal.

255. [4301] *Mary Leman to Sir John Holt, 2 April 1689 «» 1710*
April the 2.
My Lord, I have receved from your Lordship a bill of fifty pounds for which I
return you the humble thanks of

Signed: Your most affectionate sister and humble sarvant Mary Leman. *Holo-graph. Seal.*
Addressed: To the Right Hon'ble the Lord Chife Justice Holt
Endorsed with various calculations.
2 ff.; fine seal impression.

256. [4302] *Charles Gibbs to Sir John Holt, 25 February 1710*
Tivetshall February 25 1709/10.
My Lord, Mr Hobbard was with me this day with the articles, which he told me,
you expected the return of by the next post; I am a perfect stranger to the quantity,
and names of the lands which belong to the Hall Farm, and particularly concern
the composition, but I take it for granted, your Lordship have examind strictly
into it, and upon that confidence alone I have signd them, not doubting, but if
there should be any mistake, it may afterwards be rectified, notwithstanding what
is already done. I hope your lordship will give leave, and assist me in alienating
some glebe lands, for the conveniency of the parsonage house. I pray God restore
your Lordship to a better state of health, and then we shall hope to be made happy
by your presence att Redgrave this summer. I am

Signed: Your Lordships most obedient [servan]t Charles Gibbs. *Holograph. Seal.*

---

[394] Presumably the fourth Baronet, Sir Edmund Bacon.

Addressed: To the Right Hon'ble Sir John Holt Lord Chief Justice of the Queen's Bench att his house in Bedford Row London
1 f., slightly damaged; traces of seal.

257.   [4303] *William Longueville to Paul Joddrell, 17 June 1710*
17 June 1710

Sir, Last night I received another letter from Lord Warrington[395] about his cosyn Nathaniel Booth's morgage. His Lordship is satisfyed that interest is to cease if the administration should not bee ready by August the 1st and therfore hee will with patience waite to the time, it can conveniently bee done; and hee hopes that notwithstanding there are many trust estates to bee transferred; yet in this particular affaire there will need no such thing, the morgage having been made to Sir John Holt himselfe. Now Sir tho' there seemes time enough for obteining the administration and first a decree on the bill pending, yet I doubt such a generall transfer by one or more deeds can scarce bee prepared and executed before the 1st of August. Somewhat you mentioned of Mr Petit and my assigning or being in trust; and providing that none of our actings bee construed an acceptance thereof I confesse that it is likely there will bee a long deed should all differ their term of yeares and inheritances bee expressed in one deed but if all such matter let consideration bee had by others. About tuesday in the evening I meane to looke at your house; Sir if perchance you by this time shall advise mee what answere I may send to Lord Warrington. I am Sir

Signed: Your most humble servant William Longueville. *Holograph.*
Addressed: For Paul Joddrell Esq. at his house.
Endorsed: Mr Holt
2 ff.

258.   [4304] *Robert Kedington to Edward Ventris, 1 February 1720*
February 1 1719

Sir, Mr Howard has bene with me severall times for me to draw up the inquisition and file this Terme or he would move the Court against me as to the woman killed att Hundon which he claimes the deodand for Mr Vernon;[396] he says he will certainly bring downe a tryall next assizes. I have drawne itt up and sent itt this day by a freind to my sonne to wait on you with itt to peruse before itt be filed. I was to wait on Mr Holt att Redgrave but had the misfortune to not to see him he being gone to Norwich but I hear he will not be in London this Terme soe as there will be noe speaking to the Duke of Wharton[397] about his gromes effects which was found a *felo de se* att Newmarket. If he should be in towne before you leave itt pray mentioned [sic] *itt* to him. When you see Mr Camel desire him if there be any thing for me to doe here before the Assizes that he would give me a line to the Draggon in Bury and itt shall be observed by

Signed: Your most humble servant Robert Kedington. *Holograph.*

---

395   George Booth, 2nd Earl of Warrington (1675–1758): on his financial troubles, see *ODNB, s.v.* Booth, George.
396   Presumably on behalf of the Duchy of Lancaster, of which Hundon formed a part.
397   Philip Wharton, Duke of Wharton (1699–31).

Addressed: To Edward Ventris Esq. Counseller att Law att his chambers in the Temple, London.[398]
1 f.; Bury frank and traces of seal.

259.   [4305] *Edmund Howard to Edward Ventris, 20 August 1720*

August 20: 1720

Hon'd Sir, Serj't Reynolds[399] tells me that Mr Holts grants and writeings that came to him were so many and not abstracted that he had not time to peruse them so as to deliver his opinion in the affaire between him and Mr Vernon, that he returned them to Mr Holt to be extracted or att least put in such order that he might readily apply to such parts of them as related to the matter in question and in case they are so returned to him, he shall be att leisure this vacation to look into the busines and will be very ready and willing to deliver his opinion theron. I begg the favour of a line from you that I may know if you are pleased to have the writeng methodized and returned to the Serj't as he desires, that I may lett Mr Vernon know whether this affaire is likely to be ended by the Serj't or not. I am Sir your

Signed: most obedient humble servant Edmund Howard. *Holograph.*
Addressed: For Edward Ventris Esq. att his house near Ipswich.
2 ff.; Bury frank and traces of seal.

260.   [4306] *James Reynolds to ?Edward Ventris, 14 February 1722*

Serjeants Inn Chancery Lane February the 14 1721

Sir, I inform'd you some time agone with the result of my enquiries into the affair between Mr Holt and Mr Vernon, and beg leave to desire you'll acquaint Mr Holt, that I am of opinion that his right to the deodands etc. within the Liberty of Bury St. Edmunds in such manner as the Abbot of Bury enjoyed them, appears by the evidence laid before me to be well derived from the Crown, to the persons under whom he claims, and that I do not find that Mr Vernon has been able to collect any evidence which can be sufficient to exempt his mannor of Hundon, as to the right now in question, out of that grant, or to entitle himself to the deodand in dispute, ag'st Mr Holt, or the person who claims itt under his title. I am Sir

Signed: your most obedient humble servant James Reynolds. *Holograph.*
2 ff.

261.   [4307] *James Welton to Thomas Thurston, 17 July 1744*

Sir, On Saturday last, old Muskitt of Stow-market sat, as coroner, on the body of a boy here at Bardwell, who was kill'd by an ox of Mrs Read's of Bardwell. The jury found the ox to be the occasion of the boy's death, but the coroner wou'd not suffer them to find or value the deodand,[400] telling them it was none of their business, but belong'd only to him and he wou'd take cure of it, so that the inquisition was drawn without any mention of a deodand. If you think proper to interpose, on the behalf of Mr Holt, and so stop the filing of the inquisition, Mr Cocksedge

---

[398]   Ventris was the son of the distinguished lawyer Sir Peyton Ventris of Ipswich, on whom see *ODNB, s.v.* Ventris, Peyton.

[399]   James Reynolds (1686–1739), serjeant at law and later judge: see no. **260 [4306]**, and *ODNB, s.v.* Reynolds, James.

[400]   A chattel forfeited to the Crown (in this case, the ox which was the cause of the boy's death) and available to be distributed in alms.

and Mr Spinluff, the two leading gentlemen of Bardwell, and myself will attest his mal-practice, on oath at the assizes. If you will give yourself the trouble to inquire *into* this affair, we should be glad, if you would call upon us at Mr Cocksedges of Bardwell, in your return to Bury, which is very little out of your way, when we will give you a perfect account of this business. I am Sir

Signed: Your most obedient humble servant James Welton Rector of Bardwell. Bardwell July the 17 1744. *Holograph.*
Addressed: To Thomas Thurston Esq.
Endorsed with notes in two separate hands: (1) Robert Barker Sir Edmund Bacon *(2)* M.B.J.I. D.G.
2 ff.; Bury frank and remains of seal.

INDEX: PEOPLE AND PLACES

All places mentioned are in Suffolk, unless otherwise stated or obvious in location.

Nunn, George, servant to Sir Nicholas Bacon I
xviii, 18, 23, 30–3, 36, 40–3, 52, 54–7
letters from   16–18, 24–5, 48
letter to   22, 49

Odierne (Hodyhorn), Mr   6
Odierne (Odyan), Gregory, servant to Sir
Nicholas Bacon I   31, 41
Ogle, …   108
Orange-Nassau, Elizabeth of (marr. Henri de la
Tour, duc de Bouillon)   letter to   93–4
Orange-Nassau, Louise Juliane of (marr.
Friedrich IV, Elector Palatine)   93
Ormesby, Thomas   34n
Osborne, John, clerk to Sir Nicholas Bacon I
xix, 57
Outwell (Nf.)   48
Oxford University   135

Padnall, William   144
Paget, William, 5th Lord Paget (d. 1628)   101
Palavicino, Toby   99n
Palfrey (Palfeye, Palferye, Perfee), Abraham,
mark of   87–8
Parham   39–40
Parker, Calthorpe   77
Parker, George   75, 104
Parker, John, servant to Sir Edmund Bacon III
112
Parker, Sir Philip   77n
letters from   63–4
Parkhurst, John, Bishop of Norwich   31
Patten, Mr   67–8
Paulet, William, Marquis of Winchester   10
Payn, Robert   74
Paynell, …   145
Peck, …   58
Pembroke, Earl of: see Herbert
Percy, Henry, 9th Earl of Northumberland, letter
from   83
Percyvall, John   52n
Petit, Mr   151
Pey, Mr   126
Peyton, Christopher, letter to   9–10
Peyton, Elizabeth (marr. Sir Anthony Chester),
letter from   146
Phelips (Phillippes), Sir Robert   121
Phillips, William, servant to Sir Nicholas
Bacon I   34
letter to   34–5
Playters, Thomas I (d. 1572)   44–5
Playters, Sir Thomas II (d. 1638)   113
Pointen, Mr   100
Poitou (France)   91
Poley, Giles   37n
Poley, Thomas   50
Poley, Sir William   107
Pope, Sir Thomas, letter from   11
Popham, Sir John   xx
letter from   76
Portugal   64n

Posford, John   98
Power, Robert   34n
Pownser, Robert   61
Prentys, William   98
Preston, Mr   24

Quarles, Mr   118

Radcliffe, Thomas, Earl of Sussex   xviii, 50
Ramsey, Mr   107
Raven, …   123
Read, Mrs   152
Reade, Mr   125–6
Redbourne (Hertfordshire)   84
Redgrave   xv, xxivn, 112n
Redgrave Hall   xiii–xvii, xxiii–xxiv, 32, 43,
51–2, 75, 90, 112, 133, 135–7, 139–40, 144,
150–1
audit at   48, 72
building works at   36–8
deer at   33, 53
demolished   ix
garden works at   29–30, 32
illustrated   frontispiece, xii, xxvii
letters addressed from   48, 66, 69, 78, 90,
109, 114
letters addressed to   30–32, 41–4, 50–1,
53–7, 63, 65, 67–8, 75, 78–9, 114–15,
120, 122, 127, 129, 132–8, 140, 142–9
Redlingfield Nunnery   10
Reeve alias Melford, John, Abbot of Bury   6n
Reve, George   147
letter from   147
Reve, Robert, letter from   122
Reynolds, James   152
letter from   152
Riccall (Yorkshire)   15n
Rich, Sir Richard   8
Rickinghall   31–32
Rickinghall Inferior, letter from inhabitants   98
Risby   102
Rivett (Rivatt), Edward   126
Rivett, John   22n, 36n
Rivett, Thomas   51n
Rochester, Lord: see Carr
Rockitt, Henry   85
Rockitt, Thomas, letter to   84–5
Rockitt, William, letter from   84–5
Rogers, Robert, letter from   60
Rolfe, …   97
Roper, Sir John   94
Rookwood, Robert   38–42, 47
Rous, Sir Edmund, letter to   11–12
Rous, Sir John   113
Rowe, Joy   xxiii
Royston (Hertfordshire)   xxii, 51n, 95, 98–9
Rupp, Thomas   146
Rush, Anthony   30
Rushbrooke   50n
Russell, Sir William   128–9
Ryburgh (Nf.)   61, 110

INDEX: SUBJECTS